MARINE CONVERSIONS

MARINE CONVERSIONS

Vehicle engine conversions for boats

SECOND EDITION

NIGEL WARREN

Drawings by Beryl Riches

ADLARD COLES LIMITED
8 Grafton Street, London W1

Adlard Coles Ltd
William Collins Sons & Co. Ltd
8 Grafton Street, London W1X 3LA

First published in Great Britain by
Adlard Coles Ltd 1972
Reprinted 1974, 1977, 1978
Second edition 1982
Reissued in paperback with minor amendments 1985

Distributed in the United States of America
by Sheridan House, Inc.

British Library Cataloguing in Publication Data
Warren, Nigel
Marine conversions.—2nd ed.
1. Motor-boats—gasoline engines
I. Title
623.8′5 VM731

ISBN 0-229-11770-8

Typeset by V & M Graphics Ltd, Aylesbury, Bucks
Printed and bound in Great Britain by
Mackays of Chatham, Kent

By the same author

Small Motor Cruisers
Metal Corrosion in Boats
The Outboard Motor Handbook

Contents

List of Illustrations

Foreword

Boats provide the ideal field for the amateur innovator—for the ingenious handyman who likes to modify, improve, extend and embellish. There are some who like merely to sail or helm their craft, but there are many more for whom the handling of the boat on the water is only a part of the pleasure of ownership: the complementary part is the devoted attention that can be paid to the beloved's physical well-being.

There are some who are not content merely to tinker but who must create the boat herself, making and assembling every part in a long labour of love. There have always been such people, and some of them (*vide* Harry Pidgeon) have made world-girdling voyages in the creations of their own hands. Nowadays there are perhaps more people than ever who take on this major work of building, or completing, or fitting out their own craft—for there are many routes to boat ownership.

But whatever the route, whether starting with a log or a ready-moulded and part-finished hull of polyester resin reinforced with glass fibre, the modern boat almost invariably has an engine. Cold mechanics intrude where art and eye were once good enough, and the amateur handyman finds himself faced with a host of problems which are outside and beyond boatbuilding.

Vibration, cooling, transmission, sound insulation, the matching of the propeller, the design of a safe fuel system, the choice of mountings and the avoidance of mutually destructive metals, are among the problems that the amateur must face and master. Fortunately he has a good friend and guide in Nigel Warren.

And I would earnestly advise any owner to pay great heed to the valuable information which is collected (for the first time, I believe) in this book. Engine failures are without doubt the greatest single cause of trouble in seagoing power craft. Sometimes the fault lies with the skipper, who has forgotten to take enough fuel—and there are no service stations on the sea! More often the engine is starved of fuel by a blockage and that is when the difference between a good and a bad installation makes itself felt. A poor fuel installation leads to other, even more frightening, dangers if a union shakes itself loose, or a copper pipe chafes away or cracks. Then fire or explosion may result.

This is not the place to list all the many causes of engine failure, but it doesn't take much sea experience to realise that repairs in a rolling boat are not at all the same thing as they are in the garage at home. Nor does one have so many tools and spares available, unless great care and forethought have been given in fitting out the boat.

The man who has installed his own engine must at least be familiar with it, and he should also have a better idea than most owners of the spares and tools that he should carry aboard. These are essentially practical matters, but they are of the first importance for safety, because a boat without any means of propulsion is automatically in a most dangerous situation. (The only thing that can be worse is a boat without the means to stop—without an anchor.)

The world seems sometimes to be divided into the chair-bound academics and the chaps who roll up their sleeves and get their hands dirty. Nigel combines both these roles. He has training and qualifications in naval architecture, which he practises in the design office of a leading shipyard where every aspect of modern technology can be brought to bear. Back at home, working on his own boats, he must look to the pennies like the rest of us, and so he knows how to make-do with bits and pieces from the breaker's yard, and the come-in-handy box under the garage bench.

Thus what Nigel writes is both practical, in the sense that you and I and the chap next door will be able to do it and can afford to do it, and technically sound because it is based on expert professional knowledge. Readers of *Practical Boat Owner* will know that this is so, for over a period of years he has been writing a most popular and useful series of articles on engines, their use and installation. But magazine articles are one thing and a book is another. We have all felt the need of a sound and sensible book for the amateur engine converter and installer. As far as I know there is nothing at all to be had in the field, so this new work is doubly welcome.

Denny Desoutter
Former Editor, *Practical Boat Owner*

Introduction

The aim of this book is to help the amateur who is marinising a car or truck engine and installing it in a boat. The aim is not only to describe what to do but also to give the whys and wherefores of the various techniques of conversion.

There is no single best way of fitting a car engine in a boat; there is a spectrum of conversion ranging from an old banger's engine dropped straight into the boat at the cost of a few pounds, to a new or reconditioned truck diesel fully converted with fresh water cooling and installed with all the sophistications, down to fine details such as twin batteries and an array of instruments.

There must be thousands of amateur-installed car and truck engines in boats, some of them weird and wonderful, some sophisticated and professional, but they all work and give hours of pleasure, which is the prime object of the exercise.

In the professional world most 'marine' engines on the market are basically automotive units intended for a variety of purposes. The basic engines, usually Ford or British Leyland, are bought by marinisers and fitted out with marine gearboxes, suitable cooling, starters, dynamos and other bits and pieces, and sold as complete marine engines. Provided the marinisation caters for a salty environment and the needs of boat propulsion there is nothing to be lost over a true marine engine. Indeed there is everything to be gained because car and truck engines are highly developed, efficient, reliable and relatively cheap as they are made in thousands, unlike true marine engines. What is more, spares are easily obtainable.

Professional converters have to cater for all types of boats, and have to provide sufficient cooling so that their engines can run indefinitely at full throttle in a confined space. The amateur is usually adapting an engine to a specific boat, and can therefore take liberties with the installation. Unlike the professional conversion, which tends to be stereotyped, the amateur can choose any number of ways of cooling the engine and driving the propeller shaft, often with unusual results, for instance Balata-belt drives, paddle wheels, running on paraffin, changing gear to go upwind, and electric or hydraulic transmission. In mentioning such unusual amateur boat propulsion arrangements I am drawing on the varied articles by individuals which appear in the monthly magazine *Practical Boat Owner*. In fact, a large number of the ideas presented in this book are based on ideas from this source, and to the people who have produced these different car engine conversions and drives and subsequently put pen to paper for *Practical Boat Owner* I hereby say Thank you.

CHAPTER ONE

General Ideas

Conversions can be split broadly into four categories. In the first as much as possible of the original mechanics is used and the cost kept down to the absolute minimum. The complete engine including the radiator, fan, gearbox, articulated propeller shaft and mountings are used. Propeller thrust is taken through the articulated joints to the gearbox, which is unmodified, and the engine is kept partially open to the elements to give sufficient cooling. An installation like this will give poor power astern, will boil over if run hard for very long, the articulated joint and rubber mountings will soon fail, salt spray will cause corrosion everywhere, and the electrics will soon give trouble.

By fitting a thrust bearing, converting the gearbox and enclosing the engine these problems will be overcome. Better ducting and a larger radiator will solve the cooling problem so long as the engine is not run too hard. These modifications cost a few pounds, but make the installation much more reliable and more compatible with the requirements of boat propulsion. For inland waters a simple conversion like this goes a long way towards perfection. An air-cooled installation is a boon on inland waters where weed can so often block the intake of a water cooling system. On inland waters not much power is needed and the engine can be run quite slowly, so that overheating is not a problem using a radiator and fan. The soft car-type rubber mounts ensure quiet and vibration-free running.

At sea, where rather more power is required to overcome wind and tide, sufficient cooling is more easily obtained by using the great cooling effect of seawater, and the following type of conversion is an attempt to make a 'marine' engine out of a car engine. The engine is cooled by fitting a pump to circulate seawater through the block. The exhaust manifold, which would get too hot without a flow of air over it, is changed for a water-cooled manifold through which salt water passes on its way to the block. The engine is solidly bolted down to engine bearers and the propeller thrust taken on the converted gearbox, or a marine gearbox is fitted instead. All aluminium parts which would be in contact with the cooling seawater have to be discarded, otherwise they would soon disintegrate. Many successful conversions have been achieved by this method, but it is a trifle crude. The engine runs very cold, below 100°F, the boat vibrates with the engine, and the gearbox is asked to take a large thrust for which it was never designed.

The fourth broad method of conversion overcomes these objections. A fresh water closed-circuit cooling system is used, as in a car, but in place of a radiator a heat exchanger is fitted. Seawater is pumped through the heat exchanger, where heat is transferred from the fresh to the salt water without the two actually mixing. The fresh water can then be kept at a healthy 180°F. Two pumps are required, but usually the original centrifugal pump fitted to the car engine can be used for the fresh water side. The water-cooled manifold and the lubricating oil can be cooled by either the salt water or, preferably, by the fresh water. Oil cooling becomes necessary when the engine is enclosed and run hard for long periods. Cooling the block, sump and exhaust manifold by the fresh water system will ensure that the whole is kept at a desirable 180°F, oil sludging, rapid cylinder wear and poor combustion being avoided. The original car-type rubber mounts, if fitted, will prevent transmission of vibration and noise to the hull, and a separate thrust bearing will take the unfair propeller thrust load off the gearbox. One can add refinements to make a 'Rolls-Royce' installation with soundproofing, single lever control of the throttle and gearbox, and by fitting an alternator and separate batteries for starting and lighting.

Which method of conversion you choose out of the many possible combinations will depend on your pocket, the type of boat and her cruising ground, and any personal preferences you may have.

Suitable engines

Practically all car, truck and tractor engines can be modified for marine use. Some make simpler conversions than others. The difficult car engines are those which drive the front wheels of an orthodox car, or the rear wheels in a rear-engined car. It is the transmission which causes the difficulty. For example, a Mini or BLMC 1100 engine would make an excellent boat engine but for the fact that the differential is in the sump, and there are two output drives to the two front wheels. The overall ratio between the engine and the output flanges, even in top gear, is around 4 : 1, and 14 : 1 in reverse—both unusable ratios. With skilled attention in a well-equipped workshop no doubt the differential could be modified to overcome these two difficulties, but there is usually little point when a similar-sized engine can be used which has a straightforward gearbox. As the gearbox of the Mini and 1100 is actually incorporated in the sump there is little scope for mating a marine gearbox. Car engines which drive the wheels directly, e.g. the Volkswagen or Hillman Imp engines, can be adapted by fitting a marine gearbox in place of the original, although again there seems little point in adopting this arrangement except in the case of the air-cooled VW engine. The fact that it is air-cooled is an advantage on inland waters where weed can be such a problem. Engines such as the BLMC transverse engines, the Hillman Imp and the VW are ready-made units for side-paddle propulsion, where the paddle r.p.m. required (up to 100) demands a large reduction ratio.

The straightforward front engine rear-wheel drive car engines make the simplest conversions. Popular ones which boat owners have used include the following:

FORD—105E, 100E, E93A, Consul, Crossflow engines
BLMC (BMC)—Austin 7, 'A' series, e.g. A30, A40, Morris Minor and the Morris 8, Austin 8 and 10 (1939/47), Triumph Herald, 'B' Series, Marina, Jaguar 2.4 and 4.2.

The choice is usually dictated by the source, but if, subsequently, you wish to buy conversion parts, then obviously the choice must be reduced to those for which conversion parts can be obtained. Appendix 1 at the end of this book gives firms which can supply parts for various engines.

The diesel field is more compact and the following engines are most popular:

FORD—4D, 6D, 2700 series, e.g. 2701E and 2701C and the 2401E and 2402E
BLMC (BMC)—1·5, 1·8, 2·2, 2·5, 3·8 and 5·7

The BLMC 1·5 litre diesel is about the smallest four-cylinder automotive diesel that is used—there is a dearth of small multi-cylinder diesels.

The Perkins 4108 is a fairly old engine but still going strong in various vans, while a relative newcomer is the Golf diesel (1·5 litre) which has a reputation for quiet running. The BL 1·8 is also a smooth runner, as is the Ford 2401/E (2·36 litre). A petrol car engine installed in a boat can be made extremely smooth and quiet running, which always impresses invited passengers. The engine will be smaller in size, much lighter, which helps greatly when transporting the engine, and is free of parts which just cannot be tinkered with at home in the garage. The diesel's injector pumps and injectors can only be worked on with special equipment.

There are industrial and automotive engines having less than four cylinders, but these are not so numerous. A four-cylinder engine is a good compromise between the smooth running in-line six-cylinder and the rough but efficient single cylinder engine. An in-line six is the smoothest running configuration without going to a far larger number of cylinders. A single cylinder engine of, say, 1 litre capacity will be more efficient, i.e. consume less fuel, than a four-cylinder of the same capacity, assuming that the compression ratio is much the same. Single-cylinder engines are naturally very rough running, and even flexible mounts are not completely effective. There are industrial single-cylinder engines used for driving pumps, generators and mini-tractors, but these are, of course, bare engines without gearboxes.

Sources

The person who is going to fit a car engine in a boat is not likely to buy a new bare engine and marinise it himself—the total cost would be more or as much as buying a complete professionally marinised engine. Car engines can be bought from all sorts of sources, and the reader will probably have good ideas himself. However, here are a few comments.

A variety of ex-army or government reconditioned engines are obtainable from traders who specialise in this type of equipment. These ex-WD units are reconditioned to a high standard and are usually complete with all the ancillaries.

A scrapyard will yield a complete engine, including gearbox, starter, dynamo, etc., fairly cheaply, depending on whether it is a 'runner' or not. Before it is worth fitting an engine like this into a boat a detailed inspection and partial or whole reconditioning will be required. Perhaps a more effective way of obtaining a good running engine in these days of the MOT test is to buy a car that has failed the test because of body corrosion. The engine, in fact, may have been reconditioned a short time before, and therefore in very good order. The snag here is that the car has to be towed home, the engine extracted together with all the 'useful' bits, and then the body towed away to a scrapyard. In this way a good engine can be obtained cheaply.

Reconditioned engines can usually only be bought in exchange for an old one. This suggests another method—a scrap engine from a breaker's yard can be stripped of its accessories and exchanged for a reconditioned block. Reconditioned engines are usually sold sans everything, sometimes even without the cylinder head (this is called a 'short' block). Charges for this exchange service are equivalent to a week's wage for a skilled man. Reconditioned engines can be bought through a dealer for the car maker or firms which specialise in this work. The *Exchange and Mart* is a good guide to sources of supply. A properly reconditioned engine will give as good service and last just as long as a new engine. All the tolerances in the bearings and all other moving parts will have been brought up to the 'new' limits. There are, of course, 'recons' and 'recons', and it is always best to enquire exactly how the reconditioning is carried out. The engine manufacturer's 'recon' is perhaps the safest.

Another possibility is to buy the engine from a relatively new but wrecked car. Prices are naturally higher in this case, but the complete engine and gearbox can be obtained, so there will be no problem or expense incurred in obtaining all the ancillaries. There are quite a number of ancillaries on an engine—dynamo, starter, gearbox, thermostat and housing, distributor, clutch, carburettor, oil filter, coil, plugs and so on—and to equip a bare engine is a costly business, even when buying from a car breaker.

When converting and installing an engine, there are some operations which demand work on a lathe or the use of welding gear. Other than these jobs, all the work can be done using simple DIY tools—and perhaps a large vice and an electric drill. When it comes to the lathe work or welding, in most areas there are small firms or garages who can tackle simple jobs. Wrought iron firms, car body repairers, or small engineering firms in industrial estates are usually very obliging. The Yellow Pages in the telephone directory provides a good guide.

Recommended practice

There are some particular points on converting an engine which I would recommend. Fresh water cooling, for example; although severe rusting of the cast iron passages of a car engine will not occur when salt water is pumped through, the running temperature will be very low, and the severe temperature gradients over the whole engine tend, for one thing, to cause gasket leaks. Other failings are rapid sludging of the lubricating oil, greater engine wear and poor combustion. Commercial purpose-built heat exchangers are rather expensive, but I think it is a desirable system for petrol engines as well as diesels. For some reason, most marine or converted petrol engines are direct cooled, which I think is a mistake.

No matter how good the basic engine or the subsequent conversion, its performance in the boat will be dictated to a large extent by the way it is installed. Without attention to the mountings, fuel feed and engine enclosure the best engine can become noisy, rough and unreliable.

Flexible mounts should, I think, always be used—they have been universal fittings in cars since the 1930s. Particularly in the case of diesels they avoid that headache drumming and blurred vision caused by a vibrating deck. Even if the engine is mated to a marine gearbox I think that a separate thrust bearing on the propeller shaft is a good feature. Obtaining and mounting a thrust bearing is not a great or costly problem.

Reliability is achieved by attention to the ignition system and the fuel feed. Inability to start, or a stoppage while under way, is usually caused by a flat battery, dirt in the fuel, fuel starvation or ignition failure. A flat battery after a week's disuse is frustrating; a change-over with the car's battery is the usual procedure. Make sure that the battery is easily accessible. Twin batteries or hand starting will solve this problem, and an alternator will make the occurrence less frequent. The other causes of failure—fuel and ignition troubles—are eliminated by regular attention to the distributor contact breaker points, the fuel filters and the carburettor jets. The variable jet carburettor (e.g. SU) is less liable to fail due to dirt in the fuel. Anti-moisture sprays are useful for the ignition circuit, but cleanliness of the whole engine is a preventive cure for many troubles.

Any engine in a boat should be well protected from the weather. Often one sees engine boxes with the gearbox poking out, or an ill-fitting top which leaks rainwater on to the engine. This leads to unreliability in the long run, as well as corrosion. Condensation is always a problem, but corrosion from this can be kept down by painting the engine. The aluminium parts of a car engine will suffer badly from salt water, so if they happen to be part of the seawater cooling system they must be replaced, but for other parts a primer coat and then two coats of polyurethane paint will make the item last for a long time. A weathertight engine casing, though, is still essential. Most engines, marine or otherwise, in pleasure boats rarely wear out—they usually have to be discarded because of corrosion or bad maintenance. Easy access to the whole engine is very desirable. An enclosure must allow the engine a supply of air, and the best way of achieving air flow with weather proofing is by fitting an extractor fan. This also lends itself to noise reduction, but a water-cooled exhaust manifold then becomes essential.

Whenever possible the fuel tank should be below the level of the carburettor and a petrol pump fitted. This is by far the safest method. Petrol in a boat can be dangerous, but the chances of fire or explosion can be reduced to virtually nil if simple precautions are followed. The chapter on tanks and feeds goes into these precautions, but the Thames Conservancy regulations are a good guide (mandatory on the Thames, of course) as are their rules on bottled gas. A petrol tap and battery master switch are, I think, very desirable items.

When the original gearbox is used the hydraulic clutch mechanism as fitted to the car is the best clutch control to fit. A marine box does enable single lever control, which is nice to have but by no means essential. An oil pressure gauge or light, a water temperature gauge and ammeter or warning light are very desirable, a rev counter and an oil temperature gauge come a close second.

CHAPTER TWO

Engine

Having obtained the engine, unless it is new, reconditioned, or is known to run well it will be necessary to strip it down and measure the wear on the moving parts. By stripping the engine yourself and examining the bearings and bore, thus ascertaining precisely what needs replacing or regrinding, it is possible to save money. For instance, if the big ends are worn, regrinding costs remarkably little. On the other hand, it may be thought easier to exchange the engine for a reconditioned one, as mentioned in Chapter 1. A professionally reconditioned engine and a written guarantee may well be worth the extra money.

It is best to take off all the ancillaries—starter, distributor, etc.—as these may have to be exchanged or repaired, and in any case removal makes it easier to clean the engine. Engines in cars get incredibly filthy, and unless the engine is cleaned off in the early stages work on the engine is for ever a dirty job. It also lessens the chance of dirt getting inside the engine when it is stripped down. Steam hosing is the easiest way to clean an engine, but otherwise a detergent/emulsifying agent such as Jizer or Gunk will help, together with a wire brush and a hose, especially a high pressure hose. Petrol is the cheapest cleaner and leaves a good dry surface for painting. Naturally the floor or ground under the engine during the operation will become fouled with grease and dirt, so cleaning is best done where dirt does not matter. All the old engine and gearbox oil and any water in the block should be drained out first, and the old oil filter discarded.

The motor manufacturer's workshop manual for the car and engine will give the wear and regrind particulars. Apart from the appropriate car distributors, the *Exchange and Mart* is a good source of supply for manuals, or otherwise many motor manuals can be obtained from local libraries on request.

The cylinder head can now be taken off, decarbonised, the valves inspected, and the exhaust and inlet ports cleaned. Incidentally, it is very desirable to put all the bolts, nuts, etc., in labelled jars or tins, as there are quite a number of them in an engine, and as it may well be several weeks before reassembly it is very easy to mislay them or forget which goes where. A spring compressor will allow removal of the split collets and hence the valves. The height of each valve spring should be checked against the manufacturer's figures and replaced if there is a significant difference. Before using the spring compressor, loosen the cotters in the spring collar by sharply tapping the collar. Keep the different valve assemblies in their correct order so that they can be replaced in the same positions. Similarly, push the valves into a piece of card and number them.

Any valves which are cracked, pitted or burned should be discarded. Check in the manual that they are not coated with another metal, because if so they must not be reground, but the seats ground with a used uncoated valve. A length of wood dowel with a rubber sucker on the end is usually used for rotating the valve in its seating. Grinding paste should be used sparingly. This can be obtained from a car accessory shop for a few pence, and none should be allowed to enter the engine. The wooden dowel is twirled between the palms of the hands, first one way and then the other. Afterwards the whole head should be washed with petrol and the valve gear assembled.

The engine can now be turned over, the sump removed and the cylinders and main and big-end bearings examined. A light alloy sump will suffer on a sea-going boat unless it is completely protected, as for instance in a glassfibre boat with a totally enclosing engine box. If an aluminium sump is allowed to come into contact with salty bilge water it will soon become severely corroded. Other than replacement with steel or iron, or anodising, the only answer is to give it a coat of chromate metal primer and two coats of polyurethane paint. An internal micrometer or a bore dial gauge is used to measure the cylinder bores. Depending on the wear that has taken place, new rings, pistons or a rebore may be required to bring the tolerances back to the manufacturer's figures. On small car engines less than 0·003 in. wear will generally require new rings only, providing that the pistons are in good condition. Between 0·003 and 0·006 in. the first size of oversize pistons cannot be fitted, and the standard pistons with oil control rings, such as Oilmaster or Cord, can be fitted. Alternatively, the manufacturer's upgraded pistons can be used. Over 0·006 in. wear means, on small car engines anyway, that a rebore is necessary, together with oversize pistons and rings.

Before fitting the rings make sure that the grooves in the pistons are cleaned out. Use a section of old ring as a scraper. A ring clamp is necessary when refitting the pistons in the bores. This can be made out of a strip of tinplate wrapped around the piston, tightened by a nut and bolt.

The crankshaft journals and crankpins should be measured with an external micrometer at several positions at right angles to each other, and the readings compared with the figures in the manual. Slight wear of, say, less than 0·002 in. will be remedied with new shell bearings, but wear greater than 0·004 in. will probably require regrinding and new undersized shell bearings, to regain the running clearance specified by the manufacturer.

The crankshaft thrust washers may need replacing with standard or oversize washers to regain the end clearance tolerances specified. The end play can be measured by using a dial gauge and tapping the shaft lightly with a wooden mallet backwards and forwards. Camshaft bearing wear is not usually a problem, but again the journal diameters can be measured and compared with the manufacturer's figures. End play should also be checked. The front end bearing (nearest the drive chain) is the most important bearing. The camshaft drive chain can well be renewed as accumulated wear in each link can cause the valve timing to lag a few degrees. Make sure that the sprockets are in the same relative positions, as otherwise the timing will be altered.

At this stage the components can be sent away for regrinding or reboring as necessary. The Yellow Pages and the *Exchange and Mart* are invaluable guides to suitable firms. The firm that does the regrinding can usually also supply the appropriate bearing shells.

Assembly is a rewarding task. The manual will give torque wrench settings to which it is vital to work. All moving parts should be given a smear of oil before reassembly, and the main bearing and big-end nuts given new lock washers or split pins as appropriate. Check that the holes in the shell bearings are in line with the oil passages in the crankcase and crankshaft. The engine may be very tight to turn if all the bearings are replaced. When the pistons, crankshaft, etc., have been replaced the sump can be bolted on after being modified with a cooling coil, if necessary, as described in the chapter on cooling. The engine can now be turned over and the cylinder head fitted, using a new gasket. Indeed it is well worth replacing all the gaskets with new ones.

The correct tightening of the cylinder head bolts is a most important operation. The sequence and torque wrench settings necessary will be found in the manual. It should be done in three stages: in the first two, gently pull the head down by screwing the nuts in the correct sequence using a socket and short bar to prevent overtightening. In the final stage use a torque wrench in the correct sequence. The rocker shaft should also be carefully tightened, since during tightening one or more of the valves will be forced open. After about 15 hours' running the cylinder head should be retightened, to help avoid gas or water leaks. Setting the valve clearances should be done according to the manual. A useful guide as to which valve is fully closed on a four-cylinder engine is the rule of 9 (or 13 for a six-cylinder engine). Turn the engine until the second valve from either end is fully open (as far down as it will go), subtract 2 from 9 (or 13) and valve 7 or 11 will be fully closed. The valve rocker cover should be replaced as soon as possible to prevent dirt settling on the valve gear.

If the starter ring is badly worn a replacement can be fitted at this stage. Usually the ring is shrunk on and a cold chisel is required to remove the old one, while the new one has to be heated to a light blue colour.

Renew the linings of the clutch driven plate if much wear is apparent, similarly the clutch release bearing. Assuming that the clutch pressure plate is in reasonable condition and not unduly scored do not attempt to dismantle the cover assembly, as special equipment is required to reassemble and reset it correctly. If necessary, obtain a reconditioned exchange cover assembly. Reassemble the clutch to the flywheel, making sure that the driven plate is the correct way round and that it is lined up to the crank/flywheel spigot by using a dummy primary shaft.

Depending on the cooling system to be adopted, the thermostat and housing and the water pump or cover plates can now be fitted, using new gaskets. Before the rest of the ancillary equipment is fitted, the engine can be painted, for appearance and to reduce corrosion and dirt collection. A coat of rust-inhibiting paint such as Rustoleum or Plus-Gas followed by a coat of polyurethane enamel suddenly makes the engine look finished and professional, and when installed in the boat, something to be proud of.

Ancillary equipment

The dynamo and starter may need attention. The commutators should be cleaned with petrol and polished with fine glass paper. New brushes are well worth their small expense. Check that the brushes are free to slide in their guides. The dynamo pulley wheels and belt can be fitted, adjusting the tension to about $\frac{1}{2}$ in. play along the largest straight length of belt. If a new belt is used it is well to re-tension it after a few hours' running. Exchange dynamos and starters are, of course, far cheaper than buying new, and these can be obtained from auto electrical firms or manufacturers' distributors.

The manifold(s) can now be fitted together with the carburettor (thoroughly cleaned out) and air cleaner. Again, exchange carburettors can be obtained. As the air which the engine will suck in during its life on board a boat will be far freer from dirt than in a car, an air cleaner is not as essential. However, it is still a good idea to fit the normal air cleaner as apart from filtration it does cut down the hissing noise which a carburettor makes. If space in the engine compartment is limited then the least that should be done is to fit a cover plate about half an inch away from the inlet, to act as a flame trap. The Thames Conservancy insist on a small drip tray underneath carburettors other than down-draught types. The tray should be covered with copper gauze to prevent petrol which has leaked into the tray from catching alight.

Carburettors are usually of a light alloy and when used in a seagoing boat sometimes suffer from corrosion on the inside, interfering with the jets. This can occur from salt water in the fuel or from salt-laden air. The answer is to anodise the aluminium parts. Painting is difficult and unsatisfactory for the parts that matter, and prevention rather than cure is the best solution—a large water trap in the fuel line, a paper element air filter and a weathertight engine box.

The ignition can now be tackled. The distributor can be cleaned and the contact breakers renewed, or an exchange distributor bought. Make sure that the vacuum or centrifugal weights advance mechanism is working smoothly by turning the assembly against the automatic advance springs. High tension cable from the coil to the distributor and from the distributor to the plugs is well worth renewing, especially in view of the damp conditions found on boats. The contact breaker gap should be set (generally 0·014–0·016) before setting the static timing. The correct timing in degrees before top dead centre must be found from the manual. A 12 volt bulb connected across the coil low tension terminals gives the precise moment when the contact breakers open. A battery must, of course, be connected to the low tension coil terminal S and the body of the engine.

Sequence for dismantling and reassembly

	Operation	*Special tools, etc., required*
1	Drain oil and water, remove oil filter bowl and discard oil filter	
2	Remove gearbox, starter, dynamo, distributor, coil, manifold(s), petrol pump	
3	Clean engine and gearbox externally	
4	Remove cylinder head and decarbonise	
5	Remove and examine valves and springs, renew or regrind and replace	Spring compressor, workshop manual
6	Remove sump and examine bearings and thrust washers	
7	Measure journal sizes and have them reground if necessary. Renew bearings as necessary	Micrometer, workshop manual
8	Remove and examine pistons and examine bores. Have block rebored if necessary	Micrometer, workshop manual
9	Examine camshaft and renew bearings if necessary	Workshop manual
10	Reassemble pistons and new rings as necessary	Ring clamp
11	Reassemble crankshaft, bearings and thrust washers	Torque wrench, workshop manual
12	Renew timing chain if necessary	
13	Reassemble sump with cooling coil if necessary	
14	Reassemble cylinder head and set valve clearances	Torque wrench, workshop manual
15	Fit rocker cover	
16	Paint engine and gearbox	
17	Fit Jabsco pump, heat exchanger, water piping, blanking plates as necessary	
18	Fit dynamo and crankshaft pulleys and belt	
19	Fit W/C manifold or original manifold(s), carburettor and air cleaner	
20	Fit distributor, coil and HT cables and set timing	
21	Fit oil filter and new filter, petrol pump and mounts	
22	Renew starter ring on flywheel if necessary and refit flywheel	
23	Refit gearbox to engine and fit up clutch slave cylinder	

A lead from the CB terminal on the coil to the terminal on the side of the distributor must also be connected. (See the chapter on electrics.)

The final items to fit are the filter bowl and a new filter, petrol pump (if mechanical), and rubber mounts or new 'solid' bearers. To prevent crankcase fumes issuing from the crankcase breather when the engine is running (due to gas blow-down between the pistons and cylinders) a rubber pipe from the breather can be led to the carburettor intake.

Testing

The gearbox adds to the engine's weight quite appreciably, so it may be best to keep them separate and fit them together on the boat. If the engine has been 'reconditioned' at home as described above, it is worth the extra time to rig up a bench test to make sure that everything is in order. The engine can be bolted to some large blocks of wood so that the sump is off the ground. Fill up with oil and fit temporary hoses to feed the Jabsco pump with water and, if applicable, fill up the fresh water side of the cooling. Rig up a temporary starter cable from a battery to the starter motor and wires for the ignition. An old tin can act as a fuel tank with a plastic pipe running to the carburettor. A pipe connection can be soldered to the bottom of the tin. Without a silencer the noise will be incredible, so if the exhaust piping and silencer have been bought they can be temporarily hooked up. Follow the manual's instructions to roughly set the carburettor. Prime the carburettor, switch on the ignition and operate the starter motor. When the engine is running and has warmed up, the carburettor can be finally adjusted and the whole engine checked for oil or water leaks. If the engine has been reconditioned it will be very tight at first and will not idle slowly. It must not be raced during the first few hours of running. Running-in can take place just as well in the boat, but an hour's run in the garage will bring to light any obvious faults.

CHAPTER THREE

Cooling

An engine in a car is considerably cooled by the ample flow of air blown over it by the fan, and of course from the forward motion of the car, apart from the cylinder jacket water cooling. The sump is exposed to a flow of air, so the engine oil is cooled on its circuit around the engine. Similarly the gearbox is cooled. Power is lost in the gearbox (only a few per cent) and this power ends up as heat which is transferred to the gearbox oil. At 70 m.p.h. the exhaust manifold, if it wasn't cooled by the air flowing over it, would probably glow red hot.

Even if the cylinders are sufficiently cooled, when a car engine is installed in a boat, in a confined space with no cooling flow of air, it is obvious that temperatures will build up to dangerous proportions. A red-hot exhaust manifold may scorch or even set fire to woodwork that is a few inches away, and in any case is not a good companion to a carburettor full of petrol. Engine oil when it becomes very hot loses its lubricating properties, apart from having a lowered viscosity which prevents the pump from producing full pressure. Heat transfer through the clutch bell housing will heat the gearbox in addition to the internal heat caused by the gears and bearings. Fourth gear will produce very little frictional heat, because the primary and main shafts are revolving as one and the layshaft is only idling around. Third, second and first gears will have inefficiencies and thus produce heat.

This is the problem: not only must the cylinders be cooled but the exhaust manifold, the engine oil and perhaps the gearbox oil must also be cooled. Having set down the problem like this, it is well to look at it from the other point of view and say how the conversion can be simplified, because many boats are running with car engines installed and cooled in the same way as in a car, with radiators and fans.

A great deal depends on how hard the engine is going to work. If it is to work flat out, as in a speedboat, then the full cooling treatment of water-cooled exhaust manifold, seawater pump, etc., must be applied. Fortunately, though, cruising boats less than 25 ft in length only need up to 10 HP for a reasonable cruising speed. Running at this low power modifies the cooling problem somewhat, because the engine will be running slowly and under light load. Even a small car engine, say 1,000 cc, can produce at least 35 HP at full throttle. A car engine producing 10 HP continuously certainly does not need gearbox cooling, and the exhaust manifold need not be cooled, especially if the engine box allows plenty of air circulation. Some people, however, prefer a water-cooled manifold in any case, on the grounds of safety. Similarly, the engine oil need not be cooled if air can always circulate. The original fan will provide this circulation of air.

Radiator and fan cooling

Many stationary engines are cooled by radiator and fan, for instance air compressors at roadwork sites, and it is a perfectly sound engineering proposition even if the engine is enclosed. A car engine, though, does also depend on a flow of air, so installation where it is going to work hard, in a speedboat, for example, will probably cause overheating. Even an installation in a river cruiser using the radiator and fan as fitted to that particular engine in a car will probably not provide sufficient cooling unless the engine is quite open to the air. Boxing-in is very desirable on a boat for many reasons, and there are several ways of forestalling cooling problems if radiator and fan cooling is adopted. The first is to adopt a larger radiator than is fitted in the car from which the engine was taken, in particular one with a deeper core. The second is to design, before starting the installation, a definite path for the hot air to be directed away. The most important point here is to prevent the hot air recirculating through the radiator—the inlet and outlet of the complete air passage must be well separated.

Another trick is to twist the fan blades so that the fan blows air through the radiator rather than sucking. This causes cold air rather than warm to flow over the engine. It's no good turning the blades back to front because the fan will still blow the same way—the blades have to be twisted. The fan can also be speeded up by fitting a smaller diameter fan pulley wheel, or a larger diameter crankshaft pulley.

Concerning the installation of the radiator cooling system, there is no need to say anything here. The usual car hoses and clips are quite adequate. The radiator will probably have to have feet bolted on in order to reach the engine bearers. It is a good idea to make sure that the drain tap on the radiator is accessible, because unless antifreeze is added during the winter, you will want to drain it at the end of the season. Incidentally, river water is just as good a coolant as tap water, providing the leaves and debris are filtered out.

The air ducting needs careful planning. The simplest way is to have an extra large radiator and allow plenty of gaps and holes around the sides and ends of the engine box, with a large grill immediately in front of the radiator. This method causes noise problems, and if you are concerned about this aspect turn to the chapter on noise.

The best method (1) causes the air to flow in one end of the box and out through the other. An open fan will suck air effectively enough through the centre portion of the core of the radiator, but not through the perimeter (2). Air will also tend to recirculate around the sides and top of the radiator. In a car, of course, the forward motion prevents this recirculation and adds to the fan's effect. What is needed is a plate right across the engine box with a hole cut for the fan (2) rather like the arrangement in a Mini. Air is then forced through this hole and cannot recirculate back. It is difficult to achieve a good scheme like this because the very fact of restricting the flow of air through the fan disc causes all the minor gaps and holes in between the radiator and the fan—especially in the bilges—to leak far more air, thus depriving the radiator. If the engine is rubber mounted then there must be sufficient gap between the tips of the fan blades and the edges of the hole in the plate to allow for engine movement, unless the radiator is mounted on the engine as in the Mini. Gaps here are very detrimental to the fan performance. Making a 'turbine' out of the fan like this is obviously the best way

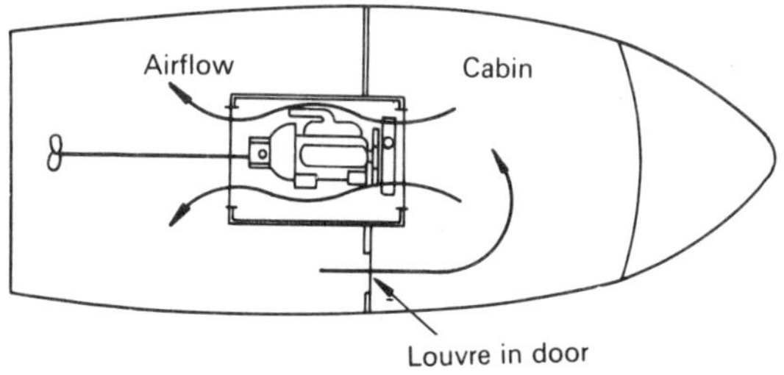

1 Through-flow ventilation

theoretically, but in practice I think the following layout is a good compromise.

What does help a great deal is to fit the radiator as close to the fan as one dares. Blanking off the gaps between the top, bottom and sides of the radiator and engine box will then create a similar continuous 'tunnel' effect (2). Recirculation is bound to occur through the core of the radiator outside the fan disc area, but at least the recirculating warm air is passing through a hot core, thus giving some cooling effect.

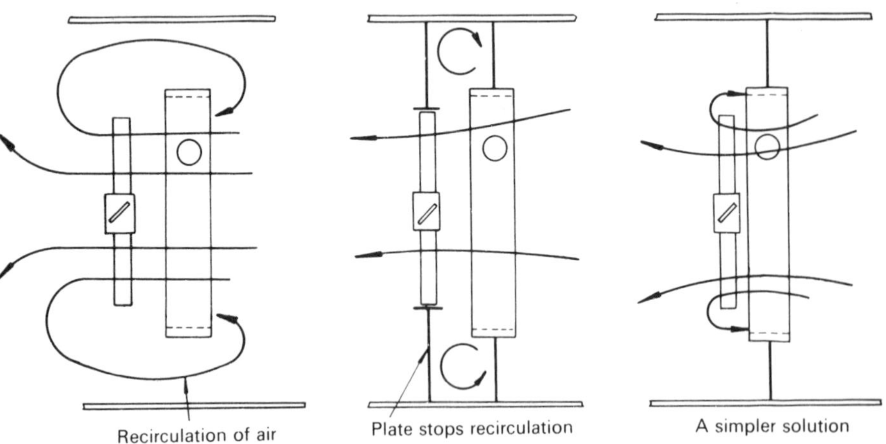

2 Improving the flow of air through the radiator

Warm air circulating around the boat can be put to good use. It's very nice to be able to warm one's feet, or dry wet clothes, or to be able to retire into a warm and snug cabin on a cool day. If the warm air is ducted into the cabin it really is no disadvantage on a warm day (in the English climate), because on such days you would not normally sit in the cabin. In any case, a warm summer's day usually becomes chilly in the evening and the warmed-up cabin and engine give out a comforting warmth for several hours after the day's run is over. Engine smells are not noticeable because of the large amount of air being circulated. Having cruised in fan- and radiator-cooled boats for many years I cannot really see any disadvantage from the hot-air point of view.

The exhaust manifold and engine oil are sufficiently cooled by the fan and therefore require no modification, with the proviso that the engine is not going to work very hard. A normal car-type exhaust system will serve quite well in a boat with a dry exhaust, i.e. one without water injection. Even in a salty atmosphere it will last longer than if it were fitted to a car. If the engine is rubber mounted it is possible not to have a flexible section in the exhaust pipe, by having the first pipe fixing some way from the engine and relying on the flexibility of the pipe itself. Alternatively, car-type rubber exhaust mounts can be used. Marine exhaust outlet skin fittings can be obtained at large chandlers. It is well to lag the pipe with heat insulation where it is within 3 or 4 in. of any woodwork or inflammable material, but otherwise leave the pipe bare to dissipate heat. Bends in the pipe should have a radius of at least four times the pipe diameter, and sea-going boats with the engine placed low down should have a swan neck just forward of the outlet, so that waves and pitching do not cause water to flood up the pipe.

The radiator and fan method is perhaps the simplest and cheapest way of tackling the cooling, as all the parts are standard car fittings and there is no extra pump or manifold to fit. There are none of the problems of possible seawater corrosion inside the engine; the water entering the block is warm and not cold, which would be detrimental to efficiency and long life; and perhaps most important, the cooling is independent of the sea or river. There is no inlet and seacock to bung-up with weed or polythene bags, a great advantage for canal boats.

Disadvantages of the system are the possibility of insufficient cooling, in that at cruising speed the water may boil after an hour or so. There is a fair chance that if no great speed or power is required, for instance in cruising boats on rivers or canals, then the cooling will be sufficient. If the cooling is not quite adequate, another dodge is to remove the thermostat, which does somewhat restrict the flow. The bypass pipe can then be blocked off.

A radiator and fan system is more bulky than a direct-cooled engine and it is more difficult to reduce the noise level. One other possible trouble is petrol vaporisation, which causes the engine to misfire and eventually stop. Heat radiated from the exhaust manifold and engine block can heat the petrol in the feed pipe and carburettor so that it vaporises. The simple remedy is to shield the pipe and carburettor with insulation material. A packing joint between the mechanical pump (if fitted) and the crankcase will also help. Vaporisation is less likely to occur with an electric pump.

Direct cooling

This is probably the most common method. Water is taken in through a skin fitting in the hull below the waterline and pumped through the block and out over the side again (3). There are several sophistications to this basic method. It is bad practice to pump cold seawater directly into the block. Also, a completely water-cooled system like this will not have a fan giving a flow of air around the sump and exhaust manifold. The oil and manifold will get far hotter, and thus a water-cooled exhaust manifold and oil cooler become

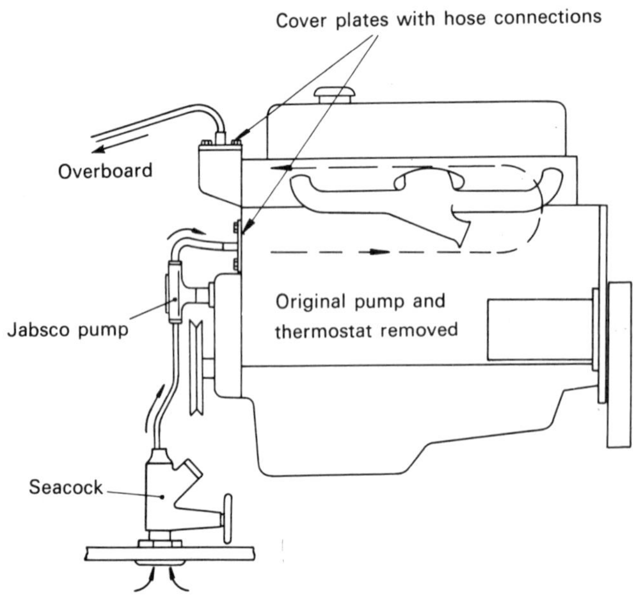

3 The simplest direct cooling system

necessary. The route the cooling water should take is from seacock to exhaust manifold, block, sump. By the time the water reaches the block it will be warmed. Often the water is passed first through the sump and then the manifold, but this may overcool the engine oil. By passing warm seawater (up to 135°F) through the sump the oil temperature will be first warmed and then kept at some temperature slightly above the seawater temperature, depending on the size of the cooling tubes. The final sophistication comes in fitting a means of controlling the outlet temperature of the cooling water. Running the

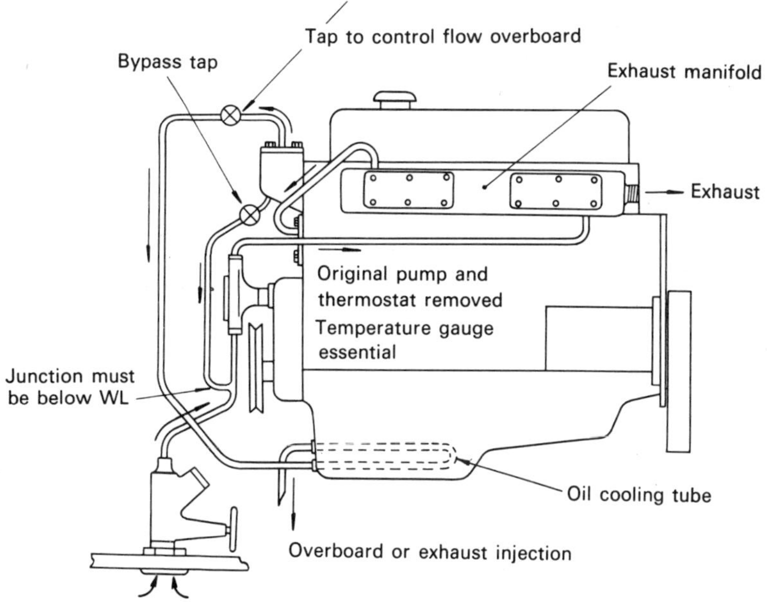

4 Hand control of temperature

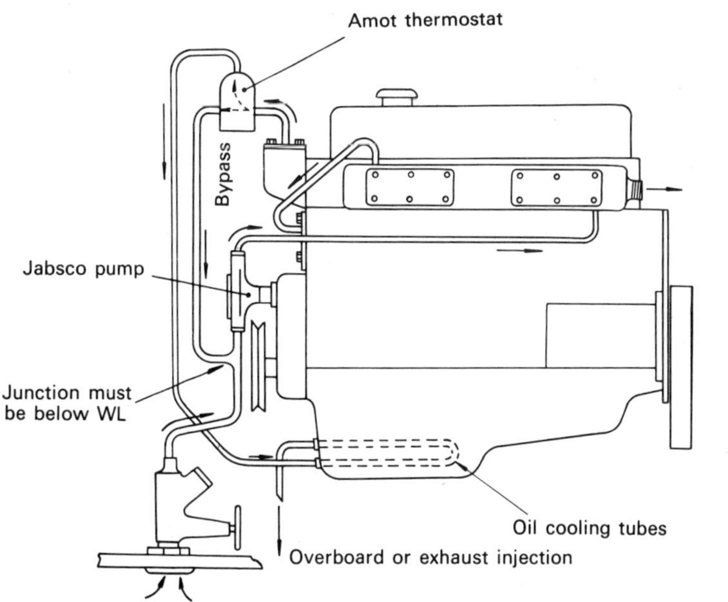

5 Thermostatic control of the temperature

engine too cool will bring condensation and corrosion. A thermostat or a hand-controlled tap will do this job and the final water circuits are as in sketches (4) and (5). The hand-controlled system will require adjustment on trials, but only occasionally thereafter. Note that with a bypass marine thermostat it is necessary to have the tee junction between the seacock and the pump below the outside water level. If it is not, the pump may well never prime, but merely pump air around the engine and bypass.

The outlet temperature should be around 135°F. Above this salt deposition may occur if the engine is cooled with seawater, and lower temperatures will cause condensation and corrosion, apart from inefficiency. Direct-cooled engines cooled by river or canal water may be run at a higher temperature, approaching the optimum 175°–185°F. In this case only the original car thermostat could be used. As a self-priming positive displacement pump must be used for direct cooling systems, a bypass pipe must be arranged similarly to the hand-controlled system so that the pump is not struggling against the thermostat when it is closed. While the thermostat is closed the water will circulate round and round the engine and prevent 'hot spots'. The car thermostat usually has a small vent hole for filling purposes, and this would work well in the above system, allowing the air inside the block and exhaust manifold to escape. For seawater cooling car thermostats open at too high a temperature and a marine type has to be used.

Most car engines have cast iron blocks and cylinder heads. Cast iron is reasonably corrosion resistant, even in salt water, and so there is no great danger of severe corrosion. Direct-cooled marine engines usually have cast iron blocks and heads, but the water passages are generally made larger to allow for silting-up. Engines with aluminium cylinder heads or blocks are not suitable for direct salt water cooling. The specification of the aluminium alloy used for these items on car engines does not include resistance to hot salt water and rapid corrosion would result. Parts like the thermostat and pump housings are often of aluminium and these *must* be replaced by steel or brass blanking plates. The original pump and probably the thermostat will not be needed in any case, so the fan, pulley and pump, together with the pump shaft and bearings, can be taken off. Blanking plates with ½ in. BSP (British Standard Pipe) connections, or tube welded or brazed on, have then to be made and fitted. The lower connection in the block where the pump used to be will be the inlet from the seawater pump, and the upper connection in the cylinder head where the thermostat used to be will be the outlet.

The water pump usually fitted to car engines is of the centrifugal type and not terribly efficient. Part of the energy needed to circulate the water comes from the thermo-syphon effect. It is not a self-priming pump, and if it happened to be just above the water level outside the boat it would, in fact, never start to pump. Nor could it pump water up above the exterior water level into the cylinder head, so unless the whole engine is installed completely below the outside water level the original type of pump is of no use.

Seawater pumps

By far the best-known seawater pumps for engine cooling systems are the Jabsco neoprene impeller pumps. The smallest Jabsco gives a sufficient flow for most small car engines cooled directly. This is the AL-$\frac{1}{4}$-200 or 6640-200. Both have the same capacity of 1·56 gallons per minute per 1000 r.p.m. with a head of 10 ft of water, the former having plain bearings and the latter ball bearings. If the pump is to be belt-driven the ball bearing model should be chosen. Vee-belt driving is the easiest method, as it can use the same belt as the dynamo, but the ball bearing model costs about twice as much as the plain bearing model. The pump should not be run at more than 2000 r.p.m. continuously, which means that the reduction from crankshaft to pump spindle should be at least 2 : 1. The camshaft revolves at half engine speed and this is often utilised for the pump drive. The pump can be mounted directly on the timing chain cover, or on a bracket attached to the cover with the drive shaft protruding inside the cover and coupled onto the end of the camshaft. Alignment has to be very good if the drive is rigid, but several firms can supply a modified timing chain case, together with the pump, for several popular engines. As the horsepower absorbed by these pumps is very small ($\frac{1}{6}$ per 1000 r.p.m.) a simple drive can be made up with rubber hose and hose clips. Belt drive demands a ball bearing pump to take the large side loads (journal loads) on the pump spindle. The pulley should be at least twice the diameter of the pulley on the crankshaft, or a shorter impeller life accepted. If the engine is to run only up to, say 2000 r.p.m. then direct drive (1 : 1 ratio) can be accepted.

Flow rates for direct cooling should be about 0·8 gallon per minute per 10 HP, which would be catered for by the smallest Jabsco pump (AL-$\frac{1}{4}$-200) running at about 500 r.p.m. for 10 HP, and 2000 r.p.m. for 40 HP. Without a bypass system and thermostat the engine will probably run cold. As these pumps are positive displacement pumps it is very detrimental to fit a throttling device in the system, for instance a tap. A bypass must be arranged. These pumps are self-priming, which is a very necessary feature for a direct-cooling pump, as the pump may be situated a little above the outside water level. Jabsco pumps must never be run dry because the neoprene impeller will soon be damaged by burning.

To avoid drive problems an electric pump can be used. Electric Jabsco pumps are available. The electrical circuit for the pump can be taken through the ignition key lock, so that it is always automatically running when the engine is running.

Water-cooled manifold

This item may or may not be necessary. The factors are the type of engine, the flow of air (if any) over the exhaust manifold, and the

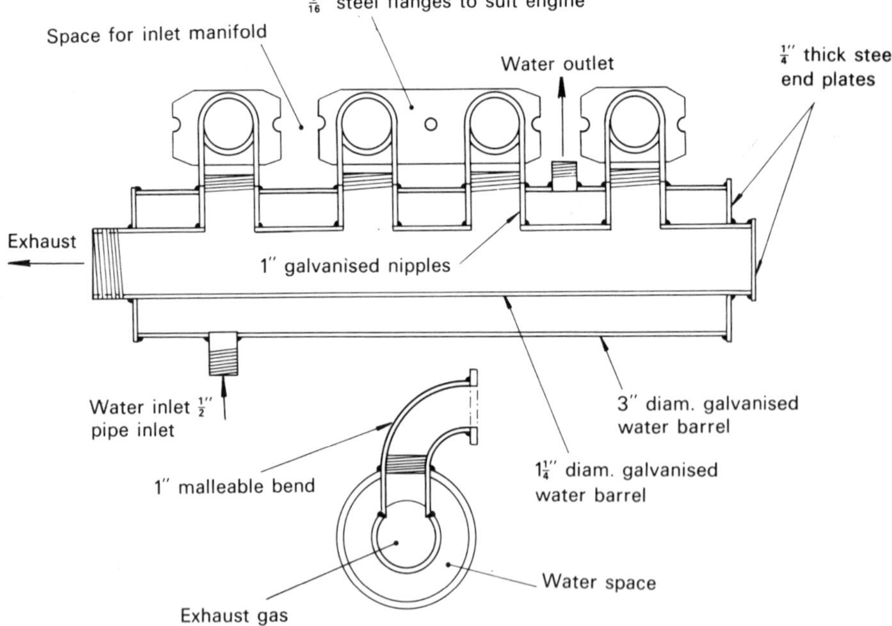

6 Fabricated welded water-cooled manifold

speed the engine is to run at. If the engine is completely boxed in and is to produce its full horsepower, then the manifold, if not cooled, will become red hot. On the other hand, many successful conversions utilising less than the full power of the engine do not have a water-cooled manifold, but rely upon a flow of air and safety precautions such as silicate insulation material on the exhaust pipe and on the inside of the engine box alongside the manifold. The original fan can be retained (with the proviso about aluminium pump housings and with a guard fitted) to create a flow of air. Alternatively, a smaller diameter fan specially made up can be fitted, vee-belt driven at a faster speed than the crankshaft, and situated directly in line with the manifold.

A commercially made water-cooled manifold is a rather expensive item but it is one which can be added fairly easily later on if, after trials, you consider that it is necessary. If you have suitable workshop equipment a water-cooled manifold can be fabricated (6). Firms producing manifolds are listed in the Appendix.

Exhaust injection and exhaust pipes

Turning all or some of the cooling water after it has passed through the engine into the exhaust pipe will further help to keep the exhaust pipe cool. The water will then come out of the exhaust outlet in dribbles and steam, producing the often-heard 'burbling' exhaust note. A car-type exhaust system cannot be used because the salt water or even hot river water would rapidly corrode the pipework. The ideal place to inject water is in the exhaust bend immediately after the water-cooled manifold. There is then no part of the exhaust system uncooled. Hot seawater and exhaust gas is a very corrosive mixture and an exhaust run made in metal does not last long (unless exotic materials are used). The answer is to use 'rubber' diesel exhaust hose and plastic or neoprene silencers and waterlocks. Rubber and plastic materials of course must only be used with a 'wet' exhaust system. In many cases simply a length of diesel exhaust hose from the injection bend to the transom is sufficient (7)—sometimes without a silencer—but only if the exhaust manifold is well above the outside water level. It is important to avoid accumulated injection water running back up the pipe when the engine is stopped. The pipe should therefore slope down as it runs away from the engine. The other danger is from waves slapping up against the exhaust outlet when the engine is stopped and water is being forced up the pipe (or simply the boat rolling or pitching the exhaust outlet underwater.) This can be prevented by a swan neck bend in the pipe close to the outlet, by a waterlock, or by an elevated mixing chamber. It is preferable to take the exhaust through the transom rather than through the side of the boat for this reason. The higher the exhaust outlet on the manifold is above the outside waterline, the less the

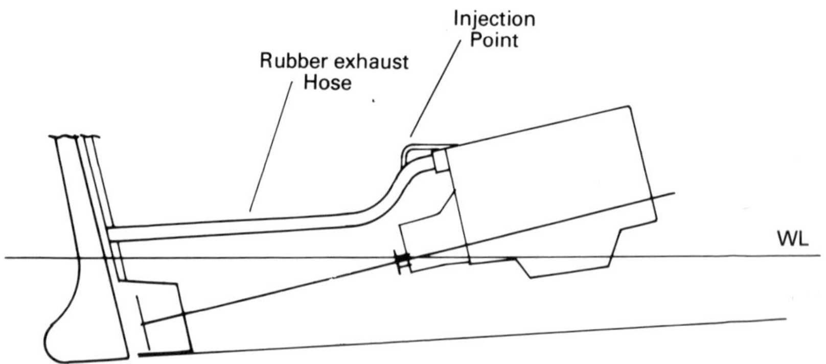

7 Simple exhaust layout

need to worry about this problem. Certainly when the exhaust outlet is only inches higher than the outside waterline then positive means must be provided to prevent water running back. In large deep draft boats the engine exhaust manifold is likely to be *below* waterline. In both cases either a waterlock system (7A) or an elevated water injection silencer (7B) must be fitted.

The waterlock system involves a normal injection bend on the end of the manifold so diesel exhaust hose can be used. There is a distinct possibility of water flooding into the engine via the water cooling circuit with a waterlock system unless the pipe to the water injection point is arranged as shown (7A). When the engine is stopped and the seacock left open water can leak back past the pump impellor and drip through the injection point. This will ultimately fill the pipe and water lock and then flood into the cylinders through open exhaust valves. A syphon break is essential—as shown. Even though

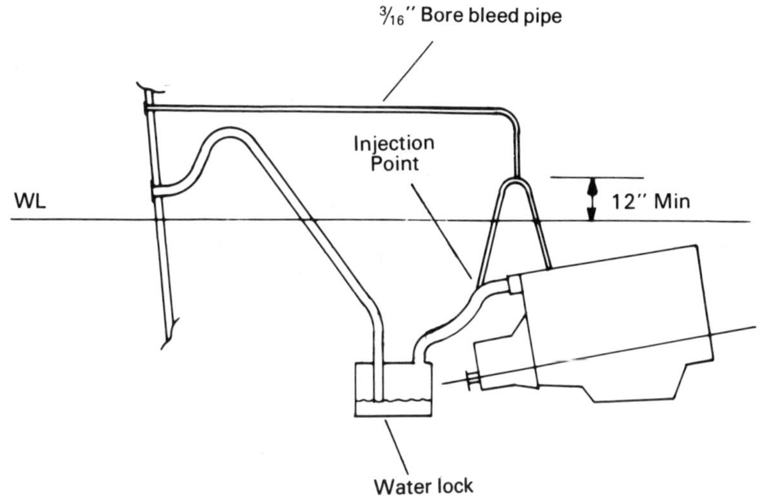

7A Waterlock system

the pipe loops well above the waterline water can *syphon* up and over and into the exhaust pipe.

The water injection silencer system involves injecting the water at a good height above the outside water level in such a way that injection water cannot get down the pipe leading to the engine (7B). The snag with this system apart from the need to find a place for the silencer is the fact that the pipe from the engine is dry (and therefore gets very hot) and needs a flexible section—a stainless steel belows. This pipe should be insulated.

Dry exhausts

With a dry exhaust there are none of the problems above, but there are problems of heat and expansion. Because of the heat, metal pipe must be used and lagging and ventilation are needed. Care must be taken in routing the pipe to avoid fire risks but the heat can be useful, if care is taken, to warm a wheelhouse or an oilskin locker. For petrol engines, piping should be of iron, steel, stainless steel, copper or brass. For diesel engines, iron, steel or stainless steel (copper and brass corrode rapidly with diesel fumes).

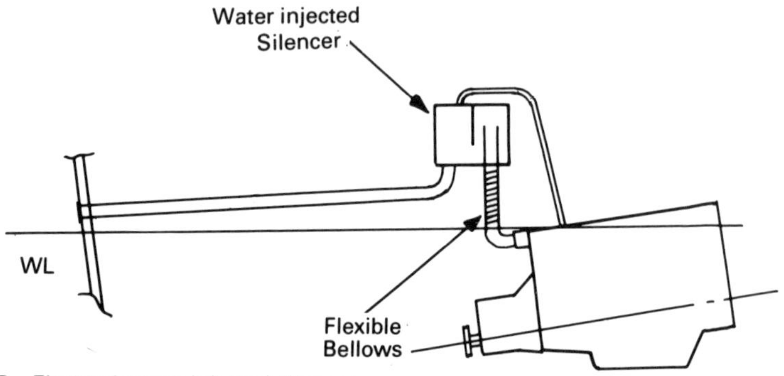

7B Elevated water injected silencer

Steels expand 0.076 inches per 10 feet per 100° F; engine exhausts can be over 1000° F, although by the time they reach the exhaust pipe this will be much reduced. But even so one can see the need for flexibility in the exhaust run. However if the engine is flexibly mounted then a flexible bellows is called for in any case. A silencer will certainly be necessary with a dry system; it should be close to the engine and of a volume 3 to 5 times that of the engine capacity. Whether the system is wet or dry it is essential that the back pressure is minimised otherwise the engine will lose power. Generous pipe diameters of straight short lengths are ideal, bends should be gentle.

Seawater piping (direct cooling)

Readers are also referred to the section headed *Pipe Size* at the end of this chapter. This is usually ½ in. nominal bore copper tubing (domestic size) or rubber hose, the latter using hose clips. Zinc-plated steel or stainless steel clips should always be used, especially on a sea-going boat. There is a very good case nowadays for dispensing with copper tubing altogether and using strong rubber hose instead. High pressure rubber hose having a bursting strength of several hundred p.s.i.

is available and makes the job much simpler. Nylon-reinforced plastic tubing is excellent for cold water piping but becomes rather soft when carrying hot water, and under these conditions rubber hose is to be preferred. Yorkshire fittings or olive compression type fittings with BSP (British Standard Pipe) fittings and threads make a simple job of connections in copper tube. Bends in pipe, unless very gentle, have to be made with a bending spring, otherwise the tube collapses. Alternatively, right angle bends can be made using a Yorkshire solder elbow. With this you fit the tubes into the elbow and apply a blow torch which melts the pre-soldered joint. Bore of $\frac{1}{2}$ in. is adequate for the salt water pipes for engines of up to 40 HP.

The inlet through the boat's bottom must be in the form of a seacock if the boat is to lie afloat. Any undetected leakage of the cooling system could well sink the boat at her moorings over a period of time if there was no means of shutting off the inlet. Seacocks are obtainable from a variety of sources. The seacock should be positioned well below the waterline so that rolling will not expose the inlet, but not so close to the keel, bow or stern that air bubbles cause trouble. It should also, of course, be readily accessible from inside the boat. The seacock should also incorporate a strainer to prevent weed entering the pump or engine. This can be cleaned out from inside the boat after turning the cock off. The pipe up to the pump, if rubber hose, should be strong enough to resist collapse. If the pump is a few feet above the waterline there may well be enough suction to collapse a weak pipe. Plastic tubing is suspect from this point of view, and it is also easily cut, damaged or burnt. Even if the engine is not flexibly mounted it is very desirable to have a section of rubber hose in each piece of pipe running from hull to engine. Vibration can soon crack copper pipe. Even pipes from, say, the pump to the block should have a short length of rubber tubing at each end close to the connections. Outlet fittings through the boat's side should be above the waterline so you can check the water flow.

Finally, on the subject of direct cooling, a few words about the gearbox oil. I have never known a case of a car gearbox where the oil requires extra cooling. Certainly very little heat is produced if 'ahead' is fourth gear (direct). If the ahead drive is taken via the layshaft by one of the usual conversion methods heat will be produced, but even under hard-running conditions this will probably be dissipated back through the clutch housing to the engine. Many marine gearboxes need oil cooling and are fitted with an integral oil cooler. Cold seawater should be passed through this cooler on its way to the engine. As the gearbox is totally enclosed contamination of the oil from condensation is avoided and it is not necessary to keep the oil at as high a temperature as the engine oil.

Heat exchange cooling

Using a heat exchanger instead of pumping raw seawater through the engine is perhaps the best method of cooling a boat engine, albeit usually the most expensive. Fresh water is pumped in a closed circuit through the engine to the heat exchanger and back again. The fresh

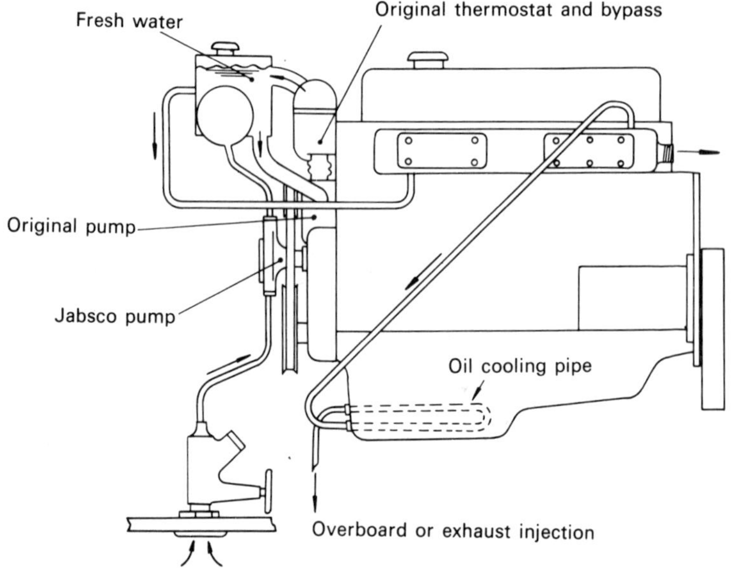

8 Basic heat exchanger cooling

water is cooled in the heat exchanger by the passage of raw seawater, pumped by a separate pump through the heat exchanger and overboard again (8 and 9). This pump is usually a Jabsco or other pump with self-priming characteristics and made from salt water resistant materials. A seawater flow rate of 1·5 gallons per minute per 10 HP is necessary as against 0·8 gallons for direct cooling. The smallest

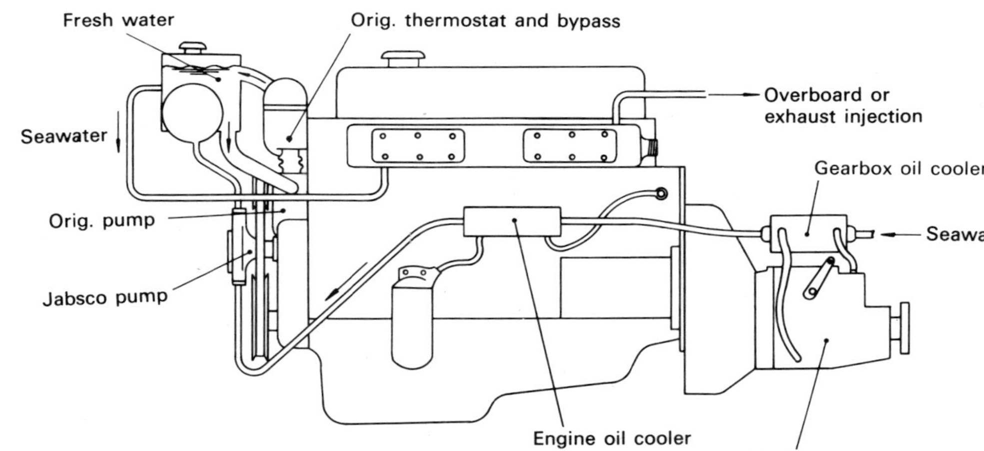

9 Usual heat exchanger circuit. Engine fitted with marine gearbox and oil coolers

Jabsco is thus adequate for up to around 20 HP. The next size up (6540-200 or 2620-200) is capable of 3 gallons per minute per 1000 r.p.m. With an increased flow the temperature rise of the seawater will be less and thus the difference in temperature between the fresh and salt water in the heat exchanger will be greater. This enables the size of the heat exchanger to be kept down.

The advantages of a heat exchanger system for car engine conversions are obvious. There are none of the engine corrosion or silting problems of a direct system, and the engine will work at a better temperature. The existing pump can be retained, together with the thermostat and any aluminium housings. Exhaust manifold and engine oil cooling problems remain, of course, and these have to be dealt with as for the direct cooling system. To enable a running temperature of 180°F to be maintained a pressure cap (about 7 p.s.i.) is necessary, as in the radiator of a modern car. This reduces the possibility of steam pockets, hot spots and undue evaporation. The pipework, connections, etc., must of course be designed to withstand this pressure.

A heat exchanger system is more usually fitted to diesels than petrol engines, because a cool-running diesel is rather more liable to soot up. There are many sources of supply for heat exchangers. Some types for specific engines fit directly onto the thermostat housing, which makes fitting easier, but these are generally intended for diesels. Most types have a header tank with filling cap incorporated in the heat exchanger. A header tank is essential in a closed system to allow for water expansion. Also it is necessary to have larger bore pipes for the fresh water circuit, because the car-type pump is not capable of creating much pressure to pass the water through small bore pipes, unlike the Jabsco pump. At least 1 in. bore pipes should be used. The heat exchanger is usually mounted high up on the forward end of the engine, so that pipe runs are short. The designed water level in the header must, of course, be above any of the water passages in the cylinder head.

A heat exchanger can be likened to an internal keel cooler with seawater pumped into the boat and around the cooling tubes. The simplest type consists of two concentric tubes welded or brazed (10). The surface in contact with the cold seawater, i.e. the outside surface of the FW tube, needs to be a little larger than the corresponding areas as given for keel cooling pipes. Heat exchanger areas should be about 19 sq. in. per HP for petrol engines and about 14 sq. in. for

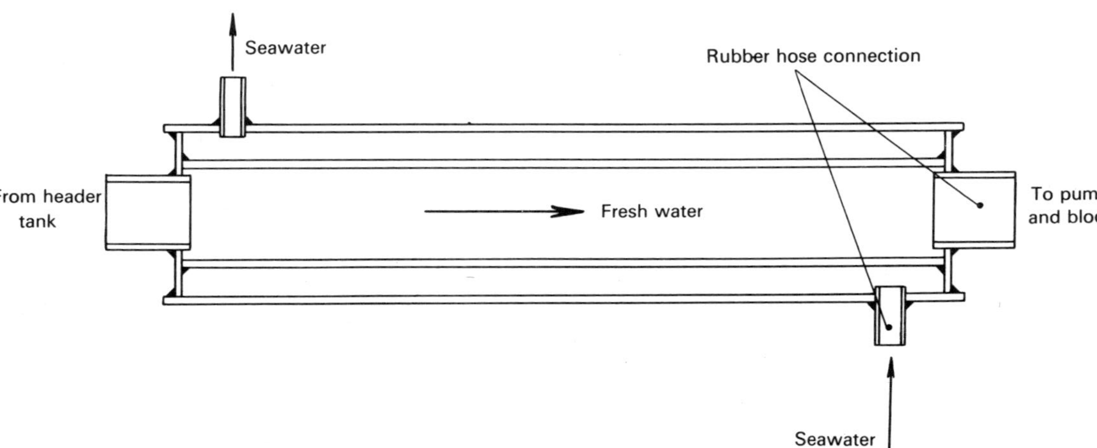

10 Simple heat exchanger made from brazed copper tube and sheet

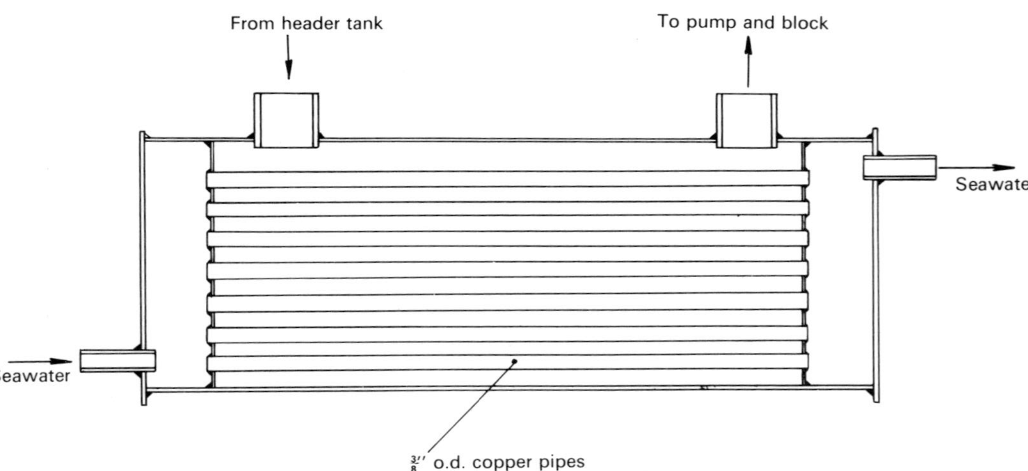

11 More efficient heat exchanger made from brazed copper sheet

diesels. A quick calculation (circumference $= 3 \cdot 14 \times$ o.d.) will show that if the engine develops 40 HP then the tube as shown (10) with a 4 in. diameter inner tube will have to be about 5 ft long, which is rather bulky. Even if the engine is not going to work hard, say in a canal cruiser, the cooling surface area necessary will not be very much less than that calculated on the full horsepower of the engine. If such a large simple heat exchanger can be accommodated, an additional Jabsco or positive displacement pump will be needed to circulate the fresh water through the necessarily long pipework.

Commercial heat exchangers are very compact: instead of a single large tube a bank of small-bore tubes are arranged in parallel, through which salt water is passed. The fresh water is allowed to filter between the tubes, thereby keeping the pressure buildup to a minimum.

By packing in a large number of small diameter tubes, the cooling area can be greatly increased for a given volume of heat exchanger. With suitable brazing or welding equipment a more complicated and efficient heat exchanger can be made up (11). When positioning the inlets and outlets bear in mind how the two parts of the heat exchanger will fill up with water. Air locks can be avoided by positioning the outlets at the top. There must be a header tank in the system, and this heat exchanger must be positioned below the level of the water in the header tank. The two can be combined by leaving more space at the top of the exchanger for a free surface. In this case the suction pipe to the engine FW pump must lead off from the bottom of the unit and the inlet from the thermostat enters at the side just below the water level. The water level must, of course, be above the top of the water passages in the cylinder head.

The home made heat exchanger (11) is a much more difficult proposition to make than the simple one (10). It is also expensive on copper, and steel tube and silver solder may be more practical. Indeed a commercial heat exchanger, especially if intended for your particular engine, is the safest solution. Certainly the original fresh water pump can then be retained.

It takes a dedicated DIY person to make a heat exchanger rather than pay for a professional one; the brazing or welding involved is complicated and must be to a high standard to avoid leaks. Nowadays there are many types of heat exchanger made to fit specific engines (manufactured notably by Bowman). The modern trend is to combine the heat exchanger, header tank and exhaust manifold in one unit.

All fresh water cooling

With a heat exchanger or keel cooling system it is possible to fresh water cool the exhaust manifold. This is preferable to salt water cooling as rust and silt accumulation are avoided and the temperature differences across the engine are reduced. Owing to the insufficient pumping capacity of the centrifugal pumps usually fitted, this is often not possible without fitting a larger fresh water pump or another Jabsco pump (12). In this sketch, which shows a completely fresh water cooled engine, the fresh water Jabsco pump has been positioned in the coolest part of the flow, as the Jabsco impeller tends to expand with heat. The oil cooler is also in the coolest part of the circuit, so

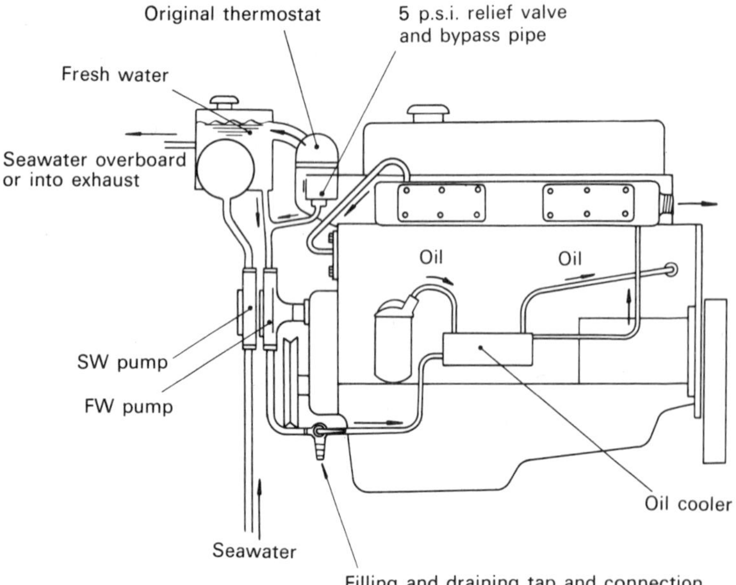

12 A fully fresh water cooled circuit

that its size can be kept down, while the block is fed with water which has been preheated by the exhaust manifold. This ensures the highest possible cylinder temperature for this circuit. The 5 p.s.i. relief valve makes the water flow round and round the block when the thermostat (original type) is closed. A filling connection is necessary in the lowest part of the circuit, because water will not flow through a stationary Jabsco pump, unlike a centrifugal pump. Subsequent topping-up is done through the heat exchanger cap.

A larger heat exchanger and oil cooler are necessary with an all fresh water system, but the benefits are more even temperatures throughout the engine, good combustion at the designed temperatures and a longer oil and engine life. However, these advantages, which are relatively small in comparison to the simpler heat exchanger method (8), are very often not worthwhile, as the attraction of the simpler method is that the original centrifugal pump can be used.

Oil coolers

The necessity of an oil cooler is debatable. Certainly, if the engine is to work hard or is totally enclosed it is desirable. There may be scope for using a car-type oil cooler kit if there is a flow of air, for instance

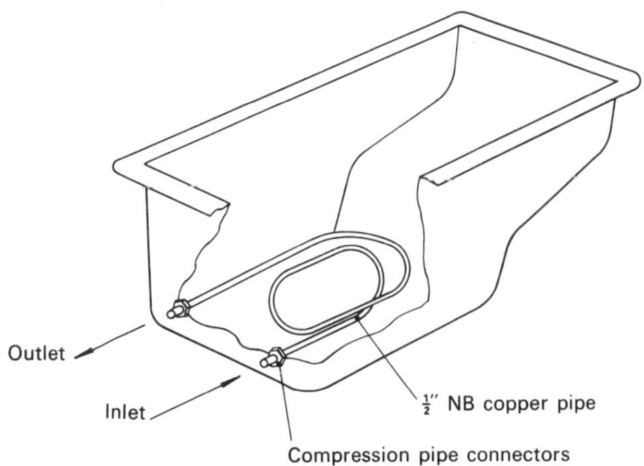

13 Oil-cooling pipe in sump

if the original fan is fitted. A simple solution is to pass the cooling water through a coil of pipe inside the sump (13). Obviously the coil must be placed well clear of the big ends and the pipe connectors must be made oil and water tight. An ideal sump temperature is around 180°F, preventing moisture from combustion being collected and yet not too high to reduce lubrication. It is just as much a sin to overcool the oil as it is to overcool the block. The engine oil will rapidly go black if both are overcooled. Often the best policy is to forget about oil cooling for the first season, fit an oil temperature gauge and see what happens.

There are many types of water-cooled oil coolers available through which the cooling seawater can be passed, to be attached to the block in a suitable place. Flexible high pressure rubber oil hoses will have to be used to connect the filter to the cooler and the block to the cooler. This is the only place in the lubricating system where the oil can be intercepted, and in this line the pressure will be around 50 p.s.i. The cooler must therefore be designed to withstand this pressure.

The lubricating oil may well be overcooled by such a system, which will be just as detrimental as overheating. It may be better, therefore, to pass the seawater through the oil cooler *after* it has been through the engine—it depends on the size of the cooler. A good method, where a heat exchanger or a keel cooler is employed, is to pass the fresh water, on the cool side of the circulation, through the oil cooler. This way the oil is quickly warmed to its correct temperature of around 180°F, and held there. It does entail a larger oil cooler because the temperature differences are less, and a larger heat exchanger to cope with the added heat picked up in the oil cooler. Also, the oil cooler must be fitted close to the heat exchanger to avoid overlong fresh water pipes, which will reduce the flow considerably if the original centrifugal pump is retained. It is possible to fit an oil cooler with large fresh water passages and connections directly beneath the heat exchanger, so that the colder fresh water drops down from the heat exchanger through the cooler and hence to the block. This ensures the minimum added resistance to flow.

Keel coolers

A method of cooling which has the advantages of the heat exchanger method without some of the complications is the keel cooler. It is a closed-circuit system with external copper tubes, usually arranged alongside the keel (14). Again a header tank must be fitted. A Jabsco pump is required to give a flow rate of about 1·5 gallons per minute per 10 HP. The HP figure to take is that of the full rated power of the engine. Because the pipework between the coolers and the engine is

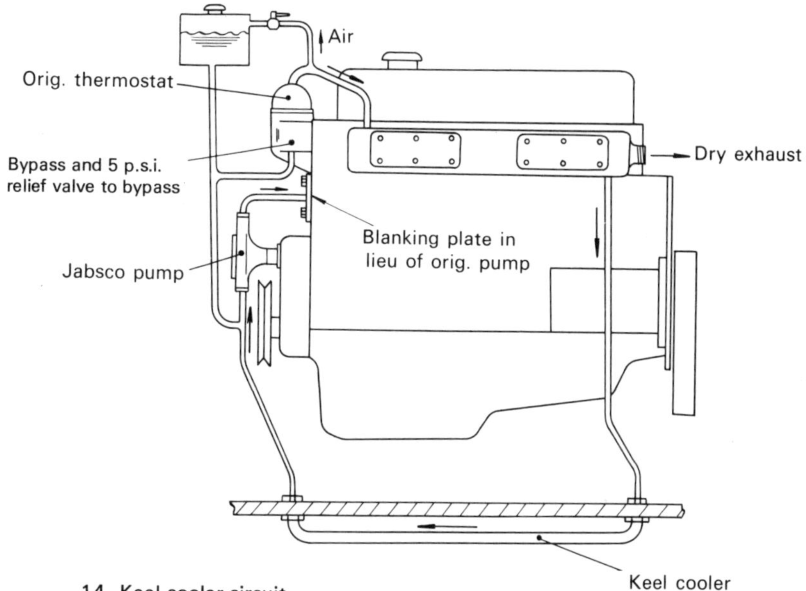

14 Keel cooler circuit

necessarily long, the pipe diameter should be generous. The pump of necessity works in warm water; this temperature should not be more than 120° F if the impeller is to give its best service life. The maximum permissible temperature is 180° F.

The existing thermostat and aluminium housing can be retained, and a bypass and 5 p.s.i. relief valve must be incorporated. The header tank need not take part in the circuit itself—indeed it is better that way, as the quantity of water involved is less and the warm-up time correspondingly shorter.

The very mimimum exposed area of the keel coolers (assuming copper pipe) is in the order of 15–20 square inches per HP (and the horsepower figure to take is the rated maximum of the engine); 30 square inches per HP is safer especially for warmer inland waters or canals, where speeds are low, both factors producing less cooling effect. In tropical waters, where water temperatures are high and fouling is rapid, doubling or quadrupling these figures may be necessary.

The surface area of a tube is found by the formula $3{\cdot}14 \times d \times L$, where d is the diameter and L the length in inches. Thus a 40 HP diesel would require 21·5 feet of one-inch tube at 20 sq. ins. per HP. This could be arranged as a parallel bank of three tubes each 7 feet long. Galvanised steel water barrel pipe has been used but allowance must be made for the poorer heat exchange properties compared to copper pipe.

Advantages of the system over a heat exchanger are that the pipework is simpler and there is no seacock to fit or to get blocked with weed. It is difficult to drain a keel cooler system if the boat is kept afloat during the winter, but antifreeze can, of course, be added. Although it is attractive from the weed point of view for canal work, the coolers themselves are very liable to damage if the boat is used on a canal. They can, of course, be fitted under the transom where they are less likely to be damaged. To avoid airlocks, which can be a nuisance when filling up, particularly if the original non-self-priming pump is used, the pipes down to the keel cooler should have a steady drop without an intermediate rise. When filling it may be necessary to slacken off the hose connections to bleed out all the air. The filling pipe from the header tank should join the closed-circuit system low down, so that the system will fill from the bottom, pushing the air out as the level rises. A bypass around the pump with a tap incorporated can be fitted for filling, or the engine can be started up and run while filling through the header tank. A vent pipe for the air can be permanently fitted, running from the uppermost part of the system to the top of the header tank. If the lubricating oil is to be cooled, the fresh water on its way up from the keel cooler can pass through a large coil in the sump, or through an oil cooler. A large oil cooler is necessary as the temperature differences are smaller.

If the level in the header tank is arranged to be several inches above or below the external waterline, then any leakage in the keel coolers themselves can be detected by the level falling or rising. A pressure cap of around 7 p.s.i. in the header tank will reduce evaporation and allow a high running temperature. Although a keel cooling system has the advantages of a heat exchanger system while being simpler in layout, there is the snag that exhaust injection is not possible.

Tank Cooling

On a metal hull one can use the bottom plating as the heat exchanger surface. A tank is welded in place through which the engine cooling water is passed; the circuit is similar to that for keel cooling.

To get the best heat exchange for the smallest tank the water needs to be encouraged to flow over the bottom surface. The tank should be baffled (14A) and shallow. Aluminium is a good conductor of heat and it keeps its surface reasonably clean and so the surface area required need not be as much as on a steel boat, but even so a tank is not so efficient as keel cooling pipes. So a figure of 30 sq. ins. per HP (the figure of HP being taken as the engine's maximum rating) should be considered a minimum for temperate salt waters. With a steel tank on inland waters allowance has to be made for rust affecting the transfer of heat, so 40 sq. ins. per HP is not unreasonable. Always allow as large a tank as practicable. A box keel makes a good cooling tank, being more efficient than a rectangular tank.

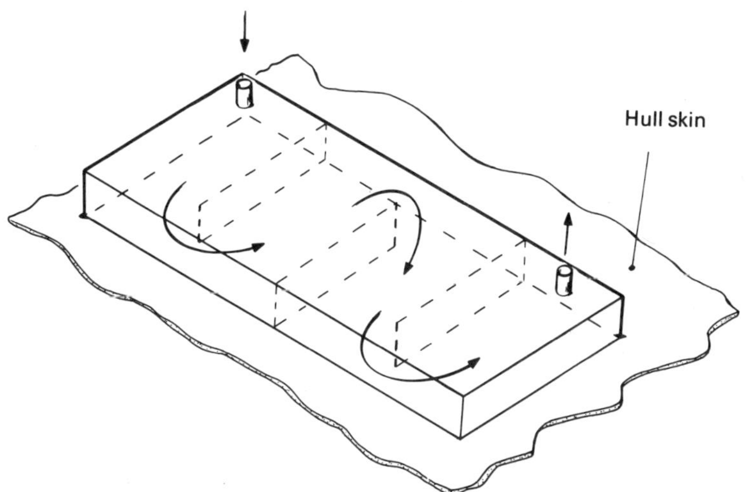

14A Tank cooling, showing the principle of a shallow allwelded tank with baffles.

Engine enclosures

To successfully enclose the engine and apply noise reduction techniques the block, exhaust manifold, and perhaps the engine oil and gear box oil must be adequately cooled. Even so, the body of the engine will be quite hot and radiate heat. In an enclosed space the air temperature will soon rise. Apart from this, an engine consumes a large quantity of air per minute. A 1 litre engine running at 3,000 r.p.m. consumes about 50 cu. ft per minute. Air will flow through natural ventilators at a speed of about 100 ft per minute, so an inlet area of at least half a square foot (50 divided by 100) must be provided in this example. Air consumption is proportional to the engine cylinder capacity and also to the r.p.m.

An electric fan is the best solution, especially if noise reduction techniques are going to be employed, because the smaller duct can be effectively silenced. In the case of a diesel the fan should blow air in. For a petrol engine the fan should extract air from low down; this ensures that petrol vapour is extracted overboard, but it does mean that the inlet to the enclosure must be made larger than is the case when air is blown in.

Whether the compartment is naturally ventilated or force ventilated, the temperature of the air inside must not exceed about 160° F, and the temperature rise over ambient should not be more than about 36° F. All engines lose power when sucking hot air (and also if working at high altitudes) and this is another reason for providing adequate ventilation. Batteries should not be sited where the air temperature is higher than about 120° F.

Pipe size

It is important to choose an adequate internal pipe diameter for the water circuit, especially if long lengths of pipe are involved with many bends and connections for example as with a keel cooling system. If the pipe bore is too small, the resistance to the flow causes the pump to work at a high pressure (or head of water) which in turn, with Jabsco pumps, means that the flow is less. Not only this but the life of the impeller will be much reduced. For instance the ½ inch Jabsco, suitable for the BL 1·5 litre heat exchanger cooled diesel, gives 8·4 gallons per minute at 1,500 r.p.m. against a 10 feet head of water. This reduces to 7·7 g.p.m. against 20 feet and 7·1 against 30 feet. For this engine one wants about 6 g.p.m. From the table below, ¾ inch pipe is just about adequate leading to a velocity of just over 4 ft/sec within the pipe, a level at which copper pipe will have a long life. Faster velocities can erode copper pipe very quickly. Aluminium brass pipe can withstand 8 ft/sec, copper nickel pipe 15 ft/sec. Faster velocities imply higher pressures and smaller bore piping.

If 4 ft/sec is adhered to, the pipe size can be chosen simply from the table below knowing the flow rate required. If a long piping system is envisaged such as in keel cooling, then a check should be made on the head of water (or pressure) that the pump will have to work against.

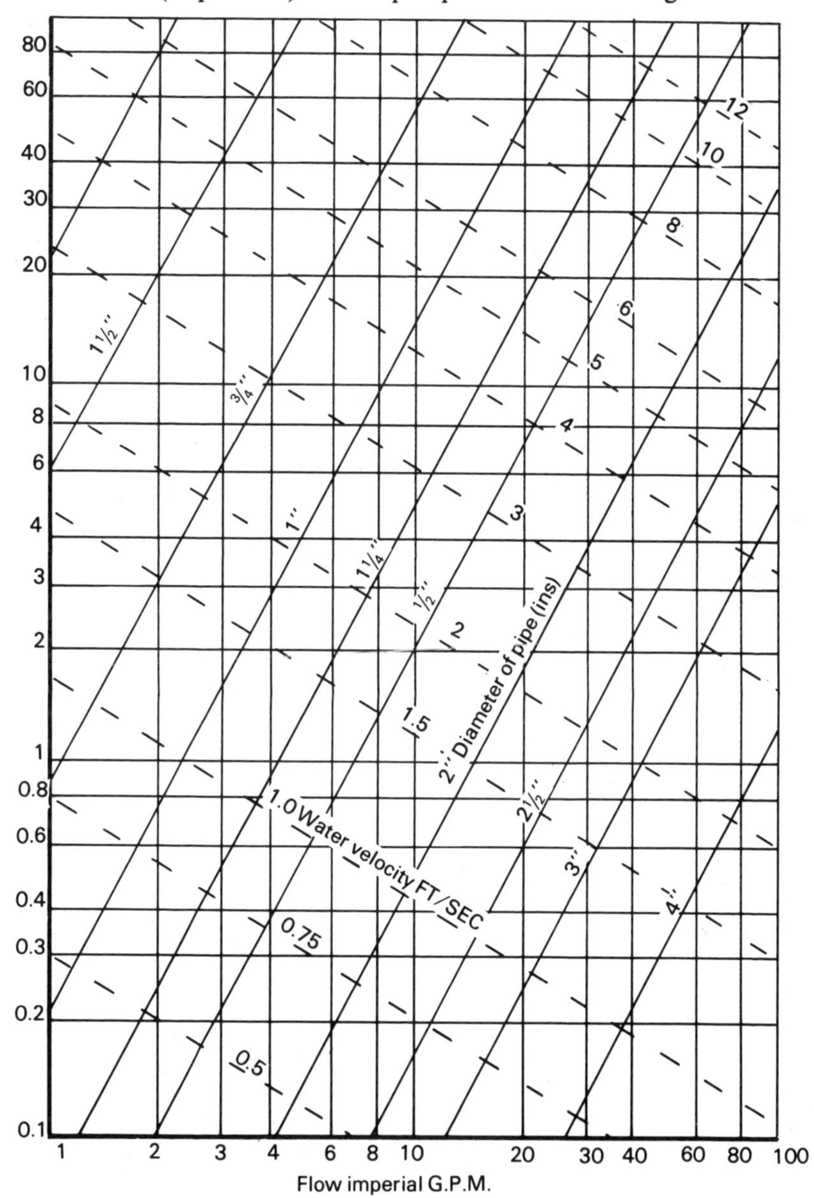

14B Friction losses in pipes

To do this, add up the total length of pipe that the water must pass through on its circulation and then add the equivalent length of pipe due to bends and restrictions according to the table below. From the figures of friction loss per 100 feet of pipe (14B) one can find the head against which the pump must work, a figure to use with the pump manufacturers catalogue. As an example suppose a BL 1·5 diesel is keel cooled and ¾ inch pipe chosen from engine to cooler. If the keel coolers are of 1 inch pipe arranged in parallel (say a bank of 3) the flow inside will be very low and the friction loss small enough to be ignored. Suppose the ¾ inch pipe length amounts to 20 feet and there are ten bends (each worth 25 diameters = 1½ feet) ten sudden enlargements or contractions (each worth 20 diameters = 1¼ feet). The total equivalent length of pipe is therefore 20 + 15 + 12½ = 47½ feet. So from (14B) at 4½ ft/sec and 6 g.p.m. the head against which the pump must work is about 11 feet. (In the general case add to this the height to which the water is pumped if the water is discharged at a higher level than sea level; but in this case, of course, being closed circuit, there is no additional head). Then one can choose a pump from the makers' catalogue that will achieve this flow against this head, and also choose the required pump r.p.m. Low speeds (below 2,000 r.p.m.) and low heads (below 10 feet of water) will prolong the impeller life.

A small change in pipe bore has a large effect on the flows and heads involved. In the above example ½ inch bore piping would lead to a very high pressure. Always be generous when choosing pipe sizes.

4 ft/sec water velocity (recommended speed) for copper pipe

Pipe bore inches	½	¾	1	1¼	1½
Flow achieved g.p.m.	2·4	5·2	9·1	14·6	21

Head loss due to bends etc

Equivalent lengths of pipe:

Square elbow	60 diameters
90° bend	25 diameters
Sudden enlargement or contraction	20 diameters
Strainer twice pipe area	15 diameters

CHAPTER FOUR

Gearbox

A marine gearbox is the ideal form of transmission between a boat engine and the propeller shaft. It gives single lever operation (no separate clutch)—pushing the lever forward engages ahead while pushing the lever aft engages astern. The central position is neutral. The reduction ratios ahead and astern are very similar and usually between 1 : 1 and 3 : 1. The larger ratios, from 2 : 1 to 3 : 1, are desirable for fast-running engines, except in the case of fast boats. Incidentally, in this book I refer to 'reducing' a ratio as coming down from say, 4 : 1 to 2 : 1 in a similar fashion to the motor-car type of nomenclature where 'changing down' means changing to a greater reduction. Generally, propeller r.p.m. should be less than 2,000. A marine gearbox is also capable of taking the considerable propeller thrust.

A car gearbox is quite a different story. Generally there are four different ahead ratios—1 : 1, $1\frac{1}{2}$: 1, $2\frac{1}{2}$: 1, 4 : 1, corresponding to fourth, third, second and first—while reverse is anything from 4 : 1 to 6 : 1. A clutch is necessary to change gears, although with a powerful synchromesh this can sometimes be avoided, and the ability to take propeller thrust is open to question. A car gearbox is a wonderful box of tricks and is quite capable of being converted to perform almost as well as a marine box, when installed with a car engine in a boat.

If you have just bought a car engine for a few pounds, you will not be very happy to spend hundreds of pounds for a marine gearbox, apart from the necessary adaptor plate and bits and pieces to make it fit. Second-hand marine gear-boxes are not easy to come by, but some of the addresses at the back of the book might help. There are quite a number of established marine gearbox manufacturers (listed in the Appendix), and bell housings are available to suit most of the popular engines. Marine gearboxes are usually either mechanically actuated (e.g. Hurth) or hydraulically (e.g. Borg Warner); the latter are usually slightly less efficient and also require a cooler. 1:1 boxes lose 3–7% of the power, those with a reduction ratio lose another 3% or so. Hydraulically operated boxes need only a small force on the control lever to engage gear, which means that push-pull cable is quite adequate for remote control. Older types of mechanically operated box needed considerable force.

The marine gearbox has to be mounted rigidly on the engine bell housing or block, and a stub shaft fitted to take the drive between the flywheel and the gearbox. The stub shaft bolts on to the flywheel using the clutch bolt holes and is splined to fit on to or over the gearbox input shaft. Obviously the stub shaft must be lined up to run true. This is usually done by turning a register in the stub shaft to locate it on the flywheel and then shimming it off the flywheel face to make it run true. The stub shaft must protrude off the flywheel face the correct amount in order for the splined end to mate properly in the gearbox.

The bell housing of the engine has to be modified to mate with the marine gearbox, and obviously it must have a register in order that location will be exact, so that the drive is in line. This is a skilled operation involving a large lathe. Alternatively, the gap between the block and the gearbox can be bridged with four heavy spacers and long bolts. The joining of the two must be absolutely rigid so the spacers should be, say, 2 in. square in section and of solid steel with machined ends. A steel plate over the gearbox face may have to be fitted to carry the upper spacers above the level of the top of the gearbox. This arrangement leaves the flywheel exposed, which does not really matter so long as the starter ring will not be continually wetted or get too dirty.

For the home convertor the fitting of a marine box will usually demand outside help unless the engine is a popular one for conversion and the gearbox manufacturers can supply the stub shaft and bell housing.

There is nothing to stop one mounting a marine gearbox separately. This way the mating problem is avoided. If the box is mounted rigidly it will be able to take the propeller thrust, and the propeller shaft can be bolted directly to it with half couplings. The drive between the gearbox and engine can then be any convenient type. A car-type articulated drive shaft would require little modification, or some other drive could be used as described in the chapter on drive.

Getting back to the conversion of car gearboxes, the big problem is the reverse gear ratio. It will be appreciated that with a 5 : 1 ratio for astern the engine is going to be racing and the propeller idling around, producing little effect. Ahead is simple, as the desired ratio, fourth, third or second, can be chosen depending on the size of propeller.

There is, in fact, nothing to prevent the use of the gearbox and clutch completely unmodified, adopting, say, third gear for ahead and reverse for astern, but after a season or two, especially on inland waters, the need for a more powerful astern becomes more and more evident. It is possible to minimise the difference in ratios between ahead and astern by using second gear for ahead, or even first in conjunction with a large propeller. The size of propeller you can fit will depend on the propeller aperture on the boat, but it is worth noting that the larger the reduction ratio and the larger the propeller fitted, the greater the efficiency. The chapter on propellers delves into this more deeply, but the following example shows the sort of size necessary in order to use first or second gear as ahead.

A 22 ft lifeboat conversion only needs 6 actual engine HP to cruise at about 5 knots. A small car engine can produce 6 HP at a very low throttle opening and an r.p.m. of, say, 1600. Suppose it was driving in second gear which had a ratio of $2\frac{1}{2}:1$. The propeller would therefore revolve at 640 r.p.m., and the required propeller would be 20 in. × 13 in. (the propeller chart in the chapter on propellers does not extend to such low revs). But 20 in. diameter is a very large propeller for a 20–25 ft boat. It would probably not fit in the aperture provided, and even if it did it would cost considerably more than, say, a 12 in. diameter propeller. If the engine were run faster to produce more propeller revs to give the same power and speed with the smaller propeller it would be noisier and running very fast and light.

After reading the propeller chapter it will be appreciated that you can knock off an inch or two from the diameter and add it to the pitch without affecting the overall result very much. If we do this, in this particular case an 18 in. × 15 in. propeller would suit the engine and reduction ratio. This is more feasible, but is still a large propeller.

Running in first gear would create an even worse situation. It is only where a car engine has to push along a heavy sea boat and produce, say, 30 HP that second gear is really of any use. To take an example: a 28 ft cruiser will manage about 8 knots with 30 HP. An 1100 cc car engine will have to run fairly fast to produce 30 HP—say 4000 r.p.m. This means that in second gear ($2\frac{1}{2}:1$) the propeller will revolve at 1600 r.p.m. and the propeller will need to be $15\frac{1}{2}$ in. × 10 in. Notice that this is a smaller propeller than the previous example, despite the much greater horsepower absorbed. In this case the second gear ratio is quite feasible—in fact, if you were fitting a marine box 2 : 1 would be desirable.

The gears in a car gearbox giving first are usually spur gears, which are noisy and wear out quicker, especially under load, and I think that this factor, together with the much greater reduction compared to second gear, excludes the use of first. In the last example above the engine ran at 4000 r.p.m. and the propeller at 1600. In reverse the reduction will be about $4\frac{1}{2}:1$, so with the engine running at 4000 r.p.m. the propeller will revolve at 900. This should give a reasonable astern power, but not of course the ideal, i.e. the same revs astern as ahead. Nevertheless, if second gear happens to be a useful ratio for ahead the box need not be converted at all, except perhaps to blank off the other gear positions so that you cannot make a mistake, for instance selecting fourth when trying to engage reverse.

Quite often it pays not to modify the box at all for the first season, but to fit the largest propeller you can, and on trials simply see what happens. Then at the approach of winter you will know more precisely what is required.

Before getting to the meat of this chapter, i.e. how to convert, it would be well to give a brief description of how a four-speed synchromesh (except bottom) car gearbox works. They almost all work on the same principle, pre-war to the latest models. A short description of how a gearbox works will help you to sort out the gears after taking off the gearcase lid. It is a little bewildering if it is the first time you have looked inside a gearbox. The description is brief—we are not concerned here with the design or details of different types of boxes, but simply how to convert them for use on boats. Incidentally, the AA *Book of the Car* has a very easy-to-understand text on gearboxes, apart from many other aspects.

The main shaft at the top of the gearbox is carried in a large ball bearing at the output end, and a needle roller spigot bearing inside the primary shaft at the other (15). All the primary shaft does is to drive the layshaft through helical gears. The layshaft, then, is always being driven. The second and third helical gears on the main shaft are in constant mesh with their partners on the layshaft, and are therefore also always being driven. They are free to rotate on plain bearings on the mainshaft, and because of the differing gear sizes rotate at different speeds.

To engage third gear there is a selector collar which can slide on splines integral with the mainshaft. This, when pushed up to the third gear, engages with a toothed wheel fixed to the third gear through a synchromesh ring. If the selector collar is pushed the other way it engages through the synchromesh directly with the driving gear, thus locking the primary and main shafts together. This is fourth gear (direct drive). Second gear is engaged in a similar fashion to third with the first/second gear selector collar, again through a synchromesh ring.

First gear is rather different. There is a large-diameter spur wheel actually mounted on the first/second gear selector collar, so that

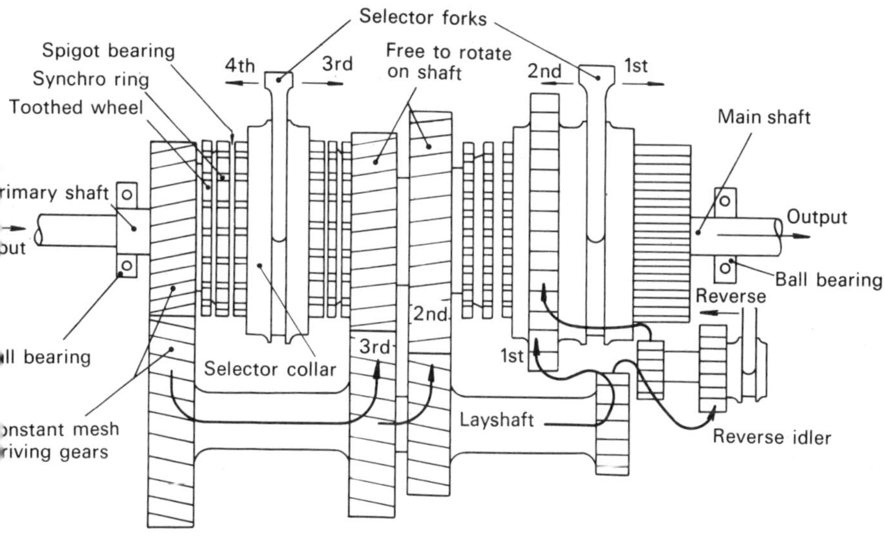

15 Typical car gearbox

when the collar is slid into the first gear position the spur wheel engages with the small pinion on the layshaft (no synchromesh).

You can see that in all these forward gears the output shaft will rotate in the same direction as the input shaft. Reverse is obtained by taking the drive from the layshaft to the main shaft via a small idler gear, so that the main shaft then rotates in the opposite direction. The short reverse shaft has two small spur gears mounted on it which, when slid to the left, engage the small pinion on the layshaft and the large spur wheel on the main shaft (15). The shift in all gears is achieved by a fork sliding along the selector rods. There are thus three forks and three selector rods. The synchromesh ring is shaped like part of a cone and is pressed up against an inner cone on the appropriate gear wheel in a wedging action by the selector collar.

The friction created speeds up the input side until the speeds are synchronised and then the selector collar splines can slide over and engage with the toothed wheel.

When stripping down a gearbox generally no special tools are required. You may be dismayed to hear bearing needles and selector rod balls fall to the bottom of the gear case, but don't despair—there are ways of putting them back. It always amazes me how clean and pristine the inside of a gearbox appears after it has been in the scrapyard mud for a few years. Gearboxes are fairly rain-tight unless someone has taken out the gear lever and allowed rainwater to trickle in. Prices from a scrapyard depend mainly on whether the gearcase is made of aluminium alloy or not. Most BLMC boxes are of aluminium, but Fords are usually cast iron, and only command a small price. Aluminium boxes may be more costly. It is rare to find bad gear damage. The first and reverse gears may be a little chipped, the aft end oil seal may need renewing and the selector rod ball springs may be broken, but these are minor details.

Having cleaned the outside and drained out the oil, the top can be taken off and dismantling begun. The selector rods can be tapped out and the forks lifted out. Make a note of which is which. Watch out for the selector rod balls and springs—these usually fall out. The main shaft will probably tap out with a wooden mallet, while the layshaft will have to be pushed out from one end with a smaller-sized rod tapped through. The layshaft and gear cluster will then drop to the bottom of the box, and clear the way for the main shaft to pass out through the output end, or the top. It is well to watch for thrust washers on the ends of the layshaft and note their number and position before they fall out of place. The reverse shaft may also have to be tapped out. In some boxes it has to be extracted one way only and a threaded hole is provided in which you can fit a bolt. If a large nut or washers are fitted under the bolt head, the shaft can be extracted by screwing the bolt home.

Naturally it pays to keep the parts free from grit and dirt. Upon reassembly the difficulty is in fitting the needle rollers in place. The layshaft usually has free rather than caged needles at each end. To make things more difficult you have to fit the main shaft in position *before* the layshaft and gear cluster is pushed home. To overcome the needle roller problem slide inside the layshaft and gear cluster a wooden dowel of the same diameter as the layshaft rod and pack in the needles. When the time comes to push in the layshaft rod it will push out the wooden dowel, leaving the rollers in place. Sometimes the main/primary shaft spigot bearing is composed of free roller bearings. This is a case for thick grease and patience. Caged roller bearings, of course, present no problem.

Methods of conversion

Converting means essentially that the reverse gear ratio is decreased from 4 or 5 : 1 to something more in keeping with a normal ahead ratio of $1\frac{1}{2}$ or 2 : 1. Basically there are three ways of doing this. First, the actual reverse gears can be changed to give a better ratio; second, the layshaft can be made to revolve faster so that the reverse gears have a faster 'input'; and third, a 'new' reverse can be created by making the layshaft revolve in the opposite direction.

Using the third gears as driving gears

The professional convertors usually use the second method. Referring to (16) the original drive to the layshaft is disconnected and the third gears are used instead. This means that the layshaft revolves faster than originally and consequently the overall reverse ratio is reduced. The intact second and first gears will also be changed in ratio. Second gear can be used as ahead and reverse as astern. For instance, the Ford 100E will give about $1\frac{3}{4}$: 1 ahead and 2 : 1 astern;

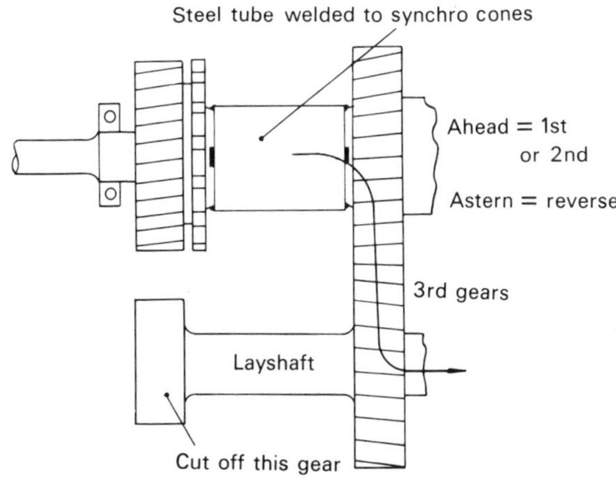

16 Conversion by driving layshaft through 3rd gears

the Ford 10 $1\frac{1}{2}:1$ ahead and 2 : 1 astern; the Hillman Minx (*circa* 1960) 1·7 : 1 ahead and 3·2 : 1 astern; the Cortina 1·75 : 1 ahead and 3·7 : 1 astern; and the BLMC 2·2 diesel 1·75 : 1 ahead and 3·4 : 1 astern.

This method is perhaps the simplest to carry out. The third/fourth splined collar carrier which is itself splined on to the main shaft is taken out, together with the sliding collar and synchro rings. The resulting gap between the toothed wheel on the primary shaft and the toothed wheel on the main shaft third gear is bridged with a short piece of tube tack-welded into place. The welding has to be done carefully to avoid heat distortion and is best carried out in situ after reassembly of the gearbox.

Alternatively, the inner splines of the third/fourth collar carrier can be ground off so that it is free from the main shaft, and this used to connect the primary shaft to the third gear. The sliding collar can be used to connect one end, or the whole thing can be welded up.

The drive gear teeth on the layshaft or the primary shaft need to be turned, ground or gas-cut off, so that the drive is disconnected. The teeth are of course hardened and need to be softened by heat treatment before they can be turned off. This will mean that the shaft itself becomes softer, which can lead to breakage. Grinding on a large wheel with adequate cooling is a slow but surer method. The selector rods of the other gears can be locked into place by small tube spacers in lieu of the springs holding the balls in the indents, and the reverse stop removed. The reverse safety stop usually fitted on a car gearbox is not necessary on a boat, but merely hinders the gear lever movement.

Second gear, being helical, is better for ahead than first gear, but then the gear lever has to be moved aft for ahead and aft for astern (imagine second and reverse in a car). In some boxes this can be overcome by locating the reverse gears on their shaft farther forward than is normal, so that the one gear is in constant mesh with the layshaft first gear (17). Thus when the first/second gear collar is moved about halfway to the first gear position it engages with the reverse pinion before the large first gear wheel comes into contact with the layshaft first gear. The reverse gear can be held in the appropriate place by pieces of tube. The first/second gear fork will have to be prevented from sliding too far into the reverse position by, for instance, a piece of tube over the selector rod, assuming that the gearbox is the type in which the forks slide on the selector rods.

The gear lever movements will then be simply forward for ahead,

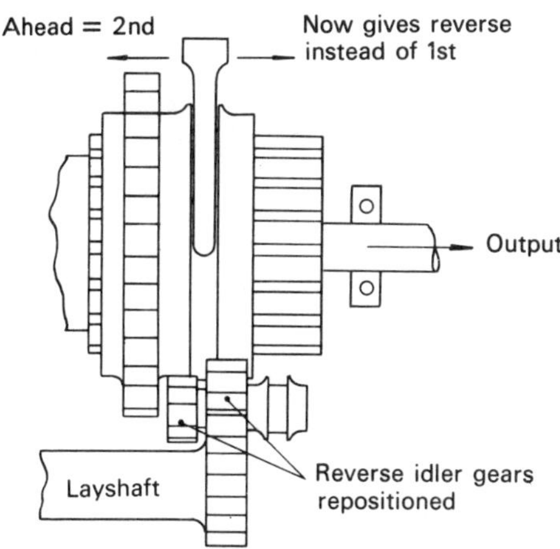

17 Obtaining reverse using the 1st/2nd gear selector

aft for astern, with no sideways movement—absolutely ideal. As I said, the possibility of this arrangement depends on the type of box, but it is worth trying. There is space between the first gear on the main shaft and the first gear on the layshaft to allow this arrangement in the Hillman Minx box.

The other two forks and selector rods can be left out, and blanking pieces bolted or welded on to the sides of the remaining selector rod lug, where the gear lever end engages, to stop the latter slipping out and engaging with fresh air.

Using the second gears as driving gears

If 1 : 1 ahead (direct) is required, the above method of conversion is no good. However, if the drive to the layshaft is taken through the second gears rather than the third, then the second gear shift will lock the main shaft solid, giving direct drive. From the input end, therefore, the flow of power will bypass the original driving gears and the third gears, and go down through the second gears to the layshaft (18). The driving gear and third gear on the layshaft must be cut off and then the only remaining gear ratios are first and reverse, both now considerably reduced in ratio (increased in speed) because the second gears increase the speed of the layshaft considerably compared to the original driving gears or the third gears. In fact, astern ratio will be 2 or $2\frac{1}{4}$: 1. The second and third gears on the main shaft

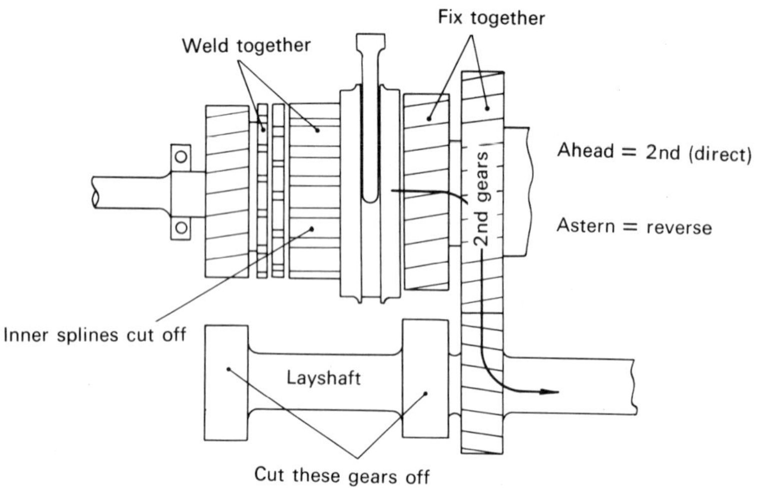

18 Conversion by driving layshaft through 2nd gears

will have to be welded together or connected somehow, or alternatively the third gear on the main shaft and the third/fourth collar carrier can be removed and tube welded directly between the driving and second gears.

To obtain a straight fore-and-aft movement of the gear lever in this case, the arrangement of (17) can be adopted if possible. If not, then the normal car-type movements for second and reverse will have to be used.

Both these methods of conversion give rise to dissimilar ratios ahead and astern, and possibly an awkward gear lever movement, so they are not ideal, but on the other hand they are the simplest methods and use the original gears, which are quite strong enough for the job.

Chain drives

The next most popular method of conversion is more trouble to do but, if properly done, makes a better job—as with most things in life. There are several combinations around chain drives. The one the professionals use is as follows. Sprockets are fitted in lieu of the driving gears, thus making the layshaft turn in the opposite direction. Then all gears other than fourth and reverse will drive astern. If the ratio of the chain sprockets is made the same as the original drive gears all the other gear ratios will be the same as originally. In choosing the sprocket diameters there is scope for adjustment of the overall ratios, so that reverse can be made the same as ahead, i.e. 1 : 1. The obvious 'gear' for reverse is third, so that the gear lever motion is directly fore-and-aft, forward to give astern and aft for ahead (19). If confidence can be had in the chain drive for full power

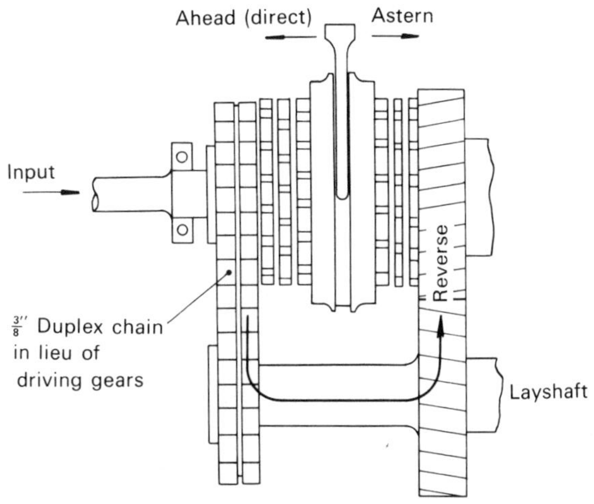

19 Conversion by means of chain giving 1 : 1 ahead and astern

there is nothing to stop you changing things around, so that pushing the lever forward gives third gear (through the chain) for ahead (with an opposite hand propeller) and aft gives astern. To obtain 1 : 1 in reverse the chain sprocket ratio should be identical, but inverse to the ratio of the two third gears. This method is pretty well ideal if you want 1 : 1 ahead and astern. The drive gears have to be turned down to suit the sprockets fitted. Standard sprockets can be bought 'off the shelf'; the Fenner sprockets are useful because of their Taper Lock locking device.

A tensioner can be avoided by carefully choosing the number of teeth on each sprocket, so that the correct ratio is obtained and yet there is not too much play in the chain when it is fitted. The Reynolds catalogue should be consulted.

The other two selector rods can be locked in position by substituting short pieces of rod in lieu of the springs holding the balls in the indents, or by tube on the selector rods if the forks slide on the rods.

Putting a chain drive in lieu of the driving gears is a popular method, but when you think about it, there are many possible places for a chain drive in a gearbox which will give the required result, especially as the ratio of the sprockets can be chosen at will. For

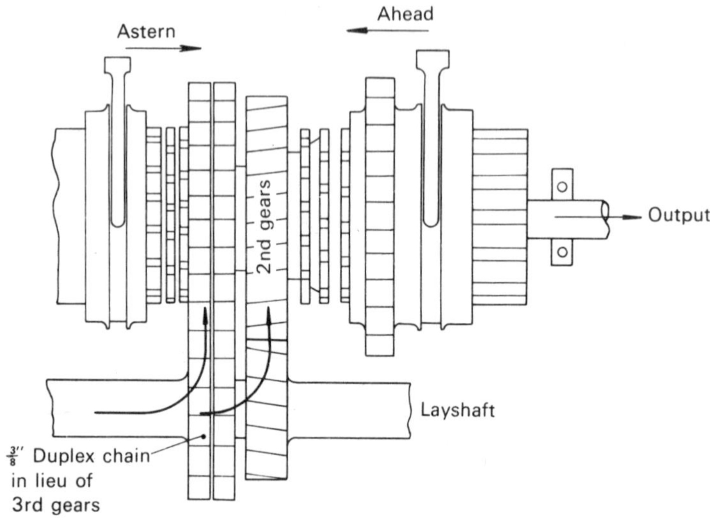

20 Conversion by means of chain giving approx $2\frac{1}{2}:1$ ahead and astern

instance, a chain can be put over the third or second gears. The result of putting a chain around the third gears is much the same as putting it around the drive gears. It may be that there is not enough room in the gearcase to fit around the drive gears. This arrangement has been used in an A40 box, but instead of direct (fourth) being used as ahead, third gear through the chain was used. In fact, the original third gear ratio was retained, so that ahead the ratio was about 1·4 : 1 and astern 1 : 1. This gave considerably more 'bite' in astern, but the engine idling speed had to be kept up a trifle so that when engaging astern the engine did not stall.

If a large reduction ratio ahead and astern is required, as in a large, heavy displacement boat where the full horsepower of the engine is required, then a chain over the third gears offers possibilities. Ahead could be second gear $2\frac{1}{2}:1$, and astern third gear with the ratio made identical to ahead by making the sprocket ratio the same as the ratio between the second gears (20). Two forks can be joined together so that the gear lever has a simple fore-and-aft movement. It is, however, back to front, i.e. to engage ahead the gear lever has to be moved aft. Remote control, however, can easily reverse this movement so that forward is 'ahead'.

Chain around the second gears

If sprockets are put in lieu of the two second gears and the ratio made the same as third gear, then ahead can be third and astern second, both $1\frac{1}{2}:1$ (21). This is a well-nigh ideal arrangement for inland cruisers which need a few horsepower only, a smallish propeller and a good reverse. A good reverse is rather more essential on inland waters than on the sea. The snag to this arrangement is that you have to go across the gate from ahead to astern. This can, however, be eliminated. The two forks are locked together so that they move as one. To avoid first being engaged as well as third, which would then happen, the first pinion on the layshaft can be ground or cut off. At the same time it is well to take out the reverse gears, fork and selector rod completely—or at least simply not to reassemble them. Similarly, to avoid fourth (direct) gear being engaged when reverse (the old second) is engaged, the fourth gear synchronising ring can be removed and the toothed wheel ground off, so that the selector collar splines do not make contact. The conversion ends up as very near

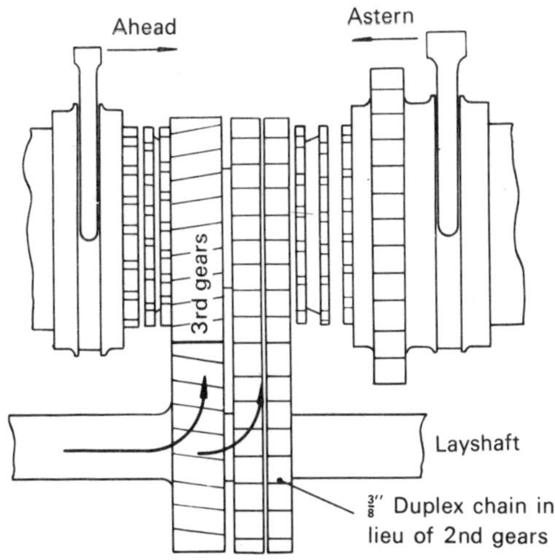

21 Conversion by means of chain giving approx $1\frac{1}{2}:1$ ahead and astern

perfect—a simple gear lever movement, forward for ahead and aft for astern, synchromesh on both gears and equal ratios ahead and astern.

Other methods

Some gearboxes have the gears splined or doweled on to the layshaft rather than in a fixed cluster. The Bedford crash box and WD trucks (1934–51) are like this and enable the gears to be shifted around more easily. For instance, the layshaft can be made to rotate in the opposite direction by the introduction of an idler gear between the driving gears on the main shaft and layshaft, after substituting for the layshaft drive gear a smaller one which does not touch its mate. Then third gear gives astern and fourth (direct) ahead. Apparently (I have not seen this) in the Bedford crash box the old reverse gear turned end for end can be used as an idler.

So far all the methods outlined have created a reverse out of gears other than the original reverse. Another method of conversion is to tackle the actual reverse ratio in the reverse gears. It is not feasible to reduce the diameter of the final reverse wheel (the large one on the main shaft) nor, in consequence, its mate on the reverse shaft. However, the other two gears, the pinion on the layshaft and the gear on the reverse shaft, which is its mate, could conceivably be swapped over. Then instead of a reduction in speed from layshaft to reverse shaft there would be an increase, and in consequence the overall ratio of reverse would be reduced. Reverse would then be about $2\frac{1}{2}$: 1 and of course all the ahead ratios would still be intact. Swapping gears like this is quite a skilled job, and I have, in fact, never seen this type of conversion carried out.

Three-speed boxes can be converted by the appropriate methods as outlined above. In addition, if 1 : 1 ahead and astern is required, the following conversion can be carried out. The driving gears are replaced by a pair of first spur gears from another box, the larger wheel being fitted on the primary shaft. This rotates the layshaft much faster than previously, and the unaltered reverse gears give an overall ratio close to 1:1. Third gear (direct) is used as ahead. One gearbox which is suitable for this type of conversion is the Ford 100E. It is obviously a skilled job turning down the upper driving gear and fitting in place the large first wheel. If this method is contemplated and you have the necessary equipment, then you will obviously have the engineering skill to carry it out. The description of the lathe work, etc., necessary for this and the chain drive methods is beyond the scope of this book.

Choice of method

This depends to a great extent on the reduction ratio required. This in turn depends on the propeller size that can be accommodated, and the speed of the boat which it is intended to drive. The table in the chapter on propellers gives a guide. The table below sums up the result of each type of conversion detailed in this chapter.

Method	Ahead			Astern			Gear lever movement	Other available gears (not original ratios)
	Approx. ratio	Gear lever posn.	Synchro.	Approx. ratio	Gear lever posn.	Synchro.		
Using third gears as driving gears	$1\frac{3}{4}:1$	Second	Yes	$3\frac{1}{4}:1$	Reverse	No	Aft-across-aft	First
Using second gears as driving gears	1:1	Second	Yes	$2\frac{1}{4}:1$	Reverse	No	Aft-across-aft	First
Chain over drive or third gears	1:1	Fourth	Yes	1:1	Third	Yes	Fore-aft (aft = ahead)	First, second, reverse
Chain over second gears	$1\frac{1}{2}:1$	Third	Yes	$1\frac{1}{2}:1$	Second	Yes	Fore-aft (aft = astern)	Fourth, first, reverse
Chain over third gears	$2\frac{1}{2}:1$	Second	Yes	$2\frac{1}{2}:1$	Third	Yes	Fore-aft (aft = ahead)	Fourth, first, reverse
Using original second and reverse	$2\frac{1}{2}:1$	Second	Yes	$4\frac{1}{2}:1$	Reverse	No	Aft-across-aft	First, third, fourth

This table relates to normal four-speed gearboxes as fitted to 'family saloon' motor-cars.

Two speeds ahead

There is the possibility in a converted gearbox of having more than one forward speed. To change up or down while going along is not as silly as it sounds. Many modern tugs have two-speed gearboxes. When idling along entering a lock, for instance, it is nice to be able to keep the propeller turning so that there is a flow of water over the rudder. Changing down to first will give a slowly revolving propeller with the engine idling. When towing another boat a low gear will prevent the engine being overloaded. Alternatively, when running with a strong following wind and sea, or motor-sailing if the boat has sails, a change up would do the same for the engine as an overdrive does in a car. Admittedly this device is not much used in practice, but it is worth bearing in mind.

Chain selection

A suitable chain size can be selected from (22). The space inside a small car gearbox for a chain drive is usually very limited. The width of the gears which are to be replaced by a chain drive cannot easily be exceeded, and the sprockets usually cannot be much greater in diameter than the original gear wheels because of the proximity of the gear case. Consequently small-pitch Duplex or Triplex chains are usually required. To fit sprockets of less than 17 teeth is not recommended for high speeds over, say, 2000 r.p.m. for long chain life. Also the drive, due to impulses from the engine and propeller, is by no means smooth and a selection factor as in (22) has to be used. The selection table is a general guide only, but basically caters for a chain life of 15,000 hours, whereas if the chain is only intended for reverse then it is permissible to take a lower selection factor. However, let us take an example 'straight from the book'. Suppose the second gears are replaced by a chain drive. The ratio needs to be more or less the same as third, therefore the layshaft gear will need to be larger and the main shaft gear possibly smaller. There may not be sufficient room to have a layshaft sprocket of more than $2\frac{1}{2}$ in. diameter, so with 17 teeth this means that $\frac{3}{8}$ in. chain is the largest size possible. A simple chain would therefore only transmit $4\frac{1}{2}$ HP at 2000 r.p.m. or 7 HP at 5000 r.p.m. The figures for Duplex chain would be 9 and 12 HP and for Triplex 11 and 18 HP. At full throttle even the smallest car engine can exceed these figures. Admittedly, the layshaft rotates at a lower speed than the engine because the driving gears give a reduction, and the long life of 15,000 hours is not required, but there is the selection factor of 2·0 which will halve the above figures. Also, in the smaller boxes it is a tight squeeze to get in Duplex chain, let alone Triplex.

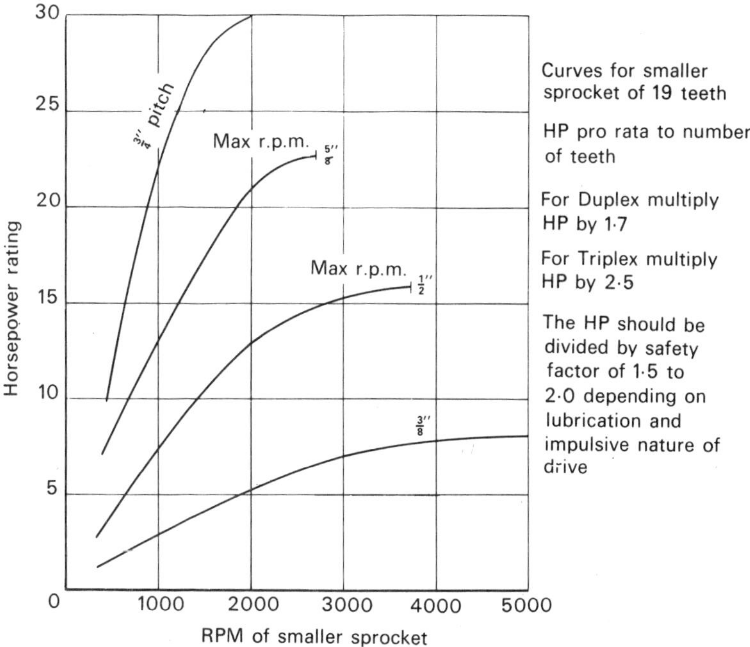

22 Chain drives

Suppose ½ in. Duplex chain could be squeezed in with 17 teeth. Ignoring the selection factor, this could transmit 20 HP at 2000 r.p.m. and 25 at 4000 r.p.m. This is approaching small car engine horsepower ratings, but you can see that to provide full power astern with a chain drive inside the gearbox is not really feasible. If the sprockets could be increased in diameter, thus allowing larger-pitched chain to be used, the horsepower capacity would leap up. Chain drives outside the gearbox, for instance between the gearbox and propeller shaft, are a sound engineering proposition.

Converting a gearbox by means of a chain drive generally means that a restriction on the transmitted power must be made. An inland cruiser with a propeller which restricts the engine revs, the engine in consequence only giving a fraction of its maximum horsepower, will be quite adequately served by a chain drive. Where the full horsepower of the engine is required, as in a fast runabout, full throttle must not be used when running astern, or the chain may stretch or even break. In a case like this it is safer not to use a chain drive but to convert the box by making the third or second gears the driving gears.

Conversion

If you are the sort of person who is contemplating installing a car engine in your boat, probably you are someone with some practical knowledge, but perhaps not the facilities at home, such as a lathe and welding equipment, to convert a box. If you dismantle the gearbox and buy the necessary parts, you then can look around for a small firm, a garage, or a friend with a lathe to tackle specific light engineering jobs. Small engineering companies abound in any country but instructions need to be very specific and backed up by a drawing.

Clutch

Some people who have used a car gearbox in a boat report that the synchromesh is powerful enough to engage gear without using the clutch, and in fact never use it. There must be a considerable 'crunch', I think, when engaging gear like this, because the synchromesh has to rotate the propshaft up to the speed of the engine at idle, and this represents quite a considerable torque. Personally, I have never had or handled a gearbox where this was possible. However, this can be found out on trials.

The choices open to you for clutch operation are foot pedal, hand lever, and combined gear lever and clutch. Older types of engines have the clutch pedal mounted directly on the bell housing clutch lever, while later engines usually have a hydraulic system. A foot pedal protruding above the floorboards is the simplest possible arrangement, but unless the steering position is closely adjacent the wheel has to be left for a few seconds while the helmsman nips around to the back of the engine and changes gear. Of course another crew member can act as 'engine-room hand' and operate throttle, clutch and gear lever on instructions from the helmsman. This is a rather clumsy way of handling a boat, and it is far better to have all the controls grouped around the helmsman. A foot pedal is not a good idea if the helmsman is standing up at the helm. It's difficult standing on one leg holding on to the steering wheel with one hand and the gear lever with the other, when the boat is rolling heavily. Sitting down on a seat with a back to it you feel 'in control' and a foot

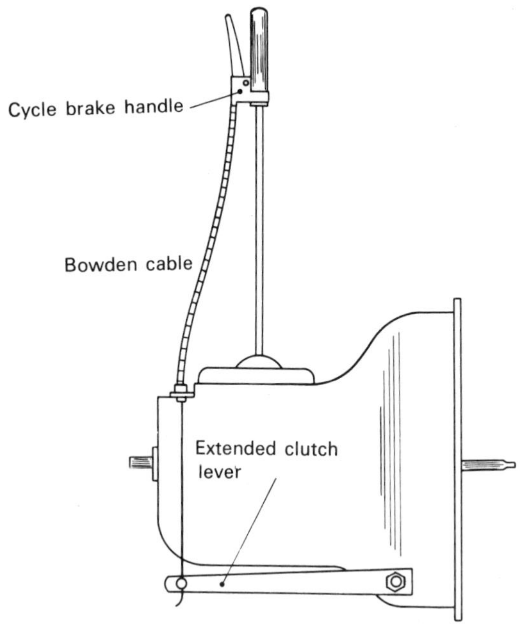

23 One handed clutch and gear lever operation

clutch pedal is then quite acceptable. This is where the hydraulic type of clutch linkage is handy, as the clutch pedal can then be sited anywhere you want. The system as taken straight out of a car is perfectly suitable.

It is possible to make gear changing a one-handed operation. A Bowden cable is run from the clutch lever to a long hand lever mounted on the gear lever (23). A bicycle brake lever is sometimes used. Considerable forces are involved in pressing the clutch plates apart, and the rig needs to be quite robust. Apart from this, a considerable leverage is required to operate a clutch by hand. Rather than give any figures on this, it is easy to see from moving the clutch lever by hand just how much leverage is necessary, and arrange it accordingly.

A more cunning method is to arrange a linkage from the gear lever itself so that when it is pressed sideways the clutch is let out (24).

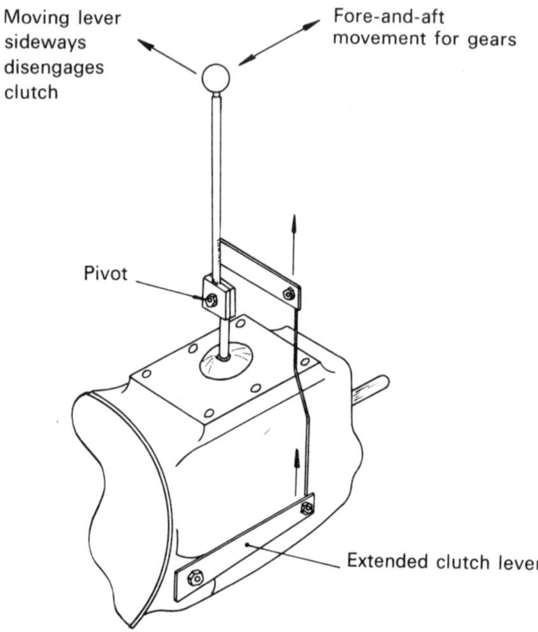

24 Single lever operation of gears and clutch

With a long gear lever very fine control can be obtained. With practice this arrangement works very well.

Quite often it is remarked that the presence of a clutch as well as a gear lever is rather a nuisance on board a boat. Personally, I find precisely the contrary, and being able to slip the clutch to inch the boat forward or take a little way off her is quite an advantage. A marine gearbox is either in or out of gear, there is no halfway mark, and unless the engine idle revs are low the boat surges backwards or forwards too fast for comfort. This perhaps does not matter on the sea, but inland, where many 'coming alongsides' have to be made, I much prefer a clutch.

Propeller thrust

Can the car gearbox take it? Strictly speaking, the answer is 'No', but in practice many car engine conversions can and do. The propeller thrust which pushes the boat along must be taken off the propeller shaft by a suitable bearing, as the magnitude of the thrust is not negligible (25).

The two large ball bearings in the gearcase are designed to take the large journal (lateral) loads imposed by the gears when the engine is running at full throttle. To impose the additional propeller thrust,

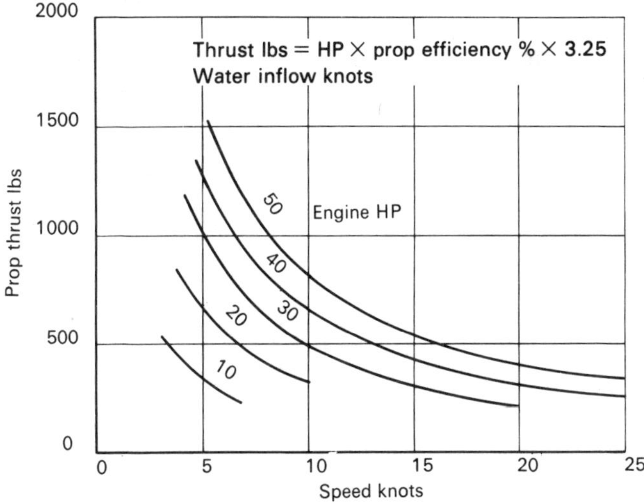

25 Propeller thrust guide

which could be as much as the gear load, is asking too much and the bearing will fail in a short time. The other question is the location of the bearing in the housing. Not being designed to take a large axial load, the bearing may only be located on one side by a circlip. Or it may not be located inside at all, in which case the bearing would creep down its housing until the load was actually being taken on the spigot bearing between the main and primary shafts. When the bearing is just pressed into the housing like this the end float is usually taken up in a thrust washer or ball inside the spigot bearing. This will certainly come to grief if the full propeller load is applied.

Having said all this, I will now look at it from the other point of view. The first thing to do is to look inside the box at the after bearing and imagine the mainshaft from the coupling forward being pushed against heavily (26). It will probably be that the half coupling transfers load through the speedometer worm and a sleeve directly on to the inner race of the bearing. The outer race may have a lip which would press against the casing—all well and good. Astern thrust will probably be resisted by the first/second gear splined hub, which presses up against the inner race. The outer race may have a circlip to prevent the bearing being pushed out aft. Obviously, different boxes have different arrangements, and it is only by careful inspection that the result of applying *axial* thrust becomes known.

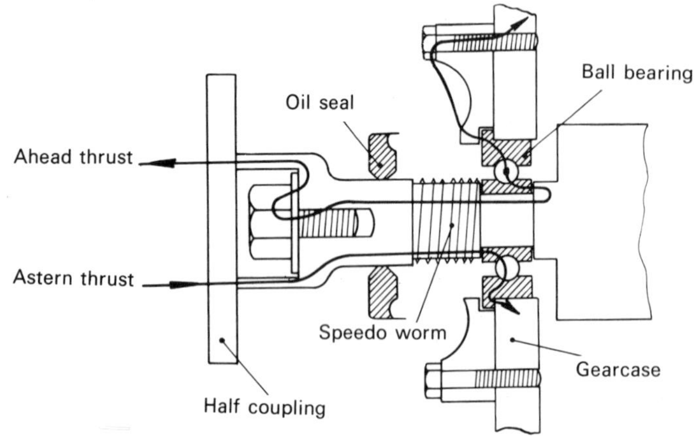

26 Example of a well retained aft-end ball bearing

For instance, the Hillman Minx box (*circa* 1960) has an after bearing which is sandwiched in position in the gearcase by the light alloy end piece. It may be quite simple to retain the bearing firmly by a bolted-on cover plate, for example.

Another factor which decides whether the after ball bearing can take the propeller thrust is which gear the box will be run in for ahead. Fourth gear (direct) will impose no journal bearing loads on the after bearing. Third will only impose a little, because the third gears are nearer to the forward end than the aft end. Second gear will be worse, and first the worst of all, because the first gears are bang up against the after ball bearing, which will take the entire journal load.

The third factor is the dynamic capacity of the actual bearing. Ball bearings are capable of taking axial and journal loads, the sum of which must not exceed a certain value depending on the size and type of the bearing. The table below gives the approximate maximum permissible load of standard rigid single row ball bearings and the RHP designation. Incidentally, bearings of the same size made by different manufacturers are interchangeable.

Bore in.	$\frac{3}{4}$	$\frac{7}{8}$	1	$1\frac{1}{8}$	$1\frac{1}{4}$	$1\frac{1}{2}$
LJ	440	440	710	710	750	1120 lb
MJ	550	600	730	1050	1200	1550 lb

These figures are for steady conditions, a speed of 1000 r.p.m. and a life of 7500 hours. For higher speeds the permissible load should be factored down, for example, at 4000 r.p.m. only 0·63 of the above load figures should be taken. Under gearbox conditions the bearing will not be operating under a steady load and the working loads above should be halved. On the other hand, a life of 7500 hours could be considered excessive in a pleasure boat, and this last factor ignored.

So—what conclusion can we reach? Take a 5–6 knot 18–22 ft cruiser where the engine is only going to be asked to deliver up to 8 HP at 2000 r.p.m. The propeller thrust would be about 220 lb, so the total would be 320 lb including the journal load, which is within the capacity of small car gearbox bearings, which are around 1 in. bore. So, providing the bearing is located securely it would be in order to allow it to take the propeller thrust in this case.

At the other end of the scale, imagine a heavy displacement sea-going craft which needed 40 HP to do 8 knots. The propeller thrust would be about 800 lb, and if the box were running in second gear the gear load would bring the total bearing load to about 1300 lb. For continuous running this is not acceptable. A light fast runabout making use of the full horsepower of the engine would not create such a large propeller thrust load, because the speed would be so much higher. This is an odd fact, but horsepower for horsepower the thrust drops as the speed increases. A runabout would probably use fourth (direct) gear, so there would be no journal load.

Incidentally, different propellers, driven through different reduction ratios but absorbing the *same* horsepower, will give much the same boat speeds and thrust. This is why propeller size has been omitted in the above examples, although a larger reduction ratio and a larger propeller will give slightly greater efficiency and therefore thrust, and therefore speed, at the *same* horsepower. The difference is only in the order of up to 15%.

If it is decided that the gearbox cannot take the thrust a separate thrust box on the propeller shaft must be resorted to. There are advantages to be had in this arrangement as discussed in the chapter on drives. Alternatively, a thrust bearing can be mounted on the end of the gearbox, but this, I think, is very rarely done, a separate thrust bearing being no more difficult.

Oil seal

The oil seal fitted at the back end of the box sometimes gives trouble when the box is operating in a boat. This occurs when the propeller thrust is taken by the end bearing in the box, because of the greater lateral wobbling that takes place. If a separate thrust bearing is fitted so that the gearbox is free from thrust and only delivers a torque, then the oil seal will be working in exactly the same conditions as in a car. The worst situation occurs when the propeller thrust is taken at an angle through an articulated joint, for instance when the prop shaft and engine are not in line and the thrust and drive are taken through a car-type universal joint. Obviously the oil seal will be asked to take up far greater deflection in the running of the shaft, and will wear out more quickly. Nevertheless, many gearboxes and drives are fitted like this and appear to work quite well. It is probably a matter of a reduced oil seal life from, say, 3000 hours to 1000 in relation to the running time of an engine in a pleasure boat of, say, 100 hours a year.

CHAPTER FIVE

Mounting and Drive

Basically there are two ways of mounting the engine on the boat's engine bearers—solidly or flexibly. The traditional method is to bolt the engine down solidly and bolt the propeller shaft rigidly to the gearbox output flange, with two half couplings. Obviously, if this is done the engine must be lined up very accurately with the propeller shaft if excessive vibration and wear on the stern tube and gearbox bearings and seal is not to take place. In motor-cars it is standard practice, and has been for many years, to mount the engine flexibly to reduce vibration and noise, and if a car engine is fitted in a boat it is very nice to take advantage of the flexible mounts already available for that particular engine. The great advantage is that noise and vibration will be much less than from a solidly mounted engine. Usually solidly mounted engines have certain engine speeds which cause the boat to vibrate badly. A flexibly mounted engine (with correct mounts) will not give unpleasant vibration at any speed, even in a lightly built boat. Car engine rubber mounts only support the weight and torque of the engine; they are not capable of taking the thrust from the propeller when the engine is installed in a boat. Marine type rubber mounts are designed to cater for this load.

There are snags to a flexibly mounted engine. The propeller thrust has to be separately arranged, a flexible drive fitted, and all connections to the engine made flexible. It is usually these problems that often cause private owners and commercial engine converters to arrange their engines for solid mounting. The biggest problem is the propeller thrust and drive. To completely isolate the engine, as it is when fitted in a car (i.e. it is free to float, and only produces a torque), a separate thrust bearing is necessary on the propeller shaft. A flexible drive is then necessary between the thrust bearing and the gearbox, to allow for engine movement (27).

If the gearbox is capable of taking the propeller thrust, then there is a way of avoiding a separate thrust bearing and yet still having the engine flexibly mounted. The engine is restrained from moving very far forward or aft by separate rubber buffer blocks and the propeller shaft is connected to the gearbox by a flexible coupling capable of taking axial load (the propeller thrust). The stern tube must have a

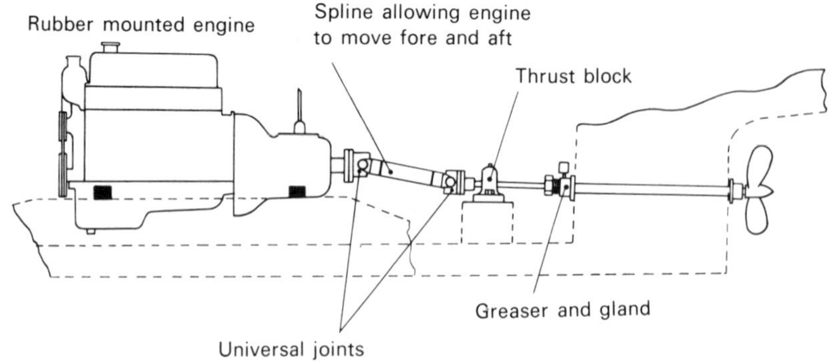

27 Using car-type components for a flexible drive

rubber after bearing and the greaser and gland connected by a rubber tube fitted with hose clips (28). Alignment must still be fairly good. The disadvantage of this method is that the engine is not fully free to move, and a flexible stern tube is essential. The car-type Hardy Spicer articulated joint can be used instead of a flexible coupling with this arrangement for low horsepower where the engine is not going to work very hard, as these joints are capable of taking a small axial load providing the angle of articulation is small.

As car engines are always flexibly mounted, the mounts, the articulated drive and the flexible exhaust, petrol pipe, water hoses, etc., can all be used complete, with advantage, in a boat. So I will consider this arrangement first.

Car engines usually have two rubber mounts at the forward end inclined at an angle, and one or two under the gearbox. Welded steel angle bar can be made up to span the engine bearers to suit the

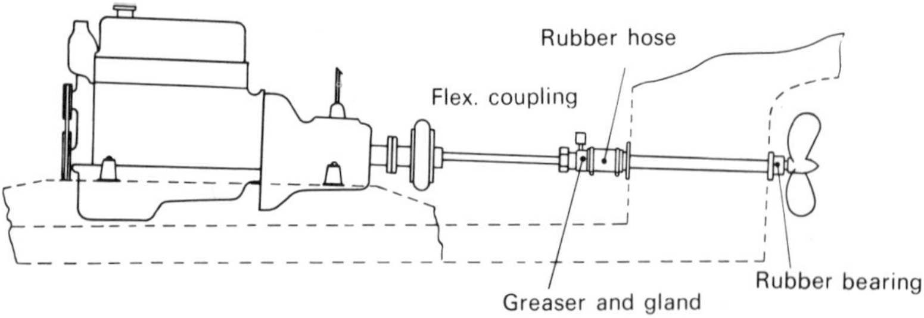

Rubber mounted engine
Mounts capable of taking prop thrust
Rubber hose
Flex. coupling
Rubber bearing
Greaser and gland

28 Marine mounts, flexible coupling and flexible stern tube

position and angle of the rubber mounts. Alternatively, wooden blocks can be bolted to the bearers to suit the mounts at the forward end (29). If engine bearers are being fitted in a bare hull they should be as massive as possible. Sheer mass and length, and numerous connections to sides, bulkheads and planks, will improve the vibration situation whether the engine is to be flexibly or rigidly mounted. In a glassfibre boat it is essential to glass in transverse stiffeners connecting to the longitudinal bearers. Longitudinal bearers are traditional, and they should run for at least a third of the boat's

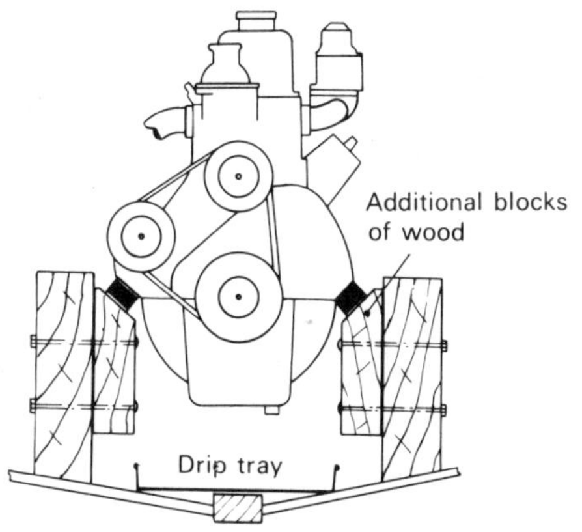

29 One method of supporting the engine on its rubber mounts

length. There is nothing against transverse bearers, providing they connect to the sides by running right up to the turn of the bilge. The steel angle bar to suit the flexible mounts can be coach-screwed to the bearers, although long bolts with recesses cut in the sides of the bearers to take the nuts are naturally a better fastening.

The maximum angle of articulation of a car-type Hardy Spicer joint is 15°, so probably the engine can be mounted more or less horizontally. In any case, a car engine should be mounted so that when the boat is under way, perhaps with a few degrees of stern trim, the angle of the crankshaft to the horizontal is no more than about 10°. The important point here is that the level of oil in the sump may be dangerously near the bottom end of the oil pump suction pipe. Another point to bear in mind when mounting the engine is how to drain the sump, the gearbox oil and the cylinder block water. The latter will probably create no difficulty, but the sump and gearbox drain plugs usually become inaccessible in the bilges of a boat. The simple solution here is to fit a hand pump with a two-way cock and pipe connections to the two drain holes (30). The existing drain hole tapping can be utilised, or another hole drilled and tapped $\frac{1}{2}$ in. BSP. A simpler method is to obtain a hand pump and fit on it a suction pipe small enough to fit down the dipstick hole. A drip tray is a sensible thing to fit underneath the engine. On the Thames this is compulsory.

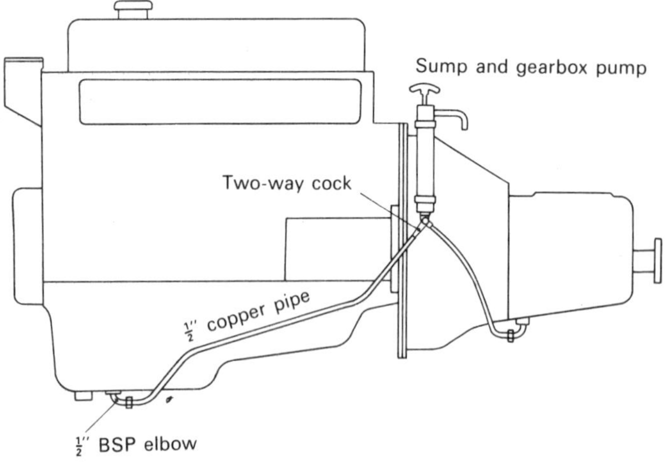

30 A way of draining the engine and gearbox oil when installed in a boat

If a stern tube and propeller shaft are already in place, then the next step is to connect the drive to the gearbox. However, if a stern tube is not fitted, then the following will not go amiss. A stern tube is basically a tube with bearings and a flange at each end, with a greaser and packing seal at the inboard end. The bearings are either white metal, lubricated by water repellent grease, or sometimes the outboard bearing is rubber and water lubricated. The tube is about $1\frac{1}{2}$ in. diameter for a 1 in. shaft, so a long auger has to be used to drill a hole, in a wooden boat. A pilot hole should first be carefully lined up and drilled. With an articulated drive accuracy in the vertical plane is not, of course, essential.

Thrust bearings

In Chapter Four the magnitude of the propeller thrust is discussed, and it is shown that standard deep groove journal ball bearings of the bore sizes to fit shafts of 1–1½ in. are capable of taking the propeller thrust, except in the case where the full horsepower of the engine is to be used. These bearings can be obtained fitted in a pillow or plummer

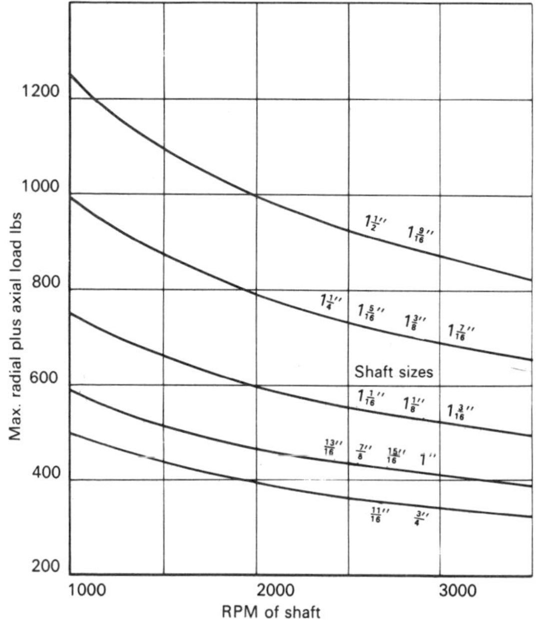

31 Basic capacity of light-type ball bearings fitted in a plummer block

block—an iron casting with mounting holes—and make inexpensive thrust bearings. They come fitted with seals and are pre-lubricated. Fitting to the shaft is usually accomplished with two grub screws which can be given a firm seating on the shaft by drilling shallow holes. Units with four grub screws can be obtained to increase the grip on the shaft. Instead of plummer or pillow blocks, flange type mountings can also be obtained.

The bearings fitted in these pillow blocks are normally of the light type ball bearing, and for high loads they have their limitations. The tables of propeller thrust given in Chapter Four (25) and bearing loads (31) should enable you to decide whether a simple bearing like this is good enough. Incidentally, Fenner and RHP are always willing to give advice on their bearings, and in any case their catalogues should be consulted, as the curves for permissible loads given here should only be used as a general guide.

For heavy duty where the engine is to be run hard for long periods, and where the boat speed is, say, less than 10 knots, a double tapered roller bearing set in a plummer block is the answer. The permissible loads for the Fenner-type plummer blocks fitted with Timken tapered roller bearings are given here (32).

The bearings described here are industrial units, but quite suitable for boats. Thrust bearings are almost unobtainable through yacht chandlers and the like, because the propeller thrust is almost always taken by the engine in professional marine engineering. In my view this is a mistaken, archaic attitude which causes may professionally built boats to have noisy and rough engine installations. Halyard Marine market a combined GKN thrust bearing and double CV joint arrangement together with very soft engine mountings.

Naturally, the thrust block needs to be bolted to a strong member in the boat, perhaps steel angle bar connected forward to the engine

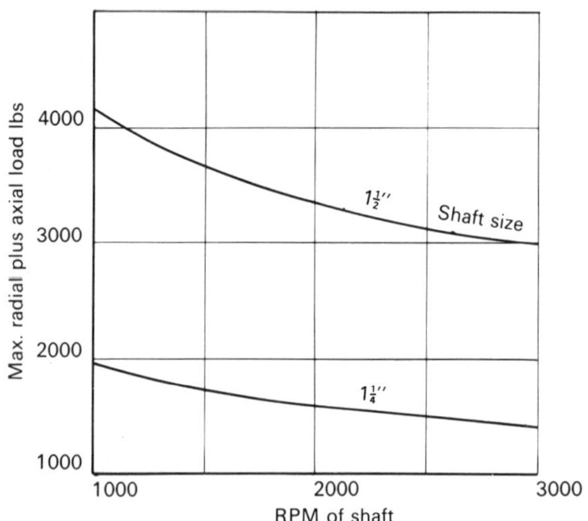

32 Load capacity of double tapered roller bearings set in a plummer block

bearers. The ball bearing types are usually self-aligning or able to accomodate small errors in line-up, so fitting these bearings is not difficult. After bolting down the shaft should turn freely. The distance between the thrust bearing and the gearbox coupling can be adjusted to suit the Hardy Spicer carden shaft. The free unsupported length of propeller shaft should not be more than the figures on page 82. It is well to keep the thrust bearing well away from the stern tube, so that it is higher out of the bilges and thus less likely to be in contact with bilge water. The half coupling connections to the after end of the Hardy Spicer shaft should be close to the thrust bearing to avoid overhang and whip.

Universal and flexible drives

The normal car-type Hardy Spicer shaft is completely suitable to connect the propeller shaft to the gearbox flange or spline. Usually it is necessary to cut the length of the tube down and reweld. Try to weld the tube concentrically to avoid vibration. This is vital if the propeller shaft is to run at more than 1500 r.p.m. To run smoothly, the angle of articulation of the two joints should be equal and their yokes should be aligned.

The alternative to a universal shaft is a carden shaft with a flexible coupling at each end. The additional advantage is that the torsional

Type of Drive	Max. Permanent Angle Between the Two Shafts	Max. Lateral Displacement Between the Two Shafts
Rigid	0·02°	0·001 in.
Single flex. coupling	2–4°	0·015–0·125 in.
Double flex. coupling with carden shaft	4–8° (2–4° each joint)	—
Articulated joints with carden shaft	15° each joint up to 1500 r.p.m. 10° above	—
Constant velocity joints with carden shaft	35° each joint	—

(twisting) vibrations will be greatly reduced, and shaft or propeller 'whistle' or 'singing' may be eliminated. The Layrub 2/4 shaft and coupling is one of the most well known. It must be appreciated that a single flexible coupling is no use whatever in absorbing the large lateral or up and down movements of the gearbox coupling relative to the propeller shaft. A flexibly mounted car engine can move on its mounts in this way at least 1 in. A single flexible coupling is only of use when the engine is rigidly bolted down, to take up small misalignments or displacements. The table on p. 70 sums up the flexibility of the different drives, but of course the manufacturer's figures for a particular coupling must be obtained.

Flexible coupling and flexible stern tube

This type of drive is often used by professional boat builders to avoid using a separate thrust bearing (28). A single flexible coupling can be used, but the engine must be lined up fairly accurately with the propeller shaft, depending on the type of coupling. The coupling must also be capable of taking the axial thrust from the propeller. The flexible car-type engine mounts must be supplemented with rubber buffer blocks sited on some part of the engine, to avoid the thrust being taken by the flexible mounts in shear. Otherwise the engine would be moved bodily forward by the thrust and probably tear the soft rubber mounts. Marine type rubber mounts designed to take the propeller thrust are readily available to suit virtually all types of diesel or petrol engine.

Solid mounting

Strong steel feet must be bolted to the engine to suit the height of the engine bearers, remembering that the gearbox output shaft must be in line with the propeller shaft (33). For many car engines you can buy cast feet which bolt on to the sides of the engine block. This does not apply to the gearbox feet because there are only one or two firms who marinise car gearboxes. However, there is nothing difficult about making up feet from heavy steel angle bar, about 3 × 3 in., or $\frac{3}{8}$ in. thick flat bar. The final lining up of the engine has to be done with large metal shims between the feet and the engine bearers. To test for alignment, assuming the gearbox has a flange coupling and the

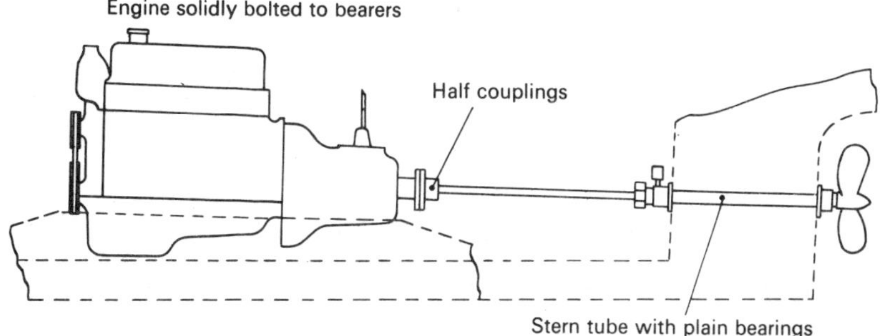

33 Solid mounting and drive

propeller shaft is fitted with a half coupling, slide the couplings together and see if the faces meet truly and concentrically. Any misalignment will quickly wear the oil seal at the back end of the gearbox and the gearbox bearings. Any boat's hull is not a rigid inflexible structure by any means, and wooden boats in particular tend to change their shape when they are put into the water. Consequently final lining up should be done afloat.

Other drives

The straightforward prop shaft is not the only way of connecting the engine to the propeller. Advantages can be gained by using other methods, such as the outdrive or Z drive. The cost of a new Z drive is many times greater than the cost of converting a car engine, so unless you are lucky and obtain a second hand unit, this method will probably not appeal. Nevertheless, an outdrive will place the engine right aft out of the way, avoid gearbox problems, and allow easy removal of weed and debris from the propeller.

The outdrive concept fits in well with fast planing boats (for which they are primarily designed) because, on such a boat, the weight needs to be aft and the hull has to have a broad flat transom for efficient planing which suits an outdrive installation. The leg of an outdrive is designed to kick up if an underwater obstruction is hit. The leg can also be tilted up to beach the boat. But outdrives are also seen on slower motor boats and on catamarans. Long legs are available nowadays especially for catamarans, the engine sitting on the centreline in a pod that just kisses the water. Another advantage is that close quarters manoeuvring is so much easier than with a conventional propeller and rudder. The stern can be pushed sideways in 'astern' just as positively as in 'ahead'.

Disadvantages of the outdrives are: 1) vague steering at slow ahead speeds. 2) rather vulnerable and prone to being bashed by the dinghy. 3) corrosion can be a big problem when it comes to dismantling parts of the leg. 4) reduction ratios are generally no more than 1·6:1 or 2:1 which means inefficient propulsion for displacement boats as the propeller diameter is restricted.

The method of taking the drive from the engine flywheel normally involves a flanged stub shaft, which is bolted on with the flywheel bolts. The outdrive usually has two universal joints and a splined shaft on to which the stub shaft slides. Outdrive manufacturers can usually supply the parts for fitting their outdrives to many popular car engine conversions. The outdrive unit incorporates forward-neutral-reverse gears in the bevel gear train at the top end of the unit.

Jet units are simpler and less expensive. The propulsive efficiency suffers over a normal propeller for slower boat speeds, but is quite good at speeds over 20 knots. In fact it is not until 35 knots or so is reached before a jet powered boat is likely to have the same speed as a propeller driven boat powered by the same engine. Consequently a jet boat needs ample power—in excess of 100 hp per ton—otherwise a disappointing performance is likely. Again the engine is right aft, and there is the advantage of safety to swimmers and skiers as all rotating parts are covered. A bucket and flap system over the jet orifice provides steering and astern power, so again no gearbox is required. The drive to the impeller shaft can be achieved with a short car-type Hardy Spicer shaft, connected direct to the flywheel. There would be some advantage to be gained by retaining the clutch, or both the clutch and gearbox, because starting and idling could then be achieved without the impeller being driven around. The clutch could be retained together with the bell housing holding the clutch fork. The primary shaft of the gearbox could be used to take the drive from the driven plate, together with the forward end ball bearing and face of the gearcase. The rest of the gearcase could be cut away, leaving a very neat stub end to the bell housing. Direct 'solid' drive would not be recommended by the jet manufacturers.

A vee drive will also place the engine right aft. It is simply a small box incorporating gears or a chain drive to enable the drive to double back on itself and pass underneath the engine. It is not now a very popular method of transmission and the gear vee drive is a costly little item.

Variable pitch propellers offer many advantages. For a car engine drive it dispenses with the need for a gearbox and clutch, although the clutch would be a desirable feature at times, so that the engine could run without the propeller turning. On a variable pitch propeller the blades can be turned by mechanical linkages from inside the boat so that the thrust can be varied to ahead, astern or neutral (zero pitch) with the shaft always revolving in the same direction.

A propeller that can be feathered (i.e. the blades are set fore and aft) offers little resistance to water flow when the shaft is stopped, and consequently a V.P. propeller is attractive for auxiliary sailing yachts. However one disadvantage is that obtaining a precise 'neutral', i.e. no thrust, is often difficult because of slack in the control system; another is cost.

The simplest and cheapest unit is by Watermota, and incorporates a thrust bearing and flange coupling. An articulated drive (car-type Hardy Spicer) could easily be fitted from this coupling to the gearbox flange, the engine flywheel or even to the primary shaft of the gearbox, after cutting off all the gearcase except the forward face attached to the bell housing.

A type of drive which has been on the sidelines for several years, as far as boats are concerned, is the hydraulic (or hydrostatic) drive. The engine drives a hydraulic pump which pumps oil at high pressure through flexible hoses to a hydraulic motor fitted directly on the prop shaft. Reverse and neutral are easily achieved hydraulically, thus dispensing with the clutch and gearbox. This drive, even using standard industrial pumps and motors, is expensive, but it may be attractive when one engine can be used to drive two propellers—on a catamaran for example. However, any hydraulic drive is composed of much more than merely a pump(s) and a motor(s). The oil needs to be cooled, the suction to the pump must be pressurised to avoid cavitation, and a relief valve and header tank have to be incorporated. Very importantly the whole system including the engine and propeller must be design-matched by a hydraulic engineer, otherwise the motors and pumps may be operating way-off their design point and be very inefficient. At very best, motor and pump efficiencies are no more than 90% so one is faced with a system 81% efficient (0.9 × 0.9) before pipe losses etc. are included. A marine gearbox in contrast is 90%–95% efficient. One chooses hydraulic drive only where a conventional drive is difficult to engineer, but it does give the added advantage of enabling the engine to be fitted in unusual places, for instance, across the transom.

Vee-belt and chain drives

There always seems to be a reluctance in the boat building world to use vee-belts or chain drives. Failure by slipping or breaking is usually due to incorrect design—asking the belts to transmit too much power. If the manufacturers' tables are used the drive will be just as good an engineering proposition as a gear drive. Chain and belt drives can be useful, for instance, where you want to tuck the engine in the stern over the propeller shaft, driving forward and down. Another instance is where the engine will not sit low enough to be in a reasonable line with the propeller shaft or perhaps it would mean the engine was too far forward with an articulated carden shaft. Obviously the engine cannot be flexibly mounted unless there is an articulated drive between the gearbox and the uppermost sprocket or pulley wheel. In this case plummer blocks (ball bearings mounted in cast iron housings) can be used to support a short shaft carrying the sprocket or pulley wheel. It must be realised that both types of drive give large journal loads (side loads) on the bearings, which must be sited close to the sprocket or wheel to avoid the shaft being unduly deflected. Belt or chain drives offer scope for a reduction ratio and 2 : 1 or 3 : 1 can easily be achieved. The chart shown in Chapter Four will give a broad indication of the sizes and types of chain required for different horsepowers and speeds. It will be noted that at higher speeds (say 4000–5000 r.p.m., at which a modern engine can revolve) the larger sizes of chain are not recommended, and consequently, the possible power transmission, even with the Triplex chain, is limited to about 10 HP (using a factor of 2 and $\frac{3}{8}$ in. chain). If third or second gear reduces the output to 3000–2000 r.p.m. maximum, the possible power goes up to 19–37 HP (using a factor of 2 and $\frac{1}{2}$ in. and $\frac{3}{4}$ in. chain respectively). These figures are assuming a 19 tooth smaller sprocket of about $2\frac{1}{4}$ in. diameter for $\frac{3}{8}$ in. chain. Probably a larger pinion could be used and the above powers would be roughly doubled if the sprocket size was made $4\frac{1}{2}$ in. in diameter. Reynolds make stock wheels and pinions for simple, Duplex or Triplex chains bored and keyed to common sizes. Fenner also make pinions and wheels and fit them with their Taper-lock. This device is a tapered bush which grips the shaft when the grub screws are turned home. In almost all cases it avoids having to key the shaft.

A 17–19 toothed pinion is the minimum to be recommended, and the faster and harder the chain is to work the greater the degree of lubrication required, otherwise the life is greatly reduced. This is one snag with a chain drive. Generally an oil bath is required, which entails a chain case to stop the oil flying around and being lost.

A vee-belt drive requires no lubrication and if correctly engineered will stand the test of time. The tables given here (34) are intended only as a guide to the number and size of belts and the size of the pulleys required for a given horsepower and speed. As with chain drives, at high speeds over 3000 r.p.m. only the smaller size of belt can be used, and this results in the necessity of using a multi-belt drive. Matched belts are then essential.

To take an example, suppose the full horsepower of the engine is required, say, 40 HP at 4000 r.p.m. (smaller pulley r.p.m.). Choose a smaller pulley diameter of, say, 4 in., making sure that it is greater than the minimum, and calculate the belt speed as $0{\cdot}262 \times 4000 \times 4 = 4200$ ft per minute. The maximum horsepower per belt (A-section) is thus about $3\frac{1}{2}$, which means that 12 belts would be required. Normally only up to five belts are used for A-section belts. There are several corrections to the allowable horsepower to be taken into account for loss of arc of contact, type of drive, etc., which would normally bring the allowable horsepower per belt down by around 25%.

Using standard belts one is again limited to something less than the full horsepower of the engine. However, there are 'higher-power' belts available, and in particular the Fenner Spacesaver wedge-belt drive, which allows far more power to be transmitted. In the above example only six belts would be required. The Spacesaver enables the drive to be very compact and the Taper Lock system is incorporated in the standard sheaves.

Obviously I can only give a broad indication of the size and type of chain and belt that is required, and the makers' catalogues should be obtained for the final choice. It is very essential in these drives to do the job properly and consult these catalogues rather than proceed by guesswork. Toothed belts are worth investigating as an alternative to vee belts or chain and again the makers' catalogue should be consulted.

Propeller shafts

Commonly used shaft materials include manganese bronze, stainless steel and monel, in increasing order of cost. Both manganese bronze and stainless steel need cathodic protection. There are many grades of stainless steel—Type 316 is the 'least' grade one should use for a shaft in seawater. Grades with a higher alloy content give a longer life. In fresh water Type 304 is satisfactory or even plain carbon steel but manganese bronze is the better alternative. Ideally shafts should be double-ended so that when they become worn they can be turned end for end.

The maximum unsupported length of shaft between bearings expressed as a multiple of the shaft diameter is as follows:

Shaft Diam ins	*Max. Shaft r.p.m.*	*Max. unsupported length (No. of diams)*
1	1,000	69
1	2,000	49
1	3,000	39
1½	1,000	62
1½	2,000	43
1½	3,000	34
2	1,000	54
2	2,000	39
2	3,000	30

This table applies to steel, stainless steel. For manganese bronze halve the number of diameters. See Table (49) for choosing a shaft diameter.

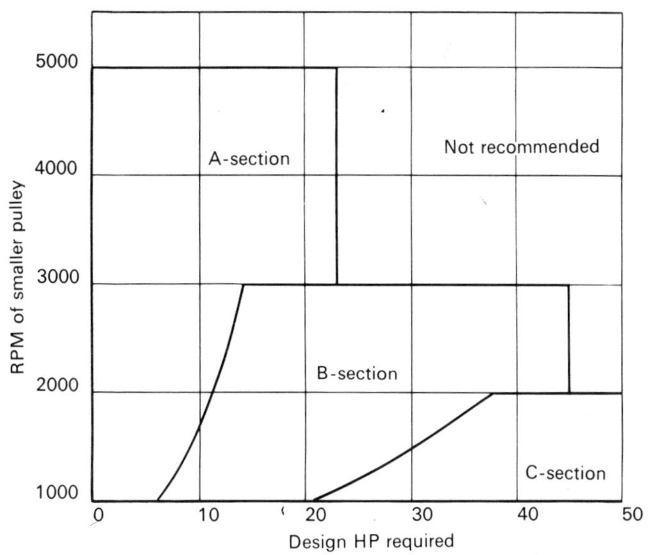
5000
4000
3000
2000
1000
RPM of smaller pulley
A-section
Not recommended
B-section
C-section
0
10
20
30
40
50
Design HP required

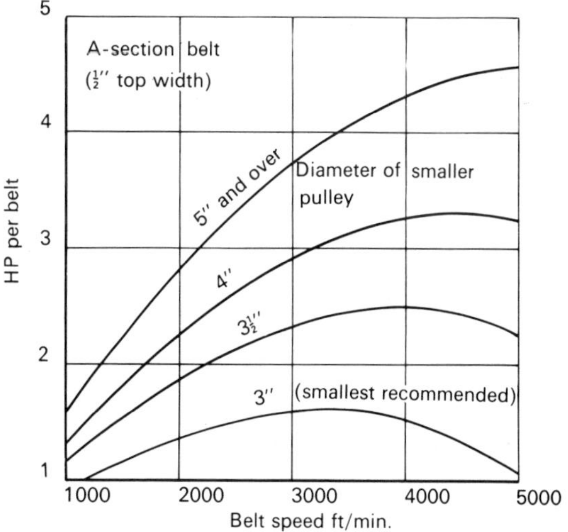
5
4
3
2
1
HP per belt
A-section belt
(½″ top width)
5″ and over
Diameter of smaller pulley
4″
3½″
3″
(smallest recommended)
1000
2000
3000
4000
5000
Belt speed ft/min.

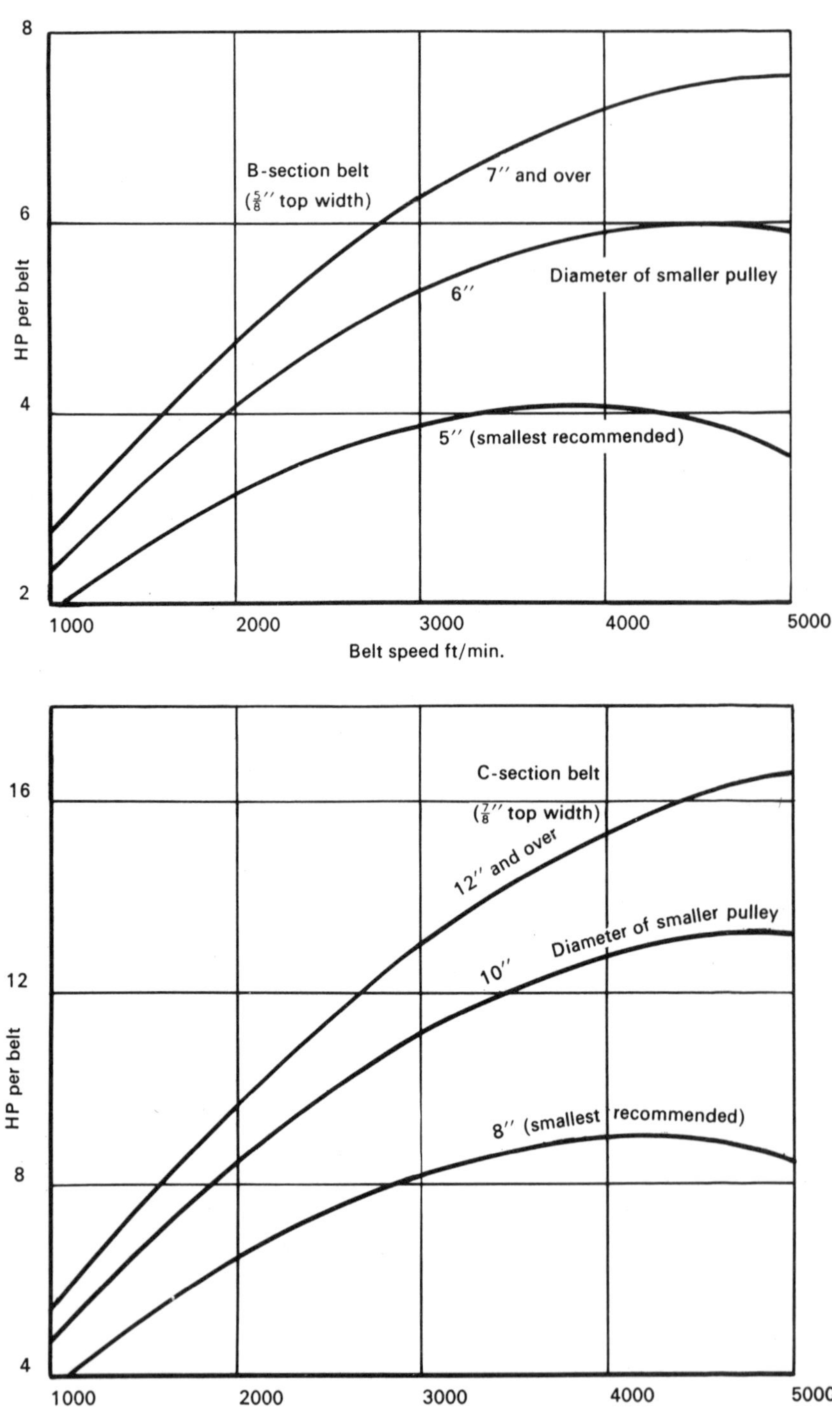

8
6
4
2
HP per belt
B-section belt
($\frac{5}{8}$'' top width)
7'' and over
Diameter of smaller pulley
6''
5'' (smallest recommended)
1000
2000
3000
4000
5000
Belt speed ft/min.
16
12
8
4
HP per belt
C-section belt
($\frac{7}{8}$'' top width)
12'' and over
Diameter of smaller pulley
10''
8'' (smallest recommended)
1000
2000
3000
4000
5000
Belt speed ft/min.

Rubber mountings

The principle is that the engine is allowed to vibrate but that the vibration is not passed into the engine bearers via the mounts. The system is flexible and will therefore have a *natural* frequency of vibration. If this occurs within the running r.p.m of the engine it will cause violent engine movement and cause more transmission of vibration to the boat than if the engine were solidly mounted. The softer the mounts the lower the natural frequency. The chosen mounts must have a natural frequency at least just below the idle r.p.m. In the case of marine mounts the manufacturers choose a natural frequency of around 550 r.p.m.

When starting or stopping, the engine r.p.m. will of course pass through this resonant frequency and the engine will shake wildly for a second (the flexibility of pipework etc. must take this into account). Conveniently the r.p.m. at the natural frequency is linked to the deflection of the set of mounts under the engine's weight. For 550 r.p.m. it is about 0·15 inches and is the stiffness usually chosen for marine mounts which have to take propeller thrust. Rubber mount manufacturers give each mount a load range within which the mounts must be loaded if it is to give the required deflection. Marine rubber mounts come conveniently with a centre stud on which there are locknuts above and below the engine foot allowing simple and precise alignment.

Car engine mounts are softer and give a greater degree of isolation. If in the boat the propeller thrust is taken by a thrust bearing on the shaft then softer mounts can be used—those designed for a deflection of 0·25 to 0·3 inches. Overloading a small mount to give a big deflection is not the way to do it because the rubber/steel bond will soon fail—the mount must be designed for that amount of deflection.

Natural frequency	Rubber mount			R.P.M.		
R.P.M.	deflection ins.	500	750	1,000	2,000	3,000
600	0·1	200	130	50	10	3
400	0.2	200	50	20	5	1
300	0·4	50	20	10	1	0

Table giving the percentage of vibration transmitted to the engine bearers. Softer mounts are obviously better.

Saildrives

Quite quickly in the 1970's the saildrive concept became popular for very good reasons. The saildrive is really an outdrive that goes through the bottom of the hull instead of through the transom. It also differs in that it does not steer nor tilt. A rudder is therefore necessary. Whatever the type of boat it is essential that there is a keel forward of the leg that will give it protection. Advantages of the saildrive include the ease of installation. The types where the leg is rigidly mounted to the engine, the whole package being flexibly mounted to the hull, give a very quiet installation. Outdrives are rigidly mounted to the transom and so pass to the hull the noise of their bevel gears.

While most saildrive legs are intended for yachts and therefore for small horsepower inputs the largest units of 60 HP or so do allow speeds of around 15 knots on small motor cruisers. Higher speeds are effectively precluded by the need to have a protective keel (which causes drag and is inappropriate on a really fast boat). On a yacht hull an outdrive is usually impossible to fit because of the shape of the stern and because the weight of the engine would be too far aft. But a compact saildrive often fits very neatly. On a transom-sterned motor cruiser hull one has the choice of outdrive or saildrive.

Twin and wing installations

RNLI statistics show that mechanical failure at sea is one of the most common reasons for a lifeboat being called. It may be a rope around the propeller or an engine failure or simply run out of fuel. It makes great sense therefore to have a second means of propelling the boat. A yacht has its engine; a motor cruiser or fishing boat also needs a second string. In boats of about 25 feet and under, an outboard is one practical answer. In boats of about 15 feet or less sensible people carry oars. A small and simple sail rig is another answer.

For fast motor cruisers, a twin-screw engine installation is the best solution, but both engines should be absolutely autonomous. Their fuel, water and starting systems should be separate. Each engine should have its own seacock and there should be two batteries each capable of starting one engine (but one battery can normally be dedicated to cabin lights etc. with the provision of bringing it into the starting circuit). Most importantly each engine should have its own tank. The two tanks can have a connecting pipe in order to transfer fuel, but there should be a valve in the pipe which is normally shut. Dirt in the fuel is a very common cause of engine stoppage; with separate fuel systems it is unlikely that both engines will stop simultaneously. It is important that the boat should steer satisfactorily on one engine otherwise the safety factor of twin engines is negated. Manoeuvring in confined spaces is delightfully easy with twin screws and to this end outward turning propellers are best.

A small wing engine is an alternative as a means of providing a second means of propulsion if the main engine packs up. This can be a considerably smaller engine (as a minimum 2 or 3 HP per ton of boat weight can be taken) driving to a 'P' or 'A' shaft bracket situated to one side of the centreline not too far outboard and not in the inflow to the main propeller. The drag of a stopped wing propeller precludes its use on a planing boat. Again it is important that the boat should steer satisfactorily on its wing engine alone. Displacement boats with large rudders are usually tolerant of the offset thrust. To this end an inward turning propeller should be fitted to the wing engine.

CHAPTER SIX

Petrol Tank and Feed

Car-type tanks can quite often be used successfully. They are not ideal, however, because they are usually an odd shape and being of thin steel plate corrode rather rapidly in a salty environment. They are sometimes treated on the inside, when manufactured, to prevent moisture forming rust particles. A few coats of polyurethene paint on the outside will prolong the tank's life. Marine petrol tanks are usually of stainless steel, aluminium alloy, tinned or galvanised mild steel, tinned copper, or Monel or copper nickel. The required size of tank depends on how hard the engine is to be run and for how long. To estimate this, a figure 0·65 pints per HP per hour can be used. In other words, an engine developing 10 HP would use about 6 pints per hour. A 6 gallon tank is usually sufficient for inland waters, while a 10 gallon tank is a practical minimum for a sea-going craft. Obviously, the tank needs to be firmly chocked into place, and very large tanks should always be positioned low in the hull to avoid top weight.

The filler tube should be extended up to a deck screw fitting by

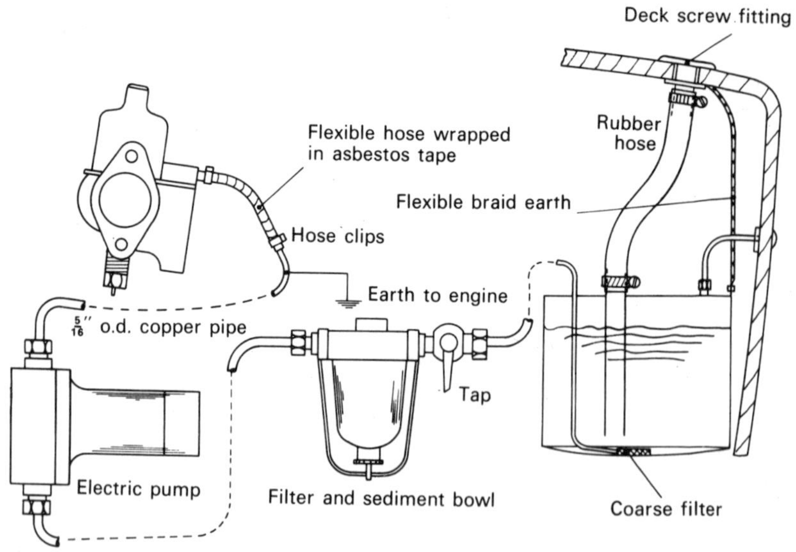

35 Tank, petrol pump and feed system involving a large tank

means of a rubber tube secured by hose clips (35). With the filler extended up to the deck any overflow will run over the deck and overboard, not down into the bilges. It is important to earth the deck screw fitting to the tank, and the tank to the engine, to reduce the possibility of sparking. Nevertheless, when filling from a petrol pump always remember to bring the nozzle of the filler hose into contact with the deck fitting before allowing petrol to flow. An even better filler arrangement is to carry the filler hose right down almost to the bottom of the tank. This minimises the generation of petrol vapour due to splashing, and it also minimises the risk of a static charge building up. A vent pipe must be arranged from the top of the tank to a point in the side of the boat to allow air to escape when filling. Also, of course, air must be able to enter the tank as fuel is used by the engine, to prevent the creation of a vacuum. Small tanks of, say, less than 10 gallons in capacity are served sufficiently by a small hole in the filler cap, unless a separate vent pipe is provided. The vent pipe, which should be fitted in any case on tanks of over 10 gallons, should have copper gauze fitted over the outlet in the boat's side.

Gravity or pump feed?

The simplest feed system is with the tank mounted in a position higher than the engine, so that the carburettor can be supplied by gravity (36). Gravity feed quite often brings problems from air locks. The petrol pipe run should be as short and direct as possible. There must be a constant fall all the way to the lowest point, and then a constant rise up to the carburettor. Intermediate rises are a sure cause of air locks. The tank is usually mounted directly underneath the deck with a gravity feed, and a position forward of the engine is better than aft, because when under way the bow tends to rise. A pump feed will allow the tank to be positioned almost anywhere, and will avoid the problem of air locks. There are two types of pump readily available, the mechanical type and the electric. Some car engines are designed for a mechanical pump to be driven off the camshaft. The mechanical pump is extremely reliable, but it only operates when the engine is turning. If the boat has been idle for a few days it will probably be necessary to pump up the petrol by means of the auxiliary hand pump, usually fitted to the mechanical pump, to prime the carburettor. Another problem is that it is subject to the heat from the engine, which can cause a vapour lock in the system. The chances of this happening can be reduced by an insulating gasket between the engine and the pump, fitting an aluminium heat shield between the pump and the engine, and wrapping the petrol pipe leading to the engine with insulation. The electric pump works as soon as the ignition is switched on, thus automatically priming the carburettor. It can be mounted away from the heat of the engine, but it should not be mounted directly underneath the tank in case the tank should leak.

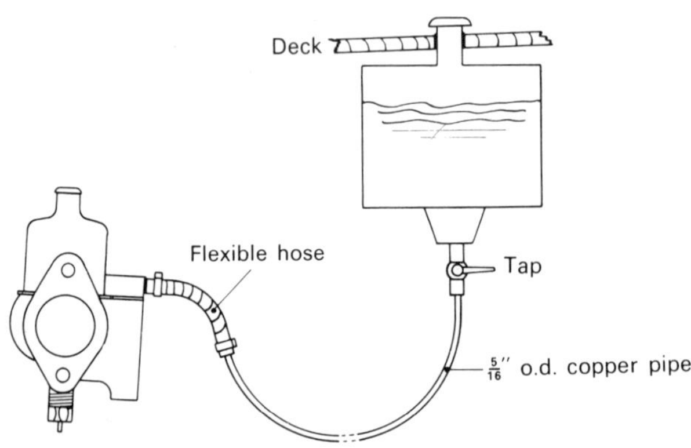

36 Simple gravity feed

The petrol pipe should be of copper; 5/16 in. o.d. is usually quite adequate, and it should be strapped in place every 2 ft or so. With a pump feed it is better to draw the petrol through the top of the tank by means of a pipe running to the bottom of the tank. With a gravity feed system, of course, the petrol must be drawn through the bottom of the tank. Connections in the copper petrol pipe must not be made by soft soldering; such a joint is very liable to crack under vibration, and in the event of a fire will quickly melt and feed petrol to the fire. Connections should be made by brazing or, more conveniently, by either a cone union or an olive union. The connection to the carburettor or mechanical pump should be by means of a flexible hose to prevent engine vibration cracking the copper pipe. Copper is rather susceptible to this. Car-type hose, especially the armoured variety, is perfectly suitable, but it is desirable to wrap it in fire resistant material. Pipe clips should be used at the connections. In a gravity feed system a petrol cock or tap should be directly beneath the tank or, if this is inaccessible, as close to the tank as possible. In a pump feed the tap can be fitted in any accessible place, bearing in mind that in the event of a carburettor fire this will be the first thing you will want to get to.

Dirt and water will inevitably enter the fuel tank in a boat. The mechanical pump, the carburettor and the tank will probably already have wire mesh filters, but it is a very good thing to have an in-line filter cum sediment bowl. This can be anywhere in the line, perhaps in conjunction with the tap. These items can be bought with a quickly removed glass or metal bowl. A glass bowl enables you to see how much dirt or water has collected, but a filter with a glass bowl should not be placed near the engine or a possible source of heat or flames, as it may well crack in the event of a fire.

A petrol tap is essential with a gravity feed, so that the flow can be stopped in the event of a fire, and possible leakage prevented by turning off the tap when leaving the boat for the week. On a pump feed with the tank below the level of the carburettor it is still a good safeguard, but obviously not so necessary. If the tank is above the carburettor with a pump feed, when the engine is switched off the pump will not necessarily stop petrol flowing by gravity if there is a leak, say in the carburettor. Whether or not the pump you fit has a non-return action can be found by attempting to blow and suck through it.

Any carburettor which can flood and overflow should be fitted with a small drip tray covered with copper gauze. A flame trap or air filter should also be fitted on the air intake. This is a requirement of the Thames Conservancy.

See the notes in Chapter Nine on diesels for diesel fuel tanks and feeds.

Safety

Petrol fumes in the bilge of a boat can turn into a bomb if a spark is made by the starter motor commutator or if there is a flame as on the pilot light of a gas refrigerator. Inland waterway authorities usually have regulations on the subject of petrol tank and fuel installations. Otherwise follow the rules of the SBBNF (see Appendix). Leakage into the bilges must be avoided at all costs, so a gravity fuel system should only be used in an open boat. In a more enclosed boat the tank should be low down and the fuel should be pumped *up* to the carburettor. There should be no penetrations through the bottom or sides of the tank. The tank must be of a metal, certainly not plastic or GRP or rubber which will melt very quickly in a fire. The whole fuel system including the deck filler connection should be earthed. One danger is when the engine refuses to start and is turned over by the starter motor with the throttle open. Often the cause is dirt in the float chamber needle valve which makes the carburettor overflow—hence the need for a good-sized drip tray under the carburettor as well as a vigilant nose.

CHAPTER SEVEN

Electrics

Generally speaking, the car-type circuit and electrical fittings can be fitted directly to the boat. Obviously the system will work, but protection from spray and damp is vital if car-type fittings such as the regulator/cut-out and switches are to last very long. This applies especially to craft on the sea. Inland, in fresh waters, there is not the same problem, and providing the equipment is kept out of the rain it should last as long as when fitted in a car. It is amazing how a salty atmosphere corrodes small pieces of unprotected mild steel found in switches and such. Once wetted by salt water, damp seems to be attracted. Condensation in boats is an ever-present problem, especially in the autumn first thing in the morning. Everything becomes wringing wet—inland or on the sea.

Marine electrics avoid mild steel parts and use brass instead. Hence they are more expensive and difficult to obtain. Dynamos and starters are usually identical to the car types, except that they are given a 'marine finish', i.e. the internals are coated with an anti-damp substance. The wonderful modern aerosol sprays that can be obtained, such as Rocket WD-40, will help to produce this 'marine finish' on all electrical equipment, especially the high tension circuit. When buying switches, for example, take along a magnet and reject anything which is attracted by the magnet, as this will indicate steel.

Circuits

The circuit shown (37) is based on standard car practice. The earth return system, one side of the electrical circuit being the engine structure, is the obvious one to use with converted car engines, as the dynamo and starter, for instance, will be earthed to the engine. Whether a negative or positive earth is used does not matter except with equipment which is marked with a correct earth polarity. Alternators and their regulators, for instance, can be ruined by reversed polarity. No fuses are necessary in this part of the system, but all other appliances such as cabin lights should be fused. On board a boat, of course, there must be wires running back to the engine block (earth), unlike the system in a car where the bodywork acts as the return. The circuit (37) shows earth returns for simplicity. The engine room fan shown in the circuit is controlled by a switch in the ignition circuit. Before the ignition and starter will operate, the fan must be switched on separately. This precludes forgetfulness and a possible explosion. (See also Chapter Eleven on noise reduction.)

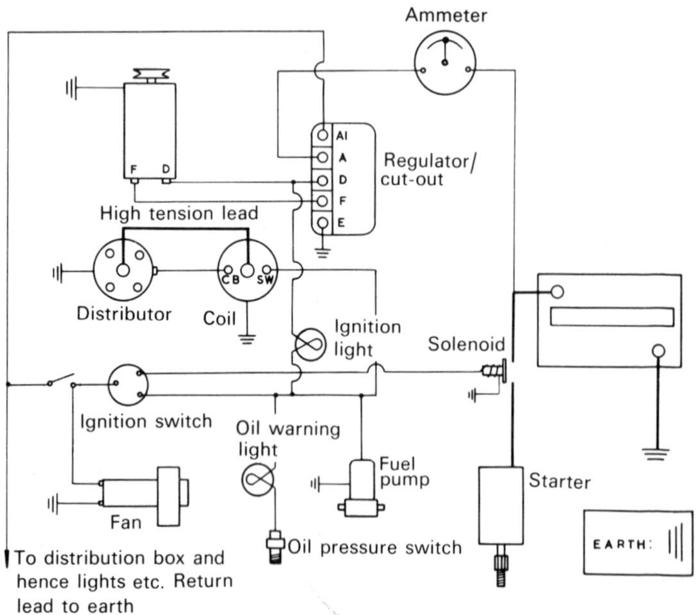

37 Basic electrical circuit

Cabin lights, navigation lights, windscreen wiper, etc., should all be fed from a distribution box, which in turn is fed from the battery. The distribution box will contain fuses and switches, and can well be placed near the wheel so that it forms part of the instrument panel. There are many compact marine switch panels and fuse boxes available through chandlers. Circuit breakers are worth considering in place of fuses. Should a rated current be exceeded a circuit breaker will trip and switch off the current. The circuit can be reconnected simply by manually switching on again. Clearly fuse boxes or circuit breakers should be positioned in a dry place.

Single pole fusing for a 12 volt system is quite acceptable, but the fuses must be in the 'live' wire and not the pole earthed to the engine.

Batteries and generators

A car electrical system does not have to cater for long periods of discharge when the engine is not running. On a boat the cabin lights may need to be on for several hours each evening. The generator and battery capacity normal on cars is sufficient for small boats and electrical loads. For instance, a cabin on a 23-footer is adequately lit by 24 watts. This is a drain of 2 amps on the battery (amps = watts ÷ volts). Car batteries are usually about 40 amp-hours (AH), which means that they can give 1 amp for 40 hours or 2 for 20, and so on. So a 24 watt bulb would drain a fully charged battery in 20 hours, and although this seems adequate for an evening's light, there must still be enough left in the battery for the morning's engine start. A larger battery and an alternator is the answer. Quite often the dynamo can be swapped for an alternator using the same bolt holes. The great advantage of an alternator is the fact that charging still carries on even with the engine idling, and much higher charging rates are possible. It does mean that heavier cables must be used. The charging circuit for an alternator is shown here (38).

One alternative to an alternator is to fit two generators, separate charging circuits and two batteries. Another alternative is to fit a

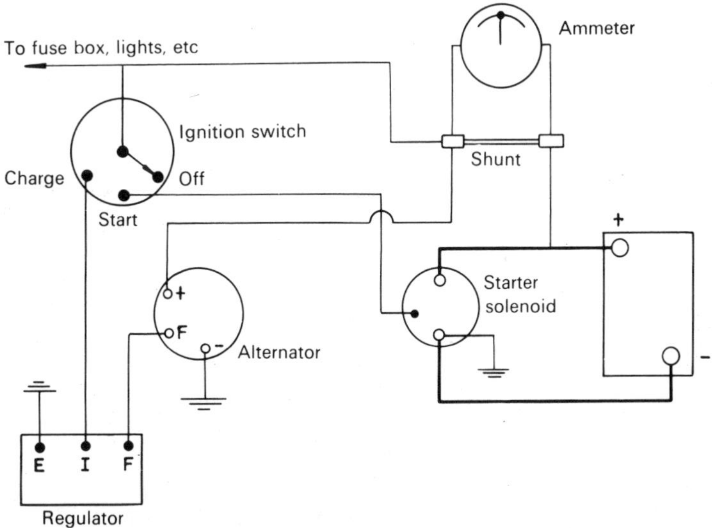

38 Charging circuit with alternator

larger dynamo feeding two batteries through a blocking diode unit. One battery is purely for engine starting, so always fresh, and the other for lights, etc. Dynamos can be picked up from scrapyards very cheaply, and when fitted with new brushes costing a few pence will give several more years' service. Similarly regulator/cut-outs can be obtained cheaply. Alternators are very expensive when new but are obtainable second-hand or from the scrap yard. Merely fitting a larger battery than is standard for the car will not give much extra capacity because the limit is then the dynamo, which will still only give the same output. Obviously, if more is taken out, more has to be put back in. Lead—acid batteries do not last as long in a boat as in a car; infrequent use and no use at all during the winter soon ruins them. Five years is an average figure even with monthly charges during the winter and regular all-the-year-round-topping-up. Nevertheless, they are the most popular type because of their low price. Alkaline batteries will last for 20 years or so, but their initial cost is considerably higher. There are many of these batteries on the surplus market at far cheaper prices. Make sure, however, that the alkaline battery you buy is suitable for engine starting, i.e. has a low internal resistance. Other advantages of alkaline batteries are that they are not damaged by high charge rates and do not need any attention over the winter.

Batteries are lumpy items and should be fitted in an easily accessible box strongly fastened to the boat. A wooden box is best for a lead-acid battery and a steel one for an alkaline battery. It must be remembered that explosive gases are produced while charging, and batteries should be situated in a freely ventilated space. They should also have a fitted top to prevent a screwdriver, for instance, dropping down and shorting across the terminals. This is a Thames Conservancy regulation. A master switch is a very good safeguard against a flat battery and possible electroyltic corrosion while the boat is moored idle during the week. Battery master switches cost only a few pounds and fit on a battery terminal.

Cables

Wiring cable should be fitted as high as possible out of the bilges, as indeed should all electrical equipment. The solenoid and coil are best fitted on the engine, with the regulator/cut-out fitted separately in a place not affected by vibration. Knowing the current which will flow in each cable the required size can be found (39).

Cable	Sectional Area mm²	Continuous current rating amps	Ohms per 100 foot of cable
Flexible single or twin PVC	0.5	3	1·25
	1	10	0·56
	1·5	15	0·39
	2·5	22	0·22
	4	32	0·14
	10	67	0·058
	16	100	0·040
	25	135	0·022
Single, PVC starter cables	40	170	0·014
	60	196	0·0092
	85	230	0·0068
	110	280	0·0050

39 Cable ratings

Stranded cable is to be preferred to solid because under vibration or continual bending a solid copper core will soon fatigue and break. PVC insulation is most commonly used. Table (39) gives ordinary commercial ratings; a boat built to the rules of Classification Society (e.g. Lloyds) would have to abide by slightly different criteria.

Apart from fitting a cable that can take the current involved it is also important to choose a cable that will avoid too much voltage drop between the battery and the electrical item. The aim should be to achieve no more than about ½ volt drop in a 12 volt circuit and no more than about 1 volt in a 24 volt circuit. Table (39) gives the resistance of the wire in ohms per 100 foot.

$$\text{Ohms (resistance over length of cable)} = \frac{\text{Volt drop over length of cable}}{\text{current (amps)}}$$

Cables should be supported with clips and bound into looms along areas that are clear of the engine, of exhaust heat or water or the scuffing of feet. Terminals and plastic clips and spiral binding are all readily available and are inexpensive.

Voltage drop in starter cables is very deleterious to the starter motor performance and consequently the battery must be placed close to the engine and the starter cables need to be of generous size. This applies particularly to diesels which need far greater cranking power than petrol engines. The starter battery size can be chosen from battery manufacturers' catalogues. Generally the size specified in these catalogues (i.e. amp hour capacity) is greater when referring to a marine engine than for the same engine in a van or truck. This is to allow for longer periods of inaction in a boat. But if two batteries are fitted, one specifically for engine starting, then this battery can be of the 'automotive' size. Two batteries are well worth having. Whereas in a petrol engined boat one can always pinch the car's battery if the one on the boat is flat, a diesel may not even turn over running from a small car battery.

There are various ways of achieving a two-battery system, but it is important to know that an alternator can be badly damaged if, while the engine is running, *both* batteries are disconnected. The simplest way is to connect the 'domestic service' battery to the starter battery (+ to + and – to –) with light cable and crocodile clips. In this way it will be charged at the same time as the starter battery and when the starter battery is switched off (after the engine is stopped) it will supply the domestic circuit. A better system is to use proper starter cable and another battery master switch. Then either or both batteries can be used for starting. Change-over switches are available to connect either battery with the circuit; some also have an OFF position and a 'make-before-break' switching arrangement so that there is no instant when both batteries are isolated when switching over. Some have an ALL position to connect both batteries with the circuit.

An automatic method involves fitting a heavy duty relay to connect the two batteries and which is only energised when the engine is running. This means that both batteries are charged, both are used for starting, yet when the engine is stopped only the domestic one remains in the circuit. The other automatic system involves using blocking diodes which act like non-return valves; marine types are readily available. Both the relay and diode system can be troublesome if inferior or underrated units are unsed. They also give no positive indication that they are actually doing their job.

Petrol engine HT systems

Damp salty air can cause a great deal of trouble to the HT circuits on petrol engines. Cleanliness, and preventing seawater (or even the fine spray which inundates a boat on a windy day) from reaching the engine, are the first lines of defence. Rubber spark plug covers and plastic boots over the distributor also help. One of the electronic ignition systems that are now sold by motoring shops are well worth while fitting. They can make the difference between firing or not firing under marginal starting conditions.

Converting a magneto to coil ignition

Some small marine engines and industrial engines have magneto ignition which can never produce such a good spark as battery-coil ignition and can 'age' gradually and cause problems when starting and when hot. Conversion to coil ignition can be easily achieved using parts of the magneto—the contact breakers, condenser, distributor rotor head and electrodes.

In principle, conversion swops a car type coil for the high tension winding in the magneto, and a battery in place of the low tension coil. In practice the new coil is bolted somewhere convenient on the engine and a HT lead taken from it to the rotor arm carbon brush inside the magneto, if necessary by drilling a hole in the case. The old HT path from the magneto coil is disconnected.

The low tension circuit follows car practice viz. battery-ignition switch-coil-contact breakers-earth (engine block). The condenser fits electrically across the CB points to stop sparking. The old LT circuit is disconnected.

I know of two engines that have been converted like this (both Stuart Turners); in the first case a dynamo was also fitted to charge the battery. In the second case the battery was taken home periodically and charged up. In this case one must be confident about the state of charge before setting sail.

CHAPTER EIGHT

Controls and Instruments

Clutch and gear lever

Even in small boats the gear lever is sometimes inaccessible, or too far away from the helmsman, so that remote control must be fitted. If the gearbox has been converted so that ahead or astern positions are in a straight line, e.g. fourth to third, then remote control is quite easy. A direct linkage to another dummy gear lever is possible (40), or a strong push–pull cable control, e.g. Teleflex.

If the gear lever has to be moved across the gate, then the control lever must duplicate this movement in a fashion similar to the remote gear change fitted to cars, for instance on rear-engined cars or cars with column change. In fact, the column change type of gearbox makes far easier remote control than the floor type. The car-type cable controls can be used complete and there will probably be no reason why the column change lever cannot also be used. Otherwise two push–pull cables will have to be arranged, one for the fore-and-aft movement and one for the athwartship movement. The dummy lever will then duplicate the action of the actual gear lever. Ordinary bicycle brake cable is not designed for pushing and heavy solid cables must be used, such as are found on some motor-cycles.

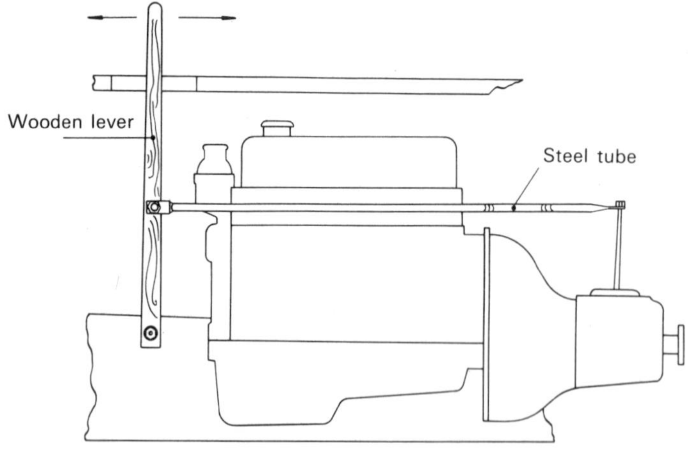

40 Simple remote control for 1st/2nd or 3rd/4th gear positions

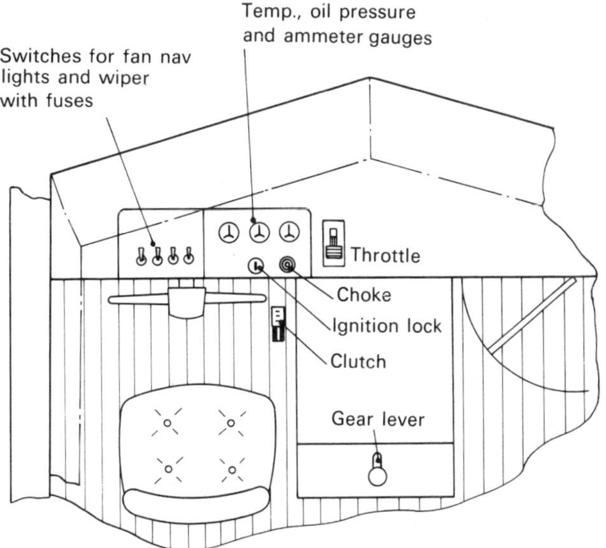

41 A good layout for the controls

The clutch control was dealt with in Chapter Four on gearboxes. A separate clutch can be an advantage, but the combination of wheel, gear lever, clutch and throttle can sometimes be too much to handle when standing in a rolling boat. If possible, it is best to arrange for the helmsman to sit down with a foot lever for the clutch (direct lever or hydraulic) and the gear lever and throttle to hand. Grouping all the other controls and instruments in front of the helmsman on a panel is a very good idea, although an undercover position then becomes necessary to avoid corrosion and electrical failure (41).

Throttle

A Bowden cable type of control is the obvious choice here. Unlike a car throttle, the lever needs to stay where it is put, despite engine vibration, and the simplest solution here is a motor mower type of lever control. Two reservations should be noted, however: over-sensitivity sometimes causes problems, and bicycle cables do not stand up to salt water very well. There are marine cables and levers available from large chandlers which overcome the last point. The length of lever fitted to the butterfly valve in car carburettors is very small, and particularly when the engine is not going to work hard it will be found that only a slight movement of the throttle lever is required for a large change in engine revs. A long lever up to 12 in. long, bolted to the butterfly valve pivot, is required to reduce the sensitivity.

Instruments

Instruments are by no means essential and it is possible to fit just an ignition lock and an oil warning light. An oil light is essential because an oil leak or oil pump failure could remain undetected and after a short time wreck the engine. The oil light works off a small pressure switch screwed into the block on car engines. An ignition warning light is not quite so essential because it only warns that the battery is not charging. It is worth fitting, though, unless an ammeter is fitted.

It is nice to be able to check the functioning of the engine at intervals more accurately than by merely looking and feeling, especially when undergoing first trials. A temperature gauge is the next necessary instrument. The electric type is generally fitted to cars where a sensor unit is housed in the thermostat casting. The temperature read is that of the hot water leaving the engine. The actual desired temperature depends on the cooling system—180°F for closed circuit or direct fresh water cooling systems and 135°F for direct salt water cooling systems.

An oil pressure gauge is a step better than an oil warning light. Car gauges usually work off the same tapping on the block as the oil pressure switch. There is little point in having both a light and a gauge, but it can be arranged with a tee-piece connector. Car engine oil pressures are generally between 50 and 60 p.s.i. dropping to about 15 p.s.i. when idling.

The next most necessary instrument is an ammeter to show charge and discharge. The ignition warning light is not then very necessary. The charging rate after engine starting should be quite high, around 15–20 amps, gradually tapering off as the battery becomes fully charged. An alternator gives much higher currents, so an ammeter reading up to 50 amps may be necessary, depending on the size of the alternator.

Car-type fuel gauges and tank units work well enough on board a boat. The tank unit consists of a float rising and falling with the fuel level which moves a lever across a variable resistance. The tank unit is bolted onto the top or side of the tank with a sealing gasket. A dipstick is a foolproof alternative, and a mechanical direct reading gauge mounted on top of the tank is another reliable solution.

A tachometer (rev counter) is useful on trials, and subsequently for finding the economical cruising speed of the boat. For fast boats it is a rather essential item to ensure that the engine does not over-speed or labour at full throttle. When optimising propellers on a fast boat to achieve maximum speed it is essential to have a tachometer.

Unless the boat is fitted with a log, recording the distance travelled, there will be no record of how long the engine has run. The mileage recorder on a car tells when a service and oil change is due, and the equivalent item on a boat is an hour meter. This gives the total number of running hours the engine has done, thus giving a better idea as to when the oil should be changed. In a car the oil should usually be changed every six months or 6000 miles, whichever comes first. Six thousand miles at 30 m.p.h. gives 200 hours. A boat engine used every weekend in the summer is unlikely to reach 200 running hours a year, so the oil should logically be changed at least once a year preferably at the end of the season so that fresh oil is in the engine over the laid-up period.

Another gauge that may be useful is an oil temperature gauge, especially if the oil is not cooled other than by a flow of air around the sump. Too high a temperature will cause loss of lubrication and oil pressure. The ideal temperature is 180°F.

The car-type ignition lock can be used, but it must not be completely exposed to the elements, although this applies to any type of electrical instrument. Gauges, if situated in the open cockpit, will soon become stained and rusted on the inside, and eventually seize up.

Marine equipment

Car type instruments certainly do not last long in a salty environment. Good marine equipment is designed to be completely watertight and suitable for mounting in an open cockpit.

While gauges give a reading of pressure or temperature they do not give a *warning* that something is wrong and the trend nowadays is to have a visual/audio alarm. A visual alarm (i.e. a light coming on) could go unnoticed in bright sunlight hence the value of a combined visual/audible alarm—a buzzer. Usually a cancel button is provided to avoid irritation while doing repairs or maintenance.

Many chandlers and marine electrical specialists can supply instrument and switch panels either tailor made or as a standard pack but as always one pays for such a service.

Marine gearboxes are usually designed for remote control via push-pull cable. A gear shift control combined with throttle control has become the marine standard and there are many varieties on show in chandlers' showrooms.

CHAPTER NINE

Diesels

There is a touch of magic in the word 'diesel': it conjures up something which is far more desirable but less easily attained in comparison to a petrol engine. Although the diesel has some undisputed advantages, it is by no means always the logical choice for boat propulsion. One of the great attractions is the far greater economy of running. A diesel will consume about 0·4 pints per horsepower per hour, compared to about 0·65 for a petrol car engine. There is not only this fact, but diesel fuel bought at the waterside is cheaper in most countries. The absence of electrical ignition and a carburettor makes the diesel more reliable, while diesel fuel is far safer than petrol because, at normal temperatures, it does not vaporise to form explosive mixtures.

Diesel engines are built to very high standards, particularly the fuel pump, and the cost of a new engine is much greater than a petrol engine of the same power. No matter how an engine is acquired and converted, new, used or from a scrapyard, the finished article will inevitably have cost more. As pleasure boats do not run for many hours each year (100 hours is more than average) it will be quite a few years before the savings in the fuel bill will pay off the extra initial cost.

Weight is another problem. A BLMC 2·2 complete with gearbox will come out at about 800 lb, whereas a 1100 cc petrol engine complete with gearbox will weigh less than half of this, yet produce the same power. This factor rules out diesels for small runabouts, and in fact it is not until the 25 ft mark is reached that automotive diesels are often used in fast craft. For the displacement type of boat the extra weight is really of no consequence, but there is still the problem of actually lifting it into the boat. Three men can lift a 1100 cc petrol engine into place, but a mechanical lift is required for all but the smallest diesels.

Noise and vibration are other disadvantages of the diesel. Unlike a petrol engine, which produces less noise the slower it is run, diesels give off a characteristic clatter even when idling—in fact, they seem to run more smoothly at high speeds. A truck diesel rigidly mounted in a hull will inevitably cause tremendous vibration and noise, especially at certain levels of engine revs, when the whole hull will vibrate in sympathy with the engine. A glassfibre hull is particularly susceptible to this sympathetic vibration, and in bad cases the hull quivers like a jelly and you wonder whether the bottom is going to fall out. The answer, of course, lies in flexible mounts and noise reduction techniques as described in Chapter Eleven.

A final disadvantage is the smell of diesel oil. Some people object to it and it does tend to soak into woodwork rather than evaporate rapidly like petrol. Attention to the tightness of the fuel lines, the fitting of a crankcase breather pipe to the air inlet and a drip tray underneath the engine will usually take care of this problem.

People who are familiar with car engines will be happier converting a petrol engine rather than a diesel, but the two types of engine are basically very similar. Mechanically, the pistons, crankshaft and valves are similar but more robust. In lieu of the carburettor there is a fuel pump, which via fuel injectors mounted in place of spark plugs injects neat fuel into the cylinders. Fuel pumps are either of the in-line type or the distributor type, and both are built with the precision of a fine watch. DIY work on these items is out of the question, but exchange will reduce the cost. Injectors, which have a life between testing of anything up to 2500 hours, can also be exchanged.

Just as a car petrol engine can be marinised and installed in a boat, so a truck or taxi diesel engine can be used. Basically the same arguments apply, but it is the differences in conversion and installation that this chapter is about. Nowadays most marine diesels are marinised automotive engines; in fact there has been a surge of professional marinisation, particularly of Ford diesels—the 2712E and 2715E—and the range of BLMC diesels. The specification usually includes heat exchanger cooling, Jabsco seawater pumps, external engine oil and gearbox oil coolers, an alternator and a hydraulically operated marine gearbox.

Overhauling

Much the same techniques apply to the diesel. The valve springs are considerably stiffer and require robust spring compressing tools. Before fitting the injectors it is best to adjust the tappets, as diesels with their high compression ratios take a lot of effort to turn over. If the fuel pump has been serviced, the fuel level will have to be topped up. The inspection cover is loosened and oil pumped up with the auxiliary hand pump until oil comes out of the level plug hole. The injector pipes must be carefully tightened and bending of the pipes avoided, or they will readily fracture. Any steadying clips on the pipes must be replaced, as long, unsupported lengths of this high pressure piping will soon crack from vibration.

Cooling

Heat exchanger cooling is most often used for diesels because the designed running temperature of the basic engine is high—about 180°F. With a direct salt water system, the temperature would have to be restricted to 135°F to avoid salt deposition in the water passages, and incomplete combustion resulting in sooting up would occur to a greater extent. This is especially true if the engine is to work normally at less than its full horsepower. With a closed circuit system the water temperature rise as it passes through a block is quite small (10°–20°F), whereas with a direct system it may be up to 80°F. It is obvious that with a direct system parts of the block or head will be overcooled, quite apart from the thermal strains inevitably set up. Direct cooling is a second rate method of cooling for any engine, and over a long period of time (several hundred running hours) diesels have atomiser troubles and experience far greater wear, due partly to quicker deterioration of the lubricating oil and partly to the lower cylinder temperatures. Noise is greater too.

The flow rate of seawater through the heat exchanger should be about 1·5 gallons per minute per 10 HP, or about 0·8 if direct cooled. Gas-blow into the water passages through the cylinder head gasket is often a problem with diesels, as it can interfere with the coolant flow. Keeping the header tank as high as possible and the fresh water circuit as simple as possible usually avoids this trouble. Many proprietary makes of heat exchangers fit directly on the thermostat housing, thus making the circuit very simple.

The factors determining whether the exhaust manifold and the engine oil require cooling are the same as for a petrol engine. If anything there is less necessity to cool the exhaust manifold because the diesel is more efficient and less heat is carried away down the exhaust pipe.

Gearbox

Smaller diesels as fitted in taxis and vans usually have four-speed gearboxes of approximately the same ratios as car gearboxes, although the reverse ratio is often much larger—upwards of 6 : 1. Truck gearboxes often have more forward ratios and even higher reverse ratios. Due to the higher reverse ratios the simple method of conversion, i.e. using the third gears to drive the layshaft, is not so effective. On the other hand diesel gearboxes tend to be more roomy inside and larger chain sprockets can be fitted in lieu of the gears, so that more power can be transmitted. A diesel gives a more impulsive torque because of the high compression ratio, and a higher shock factor must be taken into account when choosing a chain drive. Conversion can be carried out as described in Chapter Four on gearboxes: fundamentally there is no difference.

Marine gearboxes are more often fitted to diesels than to car engines, perhaps because the cost of a marine box becomes comparatively less after spending more on buying and converting a diesel engine. Because the horsepowers are no greater the same boxes can be fitted. The marine boxes most often adopted are the Borg Warner, PRM and TMP. Several firms who marinise engines can supply adapter plates to fit popular engines such as the BLMC 1·5 and 2·5 and Ford 2400 and 2700 series.

The clutches on diesels inevitably need more force to disengage and a robust system of control is necessary. A hydraulic system is undoubtedly the best.

Mounting and noise

As mentioned earlier, the diesel is heavier and rougher than its petrol cousin. Rigidly mounted lorry diesels, in boats of less than about 30 ft length, almost always cause a disgraceful amount of vibration and noise. The answer is to fit marine type rubber mounts of which there is plenty of choice. Because of the extra weight the engine bearers need to be massively constructed.

Fuel supply

It is absolutely imperative that the engine is fed with clean fuel, especially if it is fitted with the distributor type of injection pump.

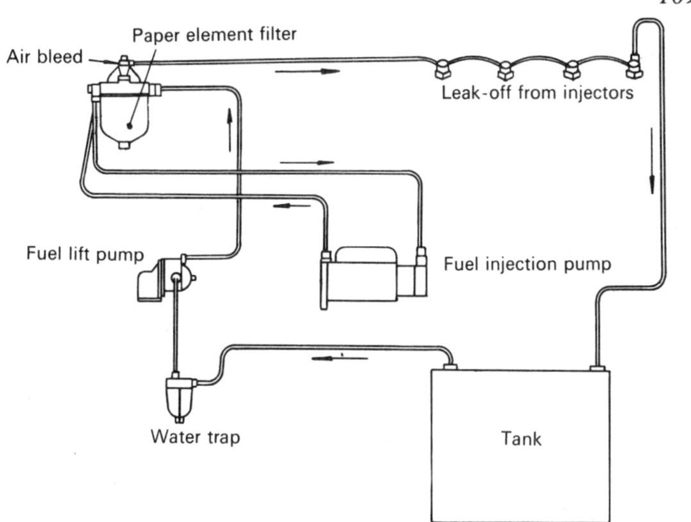

42 Fuel system layout with DPA injection pump

Dirt in the fuel plays havoc with the injection system, and is the diesel's Achilles' heel as far as reliability goes. Copper gauze and a water trap is not a good enough system: the fuel must be micro-filtered. A 3 micron filter is usually required. These are readily available through commercial vehicle dealers (e.g. CAV or Simms), the actual filter element being renewable. The element should be changed every season or every 150 hours' running. It will also remove water droplets and air bubbles, which cause erratic running. Quite often a fuel micro-filter is fitted to the engine. Two micro-filters are a very worthwhile precaution. Although the first in the line will take out 99% of the dirt the second will cater for the times when the first filter is replaced and the bowl cleaned out—in the process it is difficult to avoid dirt bypassing the first filter. The second filter will only need replacing very infrequently. In any case, it is well to have a simple bowl-type water/dirt trap in the line. Air bubbles in the system will cause erratic running or stoppage, and if air gets into the line, either through running out of fuel or when part of the system is disconnected, the whole system has to be bled. This must be done in strict sequence according to the engine manual.

The filter is usually bled first by slackening off the bleed screw mounted on top while pumping fuel through, using the fuel pump priming lever. The fuel pump is done next using the bleed valves in

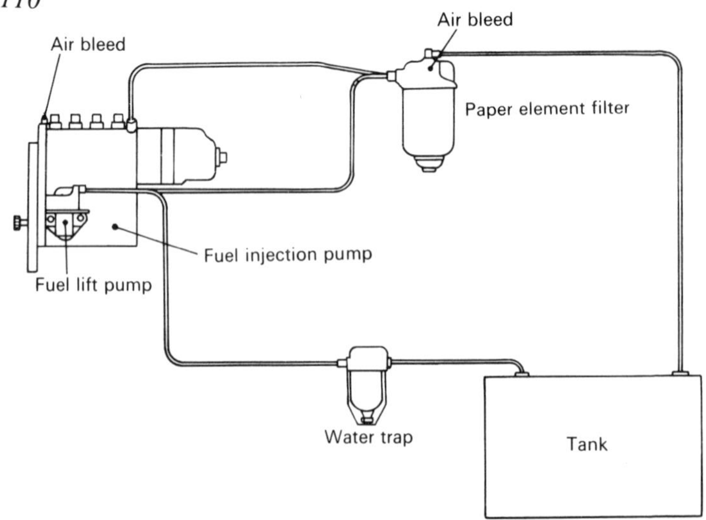

43 Fuel system layout with an in-line injection pump

the pump. Finally, the injector pressure pipes should be slackened off at the injectors and the engine cranked over with the speed control open, until all air bubbles have dispersed. The heater plugs can be removed to release the compression. If no heater plugs are fitted, the injectors can be removed, but be careful not to let the high pressure spray from the injectors impinge on your hand—it can cause dermatitis. Whenever replacing injectors make sure that the copper sealing washers are in good order. Also, never bend the pipes—take off both end connectors. Electric heater plugs, when fitted, are used for cold starts. They are left on for about a minute before operating the starter. The current taken is about 10 amps per cylinder.

Stopping a diesel is achieved by cutting off the fuel supply at the fuel injection pump. A separate pull cable with spring return, leading to the control position is usual. However an electric solenoid working on the cut-off lever on the pump and operated via the starter key is more convenient. A cable stop control can always be left pulled out unintentionally!

A diesel must never be stopped by turning off the cock in the fuel pipe, because air will be forced into the system and it will have to be bled again. A cock is useful at the tank if you want to disconnect part of the system, or if there is a fire. Normally, it is best never to shut the cock off because it is so easy to forget to turn it on again. The safety aspect of the fuel system is not nearly so critical as in a petrol-engined boat.

Diesels need a return pipe to the main tank because the injection pump takes far more fuel than it needs for injection. This flow cools the pump so the return fuel flow is warm which means that the return must not go back to a small header tank because the contents would gradually become hot.

Plastic fuel lines must never be used partly because of the fire risk and partly because leakage is more likely. If the tank is below the level of the fuel lift pump then the fuel in the pipe will be under suction and any leak will leak *air* into the system causing erratic running and non-starting. For this reason a higher tank level is desirable even with a metal pipe. Car engine lubricating oils are not usually suitable for diesels. A heavy duty oil at least to US Ordnance Specification MIL-L-2104B is most often called for (see page 184). If the engine is new or reconditioned, the oil filter must be discarded and a new one fitted after the first 15–20 hours' running. It is amazing how much metal swarf and bits are trapped in the filter at first. The filter should be changed at least once a year, or after every 150 hours' running, although obviously the handbook's recommendation must be used.

Most automotive diesels are fitted with mechanical fuel lift pumps. The disadvantages of a mechanical pump as fitted to a petrol engine disappear because the diesel fuel does not and cannot, in fact, evaporate out of the system, and vapour locks cannot be formed.

Tanks may be made of steel (but lead coated), stainless steel, aluminium alloy or glassfibre, using self-quenching resin to BS S476 Part 1. Copper and galvanised steel are best avoided as they tend to form sludge over a long period of time.

Electrics

Naturally, without an electrical ignition system the electrics are simpler. With a dynamo, regulator and cut-out, an ignition switch is not strictly necessary. However, there are still the starter solenoid switch, instruments and appliances which need to be switched off with the engine, so a normal starter lock is convenient. The basic circuits, therefore, remain the same as for the petrol engine (37) apart from the omission of the ignition side. If the engine is fitted with heater plugs, then a diesel key lock can be bought (e.g. Lucas) which has a heater position incorporated (44).

Dynamos have their limitations, and as a diesel requires far more cranking power more electrical starting power is needed. Today alternators are usually fitted to truck diesels and these are an advantage on a boat. There must be a switch to switch off the field circuit of the alternator when the engine is stopped, otherwise the battery is discharged at the rate of 2 or 3 amps. This can be arranged again with a key switch (44).

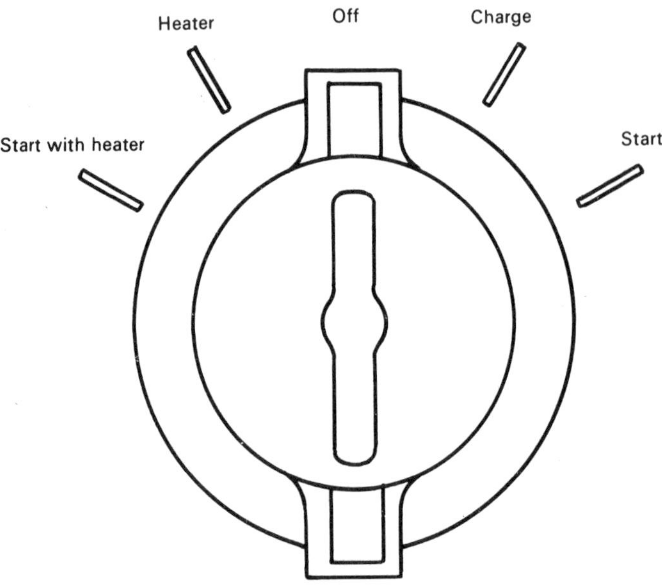

44 Diesel starter keylock switch

Engine starting batteries need to be of a greater amp-hour capacity than those for petrol engines. A $1\frac{1}{2}$ litre diesel needs a battery capacity of at least 75 AH, while a 4 litre engine needs 130 AH. Hand starting is not really feasible, except perhaps on the smallest automotive diesels—the cranking effort is too great, and decompression is not fitted. To avoid being stuck with a flat battery, two batteries can be fitted, one for starting and one for all the other systems, as described in Chapter Seven on electrics. Other alternatives are the Simms Spring Starter and the Bryce Berger Handraulic starter. These are devices whereby energy is stored by working a lever. The spring or hydraulic mechanism is then released to spin the engine.

Instruments, e.g. temperature, oil pressure, ammeter and tachometer gauges, are rather more necessary on a diesel, not because things are more likely to go wrong but because, if they do, it will be a more costly affair.

Turbocharging

Several of the larger truck diesels can be found in turbo-charged form. Essentially a turbo charger is a turbine in the exhaust flow which drives an air compressor ramming air into the engine. The two elements are combined into one compact unit called the turbocharger. Since a greater quantity of air is pushed into the cylinders under pressure more fuel can be injected without creating smoke and hence the power is increased. Engine rpm usually remains the same. The turbocharger does not 'come in' until quite high revs are achieved, usually it can be heard as a high pitched whine. The extra power—for very little extra weight—makes a turbocharged engine attractive for planing boats.

Additional power can be achieved if the air rammed into the engine is cooled (thus increasing its density and increasing the mass flow). This is achieved with an intercooler (or charge air cooler)—an air/sea-water heat exchanger.

Increasing 'amounts' of turbocharging (i.e. increasing the boost pressure) creates more power but increases the need for intercooling and the need to modify the compression ratio.

Needless to say turbochargers are expensive little items and need to be matched to the engine. Also the engine has to be suitable for turbocharging so if a turbocharged engine is what is wanted it is best to marinise an engine already fitted with a turbocharger or at least to choose an engine for which turbocharging parts are available.

See next page for table of current diesels suitable for marinisation.

Current popular diesels for marinisation

		Capacity cc	HP	R.P.M.	No. of Cylinders	
2401E	Ford	2360	59	3600	4	
2402E	"	3540	87	3600	6	
2712E*	"	4150	80	2500	4	
2715E	"	6220	120	2500	6	
2704E*	"	5945	150	2400	6	
1.5	BL	1489	36	3500	4	
1.8	"	1799	50	4000	4	Sherpa
2.5	"	2520	60	3500	4	
3.8	"	3770	74	2500	4	
5.7	"	5660	113	2400	6	
4.108	Perkins	1760	47	3600	4	
4.236*	"	3860	72	2500	4	
6.354*	"	5798	115	2800	6	
OM636	Mercedes	1767	42	3300	4	
GOLF		1500/1600	45	4000	4	
XLD416	Ford	1600	54	4800	4	Escort
FSD425	"	2500	70	4000	4	Transit

* can be turbocharged.

CHAPTER TEN

Propeller

The object of this chapter is not only to enable you to choose a propeller size which will suit the engine and boat but also to show how to choose a reduction ratio for the gearbox in the planning stage.

Choosing a propeller

There are three governing factors which determine propeller size. These are the speed of water in way of the propeller assuming the propeller is not there, the horsepower the propeller is given, and the propeller shaft r.p.m.

The first factor, water speed, is the most difficult to estimate. It depends on two things, the boat's speed and the nature of the water flow aft. The boat's speed is dictated largely by the horsepower of the engine and the waterline length of the hull (45, 46). The propeller

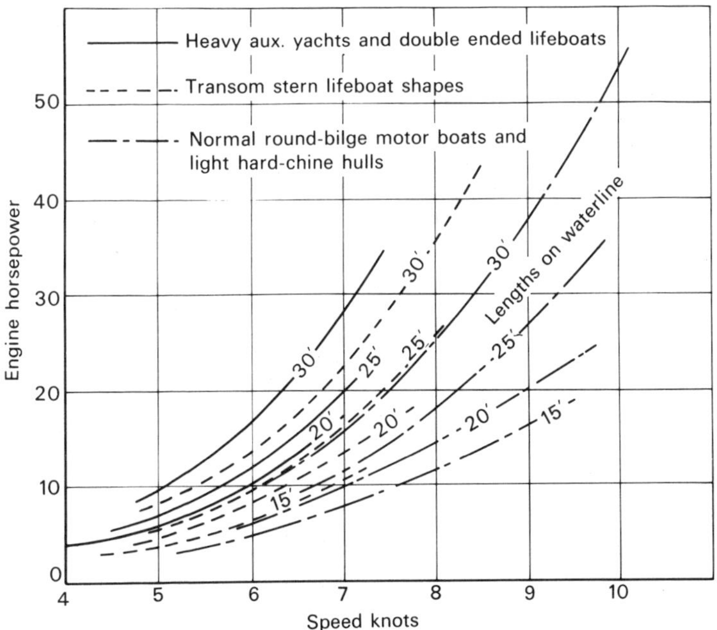

45 Curves for speed estimation; displacement boats

does, of course, have an effect because of its varying efficiency, but for propeller selection this can be ignored. Fortunately correct propeller size is not very sensitive to inaccuracies in speed estimation.

The nature of the hull aft varies the speed of flow into the propeller. If the propeller is completely below the bottom of the boat, as on a hard chine speedboat, the speed of water ('velocity' in the Propeller Tables) can be taken as the speed of the boat. On the other hand, in the case of a deep-keeled yacht with the propeller fitted in an aperture the water flow to the propeller will have been slowed down by friction on the bottom, so that the propeller will be working in the wake which is, in fact, being dragged along with the hull. Consequently although the boat may be doing 8 knots, as far as the propeller is concerned it may only have an inflow of 6 knots—a 25% reduction (47).

The engine HP must also be estimated. If the full HP is to be used, obviously the manufacturer's figures will do. It is best to lop off about 10% from their figures to allow for losses in the gearbox and transmission. The corresponding rated r.p.m. reduced by the reduction ratio should be used as the propeller r.p.m. in the table. Where the full HP of the engine is not going to be used, then a careful estimate has to be made, together with a realistic engine r.p.m. It is

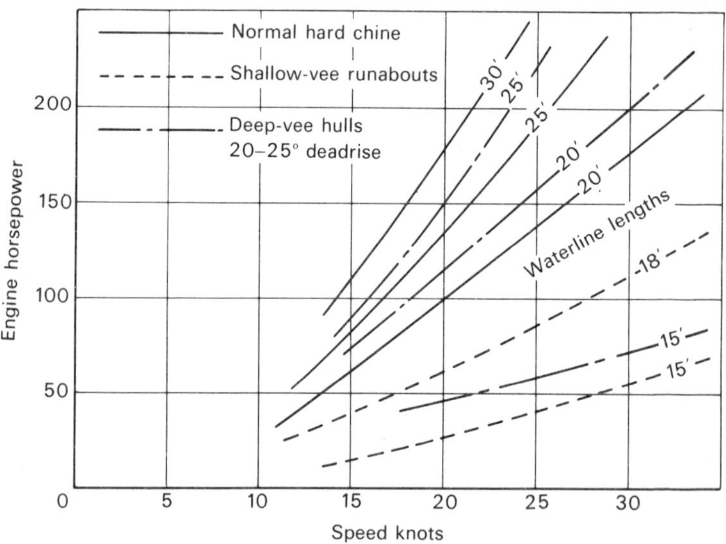

46 Curves for speed estimation; planing boats

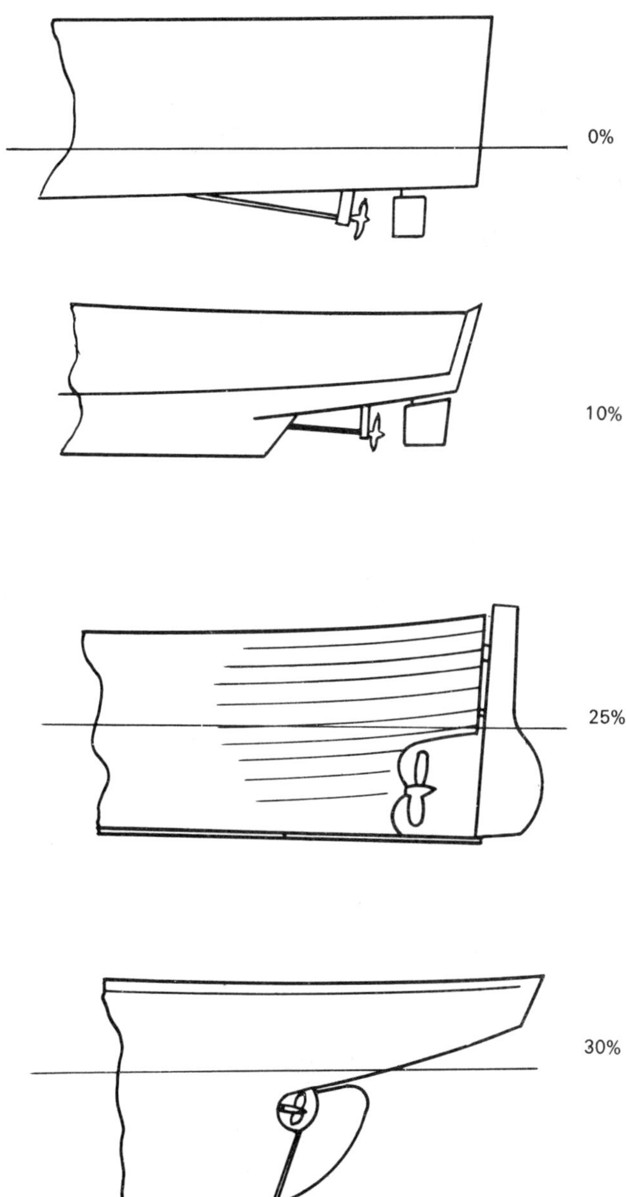

47 'Wake' reductions for use with the propeller tables

no use asking an engine to produce more power at a restricted r.p.m. than it is possible for it to produce. A safe rule of thumb is that the maximum HP is pro rata to the r.p.m., for instance, if the manufacturer's figure is 40 HP at 4000, then the maximum at 2000 will be 20, and so on. This will be at full throttle. At half throttle it will produce 10 HP at 2000 r.p.m.

Craft on inland waters do not need much power. Speed is usually restricted by law in any case, and a 22 ft heavily built cruiser will only need 10 HP to make a comfortable cruising speed of 5½ knots. This may sound slow, but it is all that you need on inland waters. It is so easy to overestimate the speed of a boat when looking over the side. It is worth mentioning at this point that a displacement boat (one that cannot plane, such as a clinker round-bilge hull) is more or less limited to speeds related to the length, no matter what power is installed. A length of 20 ft means a maximum of around 7 knots, and 25 ft around 8 knots. At these speeds the wash behind will be terrific and create havoc among craft moored along the bank, while easing off a knot or two will bring the wash and fuel consumption down enormously.

The curves (48) give an idea of what horsepower to choose for different types of boat and different conditions.

The figure to put into the Propeller Table should be the maximum that you will ever want. Bear in mind that sea-going boats may need a little in hand to counteract strong tides or winds. An appropriate engine r.p.m. which will allow this horsepower to be developed should be selected using the rule of thumb given above. To find the propeller r.p.m. divide the engine r.p.m. by the reduction ratio.

To demonstrate the preceding paragraph and the use of the Propeller Tables, let us take three examples.

An inland 20 ft ex-lifeboat cruiser with a Ford 100E and 2 : 1 reduction: 10 actual HP will give a speed of 6½ knots (45) and the engine should be able to comfortably deliver this at 2000 r.p.m. The engine will be running lightly and quietly. In fact, normal cruising could be less than this, say 1500 r.p.m. The hull will give an appreciable wake (47), say 25%, so the figures to use in the propeller tables are 4·8 knots (6½ knots less 25%). 10 DHP (delivered HP) and 2000 ÷ 2 (reduction ratio) = 1000 propeller r.p.m. Look down the columns to 4, 10, 1000 and 6, 10, 1000 giving propellers 16·7 × 10·2 and 16·5 × 11·7 (diameter × pitch in inches). Therefore for a speed of 4·8 knots a propeller size of 16·6 × 10·9

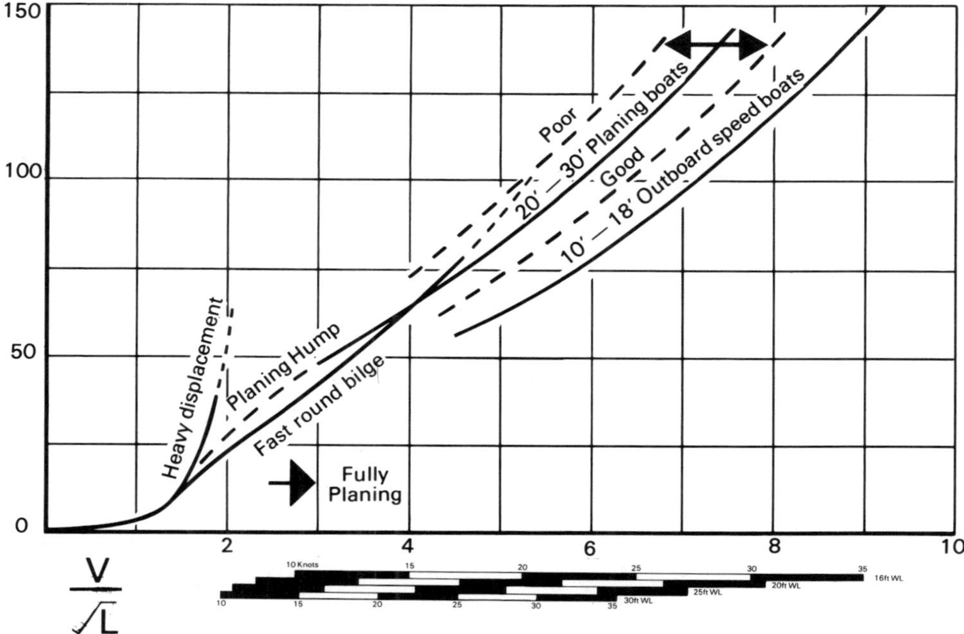

48 Guidelines for choosing engine power. To plane properly at least 50 HP/ton is necessary, although it is always better to have a margin of power to cater for rough water, a fouled bottom or the weight of extra passengers and gear. HP is total maximum, TON is all-up weight of boat plus fuel and crew, V is speed in knots, L is length on waterline in feet

should suit. This can be rounded to 16·5 × 11. This propeller will restrict the engine r.p.m. at full throttle to about 2600 r.p.m. when the engine would develop about 25 HP. This does not matter, as even the fastest cruise contemplated involves only 10 HP and 2000 r.p.m. If a smaller propeller were fitted the engine would be able to rev faster at full throttle, thus producing more power and a little more boat speed. But this would then mean that to absorb 10 HP, i.e. to travel at 6½ knots, the propeller and thus the engine would have to run faster than 2000 r.p.m., thus running very light and producing more noise. It's a delicate compromise between overloading and underloading the engine. A 16·5 × 11 propeller is fairly large for a 20 ft boat, but is very efficient (about 50%) for the low speed. If the aperture only allows, say, a 15 in. propeller then it will not affect the 'mating' of the engine to the propeller very much if 1½ in. is knocked off the diameter and added to the pitch, making the propeller size 15 × 12·5.

A displacement type sea-going 22 ft glassfibre transom sterned cruiser, with a BLMC 2·2 litre diesel and 1½ : 1 reduction. The engine develops a maximum of 42 HP at 3000 r.p.m., which is excessive power for a boat of this size (48). In this case, rather than fit a propeller which restricts the full throttle r.p.m., thus restricting the horsepower, it is better to choose a propeller that can absorb the full HP at the full r.p.m., and normally run the engine at less than full throttle. The speed of the boat with 42 HP would be about 10 knots (45), although cavitation may well set in, and in any case the boat would be trying to climb an enormous self-induced wave. However, this is just the design case, and assuming 20% wake (47) the figures to find in the tables are 8, 38, (10% off for transmission loss) 2000. The nearest line gives a propeller of 14·6 × 9·2. It would be better to err on the large size in this case, when rounding the figures, so a 15 × 9 should suit.

An 18 ft hard-chine runabout with a 1600 cc Ford petrol engine developing 60 HP at 4500 r.p.m. This is a light boat with a shallow vee bottom and will achieve a maximum of about 26 knots (46). The propeller will be in 'open' water so there will be no wake reduction, and as the drive is direct the propeller r.p.m. will be 4500. DHP will be 54 assuming 10% losses. The nearest to these figures in the Tables are 25, 50, 4000. Judging the extra 500 r.p.m. gives a propeller 8·5 × 9. The high speed section of the Propeller Tables has not been divided into such fine steps as the lower speed sections, because propeller choice for high speed is very much more a process of trial and error. However, the tables do give a starting point. If on trials the r.p.m. do not get up to 4500, then you would reduce the size a little, either by cutting off the tips or exchanging the propeller for another. If the engine 'ran away' and overspeeded, the propeller size would need to be increased. The correct propeller will give 4500 r.p.m. and the best boat speed.

Reduction ratios

The preceding paragraphs show how to choose a propeller size when the boat, engine and gearbox are already there or decided upon. In the planning stage it is possible with these Propeller Tables to determine the optimum reduction ratio from those available in the car gearbox or the marine box.

The larger the propeller the greater the efficiency, i.e. the greater the thrust given to the boat for each HP absorbed. To take an example from the tables, compare the efficiency figures given for 6, 40, 2000 and 6, 40, 1000 (38·8% and 46·2% respectively). Both propellers absorb 40 HP at a water inflow speed of 6 knots, but one revolves half as fast as the other, and is, of course, a much larger propeller. The low-speed one is 7·4% more efficient and will give that much more push. If the whole table is studied it will be seen that as the boat speed increases the general order of efficiency increases and the gain of a reduction ratio becomes less. Also at slow speeds as the power increases, the efficiency drops rapidly to around 30–40%, which is low. Generally, 50% is an average figure and 60% very good. The need, therefore, for a low propeller r.p.m. and consequently a reduction ratio becomes more important at low boat speeds and high powers, e.g. a heavy canal boat or heavy seagoing fishing launch. To generalise, it is best to keep the propeller r.p.m. below 2000 for speeds below 10 knots. This entails a reduction of at least 2 : 1 when powering the boat with a car engine, unless the full revs and horsepower of the engine are not required.

The governing factor for a low propeller r.p.m. is usually the size of the propeller aperture. It is well to allow a clearance of at least 15% of the diameter of the propeller between the tips and the hull. This is particularly important where there is a flat surface of hull directly above the propeller. A double ended hull like an ex-lifeboat is not in this category, but these hulls do have a problem which is worth mentioning here. As there is no area of hull directly above the propeller, air tends to get sucked down, resulting in engine racing and loss of thrust. Pitching in a seaway also brings the propeller tips out of the water. A 'cavitation' plate is the answer. This is usually a horizontal galvanised steel plate faired into the hull and fitted directly over the tips of the propeller.

Getting back to the selection of a reduction ratio, the largest diameter propeller that can be fitted is the starting point. Having chosen an engine horsepower an approximate boat speed can be found (45). Now look down the Tables until the appropriate water flow speed and horsepower are found. It will be noted that as the propeller r.p.m. comes down, the propeller diameter goes up. Choose, therefore, the propeller r.p.m. that gives the largest propeller diameter that can be fitted. This r.p.m. divided into the engine r.p.m. gives the optimum reduction ratio. By experimenting with a few figures you will soon see what I mean. In the planning stages, it is possible to look into and decide engine and propeller revs and propeller size, so that problems do not occur later on. It is sometimes found on trials that the reduction ratio fitted is too great and there is not enough space for the correspondingly large propeller to be fitted. To generalise once again, for an ordinary car engine fitted in an inland cruiser $1\frac{1}{2}:1$ is usually a good compromise, although 1 : 1 or 2 : 1 can sometimes be used. A seagoing boat using more horsepower should have at least 2 : 1, possibly 3 : 1, while a fast runabout could have 1 : 1 or possibly $1\frac{1}{2}:1$.

Cavitation

This occurs when the propeller is overloaded, i.e. asked to produce too much thrust for the area of its blades. The water on the forward faces of the blades literally boils, the cavitation thus formed spectacularly reducing the thrust and giving rise to tremendous noise and vibration. It usually occurs in two cases, firstly a heavy, slow boat being pushed too hard by a big engine coupled to a fast-running propeller, and secondly, in high speed boats. The best cure in the first case is to fit a reduction ratio and, in the second one, to fit a propeller with wider blades, thus increasing the blade area. Fitting a propeller with a greater number of blades is another way of increasing the area. It is easy to mistake air being sucked into the propeller from the surface for cavitation, and the term 'anti-cavitation plate' is rather a misnomer.

The least blade area (total area of one side of all blades) to avoid cavitation is approximately as follows (although at 5 knots it is more a question of avoiding excessive slip).

Max speed of boat knots	sq. ins. per max engine HP (per shaft)
5	5.6
10	2.7
20	1.25
30	0.63

It is easy enough to measure the area of one blade of an existing propeller by pressing a 1-inch squared piece of graph paper onto the blade and then counting the whole squares and estimating the part squares. Multiply this area by the number of blades.

The area of the circle described by the tips of the blades is found by the formula 0·78 (Diam″)^2. The area of the blades will be some fraction of the circle area. This ratio is called the blade area ratio (BAR). If the blade area is half the circle area the BAR is 0.5 which is a common BAR for fast craft or for slower ones where the prop revs are rather too high (1:1 or $1\frac{1}{2}$:1 reduction being employed rather than the more efficient 2:1). Yachts with small engines and 2-bladed props usually have a BAR of 0.2 or 0.3. Anything more than 0.5 is usually a 'special' and not available ready cast.

In the propeller tables on the following pages it will be noticed that the efficiency column is left blank at 20 knots and above. This is because the efficiency at higher speeds is always good, and this factor is therefore not such an important constraint as the level of cavitation. In choosing a propeller on a fast boat one should check that the blade area is sufficient. If it turns out that a very large BAR is required then a greater reduction ratio (slower propeller rpm) will be needed to give a larger diameter propeller which of course, for the same BAR, gives more blade area.

To finish off this chapter, here are a few practical points on propellers and stern gear. Propellers are usually three-bladed and are termed either left-handed or right-handed. A left-handed propeller revolves anti-clockwise when looking forward at it from behind the boat. A right-handed propeller is the opposite. The size (diameter × pitch) is usually stamped on the boss. The thinner the blade section and the sharper the edges the more efficient it will be, but the increase in efficiency is small. It will, of course, be less robust. Propellers usually come in inch or half-inch sizes, so probably all the figures in the tables, after any necessary adjustment, will have to be rounded up or down. Part exchange of propellers is quite common.

The angle of the propeller shaft to the horizontal should not be more than 10°. The deadwood or stern post immediately in front of the propeller should be faired to an edge, so that the inflow of water will not be so turbulent. Cavitation is often induced by a square-ended stern post on heavy auxiliary yachts.

The minimum shaft size is dependent on the horsepower and shaft revs (49). It is always best to be generous with shaft diameters, and for car engines 1 in. is usually a suitable size. Stern tubes are described in Chapter Five, on mounting and drive; so too is the subject of bearing spacing.

HP per 100 shaft rpm	shaft diameter ins.
1	$\frac{7}{8}$
$1\frac{1}{2}$	1
2	$1\frac{1}{8}$
$2\frac{1}{2}$	$1\frac{1}{4}$
$4\frac{1}{2}$	$1\frac{1}{2}$
10	2

49 Minimum propeller shaft diameters. The figures relate to manganese bronze or mild steel shafts. For stainless steel the diameter can be reduced 5% and for Monel 19%.

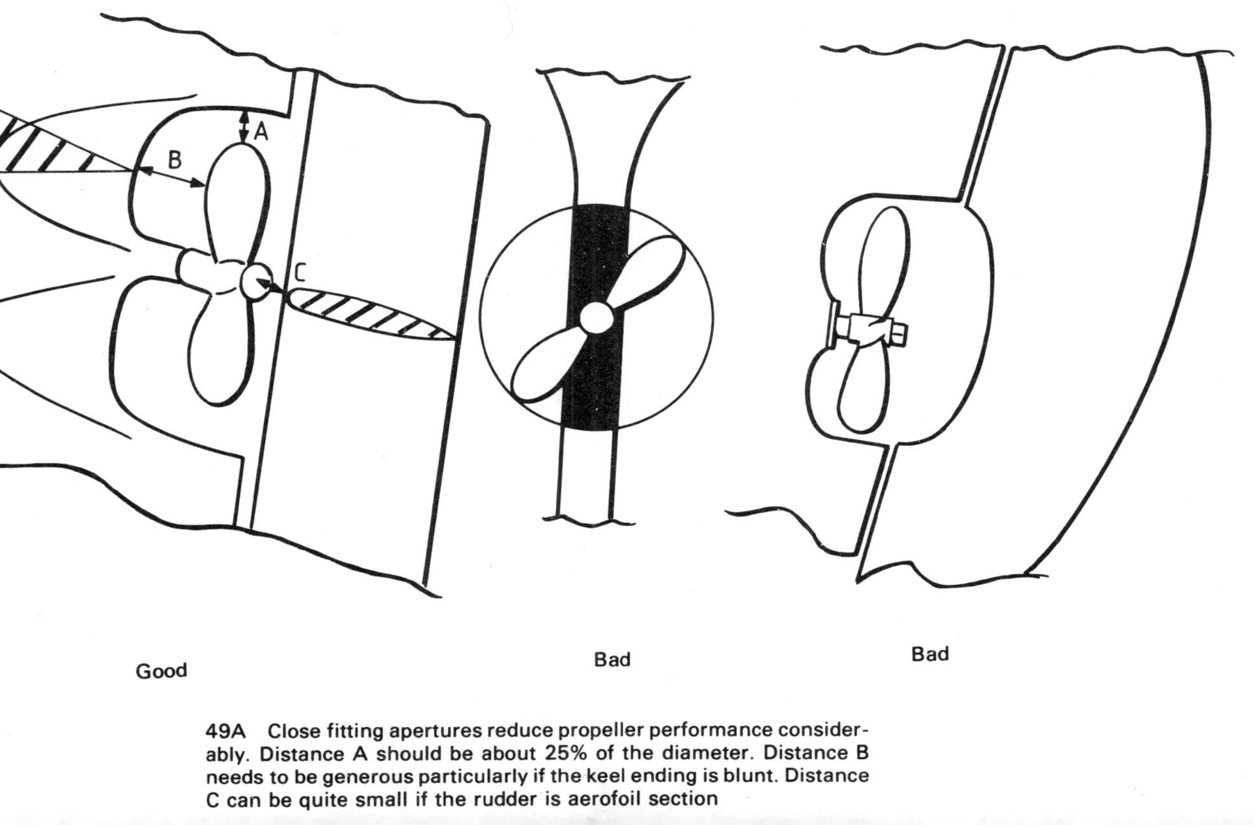

49A Close fitting apertures reduce propeller performance considerably. Distance A should be about 25% of the diameter. Distance B needs to be generous particularly if the keel ending is blunt. Distance C can be quite small if the rudder is aerofoil section

Propeller Tables

The tables progress from column to column, the speed gradually increasing 4, 6, 8 . . . knots. With each speed the power (column 2) is gradually increased 4, 6, 8 . . . hp.

Velocity knots	HP	Prop. RPM	Per cent. efficiency	Diam. in.	Pitch in.
4	4	800	50·5	16·0	10·5
4	4	900	49·3	14·9	9·6
4	4	1000	48·0	13·9	8·9
4	4	1100	46·7	13·2	8·3
4	4	1200	45·7	12·5	7·8
4	4	1300	44·9	11·9	7·4
4	4	1400	44·2	11·4	7·0
4	4	1500	43·5	10·9	6·7
4	4	1600	42·8	10·5	6·4
4	4	1700	42·2	10·1	6·2
4	4	1800	41·6	9·8	6·0
4	4	1900	41·1	9·5	5·8
4	4	2000	40·5	9·2	5·6
4	4	2100	39·9	9·0	5·5
4	4	2200	39·2	8·7	5·3
4	6	800	48·3	17·3	11·0
4	6	900	46·7	16·1	10·2
4	6	1000	45·5	15·1	9·4
4	6	1100	44·6	14·3	8·8
4	6	1200	43·8	13·5	8·3
4	6	1300	42·9	12·9	7·9
4	6	1400	42·1	12·3	7·5
4	6	1500	41·4	11·9	7·2
4	6	1600	40·5	11·4	7·0
4	6	1700	40·0	11·0	6·7
4	6	1800	39·2	10·7	6·5
4	6	1900	38·7	10·4	6·3
4	6	2000	38·3	10·1	6·2
4	8	800	46·4	18·3	11·5
4	8	900	45·1	17·1	10·6
4	8	1000	44·2	16·0	9·8
4	8	1100	43·1	15·1	9·2
4	8	1200	42·2	14·3	8·7
4	8	1300	41·4	13·7	8·4
4	8	1400	40·5	13·1	8·0
4	8	1500	39·7	12·6	7·7
4	8	1600	38·9	12·2	7·4
4	8	1700	38·5	11·8	7·2
4	8	1800	38·0	11·4	7·0
4	10	800	45·1	19·2	11·9
4	10	900	44·1	17·8	10·9
4	10	1000	42·9	16·7	10·2
4	10	1100	41·9	15·8	9·6
4	10	1200	41·1	15·0	9·2
4	10	1300	40·3	14·4	8·8
4	10	1400	39·2	13·8	8·4
4	10	1500	38·6	13·3	8·1
4	10	1600	38·1	12·8	7·8
4	12	800	44·3	19·9	12·2
4	12	900	43·1	18·5	11·3
4	12	1000	42·0	17·4	10·6
4	12	1100	41·1	16·4	10·0
4	12	1200	39·9	15·6	9·5
4	12	1300	39·0	15·0	9·1
4	12	1400	38·4	14·4	8·8
4	14	800	43·6	20·5	12·5
4	14	900	42·3	19·1	11·6
4	14	1000	41·2	17·9	10·9
4	14	1100	40·1	17·0	10·4
4	14	1200	39·0	16·2	9·9
4	14	1300	38·4	15·5	9·5
4	16	800	42·8	21·0	12·8
4	16	900	41·6	19·6	12·0
4	16	1000	40·5	18·5	11·3
4	16	1100	39·2	17·5	10·7
4	16	1200	38·5	16·7	10·2
4	20	800	41·7	22·0	13·4
4	20	900	40·3	20·6	12·5
4	20	1000	39·0	19·4	11·8
4	20	1100	38·3	18·4	11·2
4	25	800	40·5	23·1	14·1
4	25	900	39·0	21·6	13·2
4	25	1000	38·2	20·4	12·4
4	30	800	39·3	24·0	14·6
4	30	900	38·3	22·5	13·7
4	35	800	38·6	24·9	15·2
4	40	800	38·1	25·7	15·6
6	4	800	62·5	14·9	13·3
6	4	900	61·3	14·1	11·9
6	4	1000	60·3	13·3	10·9
6	4	1100	59·3	12·6	10·0
6	4	1200	58·3	12·0	9·3
6	4	1300	57·2	11·5	8·6
6	4	1400	56·4	11·1	8·1
6	4	1500	55·6	10·7	7·7
6	4	1600	54·8	10·4	7·3
6	4	1700	54·0	10·1	7·0
6	4	1800	53·3	9·8	6·7
6	4	1900	52·6	9·5	6·4
6	4	2000	51·9	9·2	6·2
6	4	2100	51·2	8·9	6·0
6	4	2200	50·5	8·7	5·7
6	6	800	60·5	16·5	13·6
6	6	900	59·2	15·4	12·2
6	6	1000	58·0	14·6	11·1
6	6	1100	56·8	13·9	10·2
6	6	1200	55·8	13·2	9·6
6	6	1300	54·9	12·7	9·0
6	6	1400	53·9	12·3	8·5
6	6	1500	53·0	11·8	8·1
6	6	1600	52·2	11·4	7·7
6	6	1700	51·3	11·0	7·3
6	6	1800	50·5	10·6	7·0

Velocity knots	HP	Prop. RPM	Per cent. efficiency	Diam. in.	Pitch in.
6	6	1900	49·9	10·3	6·7
6	6	2000	49·4	10·0	6·5
6	6	2100	48·8	9·7	6·2
6	6	2200	48·3	9·4	6·0
6	8	800	59·0	17·5	13·8
6	8	900	57·5	16·5	12·4
6	8	1000	56·3	15·6	11·4
6	8	1100	55·2	14·9	10·6
6	8	1200	54·0	14·2	9·9
6	8	1300	53·0	13·6	9·3
6	8	1400	52·0	13·1	8·8
6	8	1500	51·1	12·6	8·4
6	8	1600	50·2	12·1	7·9
6	8	1700	49·6	11·6	7·6
6	8	1800	49·0	11·3	7·3
6	8	1900	48·3	10·9	7·0
6	8	2000	47·7	10·6	6·7
6	8	2100	47·0	10·3	6·5
6	8	2200	46·4	10·0	6·3
6	10	800	57·6	18·5	13·9
6	10	900	56·2	17·4	12·7
6	10	1000	54·9	16·5	11·7
6	10	1100	53·7	15·7	10·9
6	10	1200	52·6	15·0	10·2
6	10	1300	51·5	14·3	9·6
6	10	1400	50·5	13·7	9·0
6	10	1500	49·7	13·1	8·6
6	10	1600	49·0	12·6	8·2
6	10	1700	48·3	12·2	7·8
6	10	1800	47·6	11·8	7·5
6	10	1900	46·9	11·4	7·2
6	10	2000	46·2	11·0	6·9
6	10	2100	45·7	10·7	6·7
6	10	2200	45·2	10·4	6·5
6	12	800	56·5	19·3	14·2
6	12	900	55·1	18·2	13·0
6	12	1000	53·8	17·3	12·0
6	12	1100	52·5	16·3	11·1
6	12	1200	51·4	15·5	10·4
6	12	1300	50·3	14·9	9·8
6	12	1400	49·5	14·2	9·2
6	12	1500	48·7	13·6	8·7
6	12	1600	47·9	13·1	8·3
6	12	1700	47·1	12·6	8·0
6	12	1800	46·4	12·2	7·7
6	12	1900	45·8	11·8	7·4
6	12	2000	45·2	11·5	7·1
6	12	2100	44·8	11·1	6·9
6	12	2200	44·4	10·8	6·6
6	14	800	55·6	20·0	14·4
6	14	900	54·1	18·9	13·2
6	14	1000	52·8	17·8	12·2
6	14	1100	51·5	16·9	11·3
6	14	1200	50·3	16·1	10·6
6	14	1300	49·5	15·3	9·9
6	14	1400	48·6	14·6	9·4
6	14	1500	47·8	14·0	8·9
6	14	1600	46·9	13·5	8·5
6	14	1700	46·2	13·0	8·2
6	14	1800	45·5	12·6	7·9
6	14	1900	44·9	12·2	7·6
6	14	2000	44·5	11·8	7·3
6	14	2100	44·1	11·5	7·0
6	14	2200	43·6	11·1	6·8
6	16	800	54·8	20·7	14·7
6	16	900	53·3	19·5	13·4
6	16	1000	51·9	18·4	12·4
6	16	1100	50·5	17·4	11·5
6	16	1200	49·6	16·5	10·7
6	16	1300	48·7	15·7	10·1
6	16	1400	47·8	15·0	9·6
6	16	1500	46·9	14·4	9·1
6	16	1600	46·1	13·9	8·7
6	16	1700	45·4	13·4	8·3
6	16	1800	44·8	12·9	8·0
6	16	1900	44·4	12·5	7·7
6	16	2000	43·9	12·1	7·4
6	16	2100	43·4	11·8	7·2
6	16	2200	42·8	11·4	7·0
6	20	800	53·3	21·9	15·1
6	20	900	51·8	20·4	13·8
6	20	1000	50·4	19·3	12·7
6	20	1100	49·3	18·2	11·8
6	20	1200	48·3	17·3	11·0
6	20	1300	47·3	16·4	10·4
6	20	1400	46·3	15·7	9·9
6	20	1500	45·6	15·1	9·4
6	20	1600	44·9	14·5	9·0
6	20	1700	44·4	14·0	8·6
6	20	1800	43·8	13·5	8·2
6	20	1900	43·2	13·1	8·0
6	20	2000	42·7	12·7	7·7
6	20	2100	42·1	12·3	7·5
6	20	2200	41·7	12·0	7·3
6	25	800	51·9	22·9	15·5
6	25	900	50·3	21·4	14·1
6	25	1000	49·2	20·1	13·0
6	25	1100	48·0	19·0	12·1
6	25	1200	46·9	18·0	11·4
6	25	1300	45·9	17·2	10·8
6	25	1400	45·1	16·5	10·2
6	25	1500	44·5	15·8	9·7
6	25	1600	43·9	15·2	9·3
6	25	1700	43·2	14·6	8·9
6	25	1800	42·6	14·1	8·6
6	25	1900	42·0	13·7	8·3
6	25	2000	41·5	13·3	8·1
6	25	2100	41·1	12·9	7·9
6	25	2200	40·5	12·6	7·7
6	30	800	50·6	23·9	15·8
6	30	900	49·3	22·2	14·4
6	30	1000	48·1	20·9	13·3
6	30	1100	46·8	19·7	12·4
6	30	1200	45·8	18·7	11·7
6	30	1300	44·9	17·8	11·0
6	30	1400	4	17·0	10·4

Velocity knots	HP	Prop. RPM	Per cent. efficiency	Diam. in.	Pitch in.
6	30	1500	43·6	16·3	10·0
6	30	1600	42·9	15·7	9·6
6	30	1700	42·2	15·2	9·2
6	30	1800	41·7	14·7	8·9
6	30	1900	41·2	14·2	8·7
6	30	2000	40·5	13·8	8·4
6	30	2100	40·0	13·4	8·2
6	30	2200	39·3	13·1	8·0
6	35	800	49·8	24·6	16·1
6	35	900	48·4	22·9	14·7
6	35	1000	47·1	21·5	13·6
6	35	1100	45·9	20·3	12·7
6	35	1200	44·9	19·3	12·0
6	35	1300	44·3	18·4	11·3
6	35	1400	43·5	17·6	10·7
6	35	1500	42·7	16·8	10·3
6	35	1600	42·1	16·2	9·9
6	35	1700	41·5	15·7	9·6
6	35	1800	40·8	15·2	9·2
6	35	1900	40·2	14·7	9·0
6	35	2000	39·6	14·3	8·7
6	35	2100	39·0	13·9	8·5
6	35	2200	38·6	13·5	8·3
6	40	800	49·0	25·3	16·3
6	40	900	47·6	23·5	15·0
6	40	1000	46·2	22·1	13·9
6	40	1100	45·2	20·9	13·0
6	40	1200	44·4	19·8	12·2
6	40	1300	43·6	18·9	11·5
6	40	1400	42·8	18·0	11·0
6	40	1500	42·0	17·3	10·6
6	40	1600	41·4	16·7	10·2
6	40	1700	40·7	16·1	9·8
6	40	1800	40·1	15·6	9·5
6	40	1900	39·4	15·1	9·2
6	40	2000	38·8	14·7	9·0
6	40	2100	38·5	14·3	8·7
6	40	2200	38·1	14·0	8·5
6	50	800	47·7	26·4	16·8
6	50	900	46·2	24·6	15·5
6	50	1000	45·0	23·1	14·3
6	50	1100	44·2	21·8	13·3
6	50	1200	43·3	20·7	12·6
6	50	1300	42·4	19·7	12·0
6	50	1400	41·6	18·9	11·5
6	50	1500	40·8	18·2	11·1
6	50	1600	40·1	17·5	10·7
6	50	1700	39·4	16·9	10·3
6	50	1800	38·8	16·4	10·0
6	50	1900	38·4	15·9	9·7
6	60	800	46·5	27·4	17·3
6	60	900	45·1	25·6	15·9
6	60	1000	44·2	24·0	14·7
6	60	1100	43·2	22·6	13·8
6	60	1200	42·3	21·5	13·1
6	60	1300	41·5	20·5	12·5
6	60	1400	40·5	19·6	12·0
6	60	1500	39·8	18·9	11·5

Velocity knots	HP	Prop. RPM	Per cent. efficiency	Diam. in.	Pitch in.
6	60	1600	39·0	18·2	11·1
6	60	1700	38·5	17·6	10·8
6	60	1800	38·1	17·1	10·4
6	70	800	45·6	28·3	17·6
6	70	900	44·5	26·3	16·2
6	70	1000	43·4	24·7	15·1
6	70	1100	42·4	23·3	14·2
6	70	1200	41·5	22·2	13·5
6	70	1300	40·6	21·2	12·9
6	70	1400	39·7	20·3	12·4
6	70	1500	38·9	19·5	11·9
6	70	1600	38·4	18·9	11·5
8	8	800	65·6	16·5	16·7
8	8	900	64·8	15·5	15·2
8	8	1000	63·9	14·7	13·9
8	8	1100	63·0	14·0	12·8
8	8	1200	62·2	13·5	11·8
8	8	1300	61·4	13·0	11·0
8	8	1400	60·7	12·4	10·3
8	8	1500	60·0	12·0	9·7
8	8	1600	59·3	11·5	9·2
8	8	1700	58·5	11·2	8·7
8	8	1800	57·8	10·8	8·3
8	8	1900	57·1	10·6	7·8
8	8	2000	56·6	10·3	7·5
8	8	2100	56·0	10·0	7·3
8	8	2200	55·5	9·8	7·0
8	10	800	64·8	17·4	17·1
8	10	900	63·9	16·4	15·5
8	10	1000	62·9	15·6	14·1
8	10	1100	61·9	14·9	12·9
8	10	1200	61·1	14·3	12·0
8	10	1300	60·3	13·6	11·2
8	10	1400	59·5	13·1	10·5
8	10	1500	58·7	12·6	9·8
8	10	1600	57·9	12·2	9·3
8	10	1700	57·1	11·8	8·8
8	10	1800	56·5	11·4	8·4
8	10	1900	55·9	11·1	8·1
8	10	2000	55·3	10·8	7·8
8	10	2100	54·7	10·6	7·5
8	10	2200	54·0	10·3	7·2
8	12	800	64·1	18·2	17·3
8	12	900	63·0	17·2	15·7
8	12	1000	62·0	16·4	14·2
8	12	1100	61·0	15·6	13·1
8	12	1200	60·2	14·8	12·1
8	12	1300	59·3	14·2	11·3
8	12	1400	58·4	13·6	10·6
8	12	1500	57·6	13·1	9·9
8	12	1600	56·8	12·7	9·4
8	12	1700	56·1	12·3	9·0
8	12	1800	55·4	12·0	8·6
8	12	1900	54·8	11·6	8·2
8	12	2000	54·1	11·4	7·9
8	12	2100	53·4	11·1	7·6
8	12	2200	52·9	10·8	7·4

Velocity knots	HP	Prop. RPM	Per cent. efficiency	Diam. in.	Pitch in.
8	14	800	63·4	18·9	17·5
8	14	900	62·3	17·9	15·8
8	14	1000	61·2	17·0	14·3
8	14	1100	60·3	16·1	13·2
8	14	1200	59·3	15·3	12·2
8	14	1300	58·4	14·7	11·4
8	14	1400	57·5	14·1	10·6
8	14	1500	56·6	13·6	10·0
8	14	1600	55·9	13·2	9·6
8	14	1700	55·2	12·8	9·1
8	14	1800	54·5	12·4	8·8
8	14	1900	53·8	12·1	8·4
8	14	2000	53·1	11·8	8·1
8	14	2100	52·5	11·4	7·8
8	14	2200	51·9	11·1	7·5
8	16	800	62·8	19·6	17·7
8	16	900	61·6	18·6	15·9
8	16	1000	60·6	17·5	14·5
8	16	1100	59·6	16·6	13·3
8	16	1200	58·6	15·8	12·3
8	16	1300	57·6	15·2	11·4
8	16	1400	56·7	14·6	10·7
8	16	1500	55·9	14·1	10·2
8	16	1600	55·1	13·6	9·7
8	16	1700	54·4	13·2	9·3
8	16	1800	53·6	12·9	8·9
8	16	1900	52·9	12·5	8·5
8	16	2000	52·2	12·1	8·2
8	16	2100	51·6	11·8	7·9
8	16	2200	50·9	11·5	7·6
8	20	800	61·6	20·9	17·8
8	20	900	60·5	19·5	16·1
8	20	1000	59·4	18·4	14·7
8	20	1100	58·3	17·5	13·5
8	20	1200	57·2	16·7	12·4
8	20	1300	56·3	16·0	11·7
8	20	1400	55·4	15·4	11·0
8	20	1500	54·5	14·9	10·5
8	20	1600	53·7	14·4	10·0
8	20	1700	52·9	13·9	9·5
8	20	1800	52·2	13·5	9·1
8	20	1900	51·4	13·1	8·7
8	20	2000	50·7	12·7	8·4
8	20	2100	50·1	12·3	8·1
8	20	2200	49·6	12·0	7·8
8	25	800	60·6	21·9	18·1
8	25	900	59·3	20·5	16·3
8	25	1000	58·1	19·4	14·8
8	25	1100	56·9	18·4	13·6
8	25	1200	55·9	17·6	12·8
8	25	1300	54·9	16·9	12·0
8	25	1400	54·0	16·3	11·4
8	25	1500	53·1	15·7	10·8
8	25	1600	52·2	15·1	10·2
8	25	1700	51·4	14·6	9·8
8	25	1800	50·6	14·2	9·4
8	25	1900	50·0	13·7	9·0
8	25	2000	49·5	13·3	8·6

Velocity knots	HP	Prop. RPM	Per cent. efficiency	Diam. in.	Pitch in.
8	25	2100	48·9	12·9	8·3
8	25	2200	48·3	12·5	8·0
8	30	800	59·6	22·8	18·3
8	30	900	58·2	21·4	16·5
8	30	1000	56·9	20·2	15·0
8	30	1100	55·9	19·2	13·9
8	30	1200	54·8	18·4	13·0
8	30	1300	53·7	17·7	12·3
8	30	1400	52·8	17·0	11·6
8	30	1500	51·9	16·3	11·0
8	30	1600	51·0	15·7	10·5
8	30	1700	50·2	15·2	10·0
8	30	1800	49·6	14·7	9·5
8	30	1900	49·0	14·2	9·2
8	30	2000	48·4	13·8	8·8
8	30	2100	47·8	13·4	8·5
8	30	2200	47·2	13·0	8·2
8	35	800	58·7	23·6	18·4
8	35	900	57·3	22·2	16·6
8	35	1000	56·1	21·0	15·2
8	35	1100	54·9	20·0	14·2
8	35	1200	53·8	19·2	13·3
8	35	1300	52·8	18·3	12·5
8	35	1400	51·8	17·5	11·8
8	35	1500	50·8	16·9	11·2
8	35	1600	50·0	16·2	10·6
8	35	1700	49·4	15·6	10·2
8	35	1800	48·7	15·1	9·7
8	35	1900	48·1	14·6	9·3
8	35	2000	47·4	14·2	9·0
8	35	2100	46·8	13·8	8·7
8	35	2200	46·2	13·4	8·4
8	40	800	57·9	24·3	18·6
8	40	900	56·5	22·9	16·8
8	40	1000	55·3	21·7	15·5
8	40	1100	54·0	20·7	14·4
8	40	1200	52·9	19·7	13·5
8	40	1300	51·9	18·8	12·7
8	40	1400	50·8	18·1	12·0
8	40	1500	50·0	17·3	11·4
8	40	1600	49·3	16·7	10·8
8	40	1700	48·6	16·1	10·3
8	40	1800	47·9	15·5	9·9
8	40	1900	47·2	15·0	9·5
8	40	2000	46·5	14·6	9·2
8	40	2100	46·0	14·2	8·9
8	40	2200	45·5	13·8	8·6
8	50	800	56·6	25·7	18·8
8	50	900	55·2	24·2	17·3
8	50	1000	53·8	22·9	15·9
8	50	1100	52·6	21·7	14·8
8	50	1200	51·4	20·7	13·8
8	50	1300	50·3	19·8	13·0
8	50	1400	49·6	18·9	12·3
8	50	1500	48·8	18·1	11·7
8	50	1600	48·0	17·4	11·1
8	50	1700	47·2	16·8	10·6
8	50	1800	46·5	16·2	10·2

Velocity knots	HP	Prop. RPM	Per cent. efficiency	Diam. in.	Pitch in.
8	50	1900	45·9	15·7	9·8
8	50	2000	45·3	15·3	9·5
8	50	2100	44·8	14·8	9·2
8	50	2200	44·4	14·4	8·8
8	60	800	55·5	26·8	19·3
8	60	900	54·0	25·3	17·6
8	60	1000	52·7	23·9	16·3
8	60	1100	51·4	22·6	15·1
8	60	1200	50·2	21·5	14·1
8	60	1300	49·4	20·5	13·3
8	60	1400	48·5	19·6	12·5
8	60	1500	47·7	18·8	11·9
8	60	1600	46·8	18·1	11·4
8	60	1700	46·1	17·4	10·9
8	60	1800	45·4	16·9	10·5
8	60	1900	44·9	16·3	10·1
8	60	2000	44·4	15·8	9·7
8	60	2100	44·0	15·4	9·4
8	60	2200	43·5	14·9	9·1
8	70	800	54·6	27·9	19·7
8	70	900	53·0	26·2	18·0
8	70	1000	51·6	24·7	16·6
8	70	1100	50·3	23·4	15·4
8	70	1200	49·4	22·2	14·4
8	70	1300	48·5	21·1	13·5
8	70	1400	47·6	20·2	12·8
8	70	1500	46·6	19·4	12·2
8	70	1600	45·9	18·6	11·7
8	70	1700	45·2	18·0	11·2
8	70	1800	44·7	17·4	10·7
8	70	1900	44·2	16·8	10·3
8	70	2000	43·7	16·3	9·9
8	70	2100	43·2	15·8	9·6
8	70	2200	42·6	15·4	9·4
10	14	900	66·6	17·1	18·1
10	14	1000	66·0	16·1	16·6
10	14	1100	65·3	15·3	15·3
10	14	1200	64·7	14·6	14·3
10	14	1300	64·0	14·0	13·3
10	14	1400	63·4	13·5	12·5
10	14	1500	62·7	13·1	11·8
10	14	1600	62·1	12·7	11·1
10	14	1700	61·4	12·4	10·5
10	14	1800	60·9	12·0	10·0
10	14	1900	60·4	11·6	9·5
10	14	2000	59·9	11·3	9·1
10	14	2100	59·3	11·0	8·7
10	14	2200	58·8	10·7	8·4
10	16	800	66·9	18·8	20·1
10	16	900	66·2	17·6	18·3
10	16	1000	65·5	16·6	16·8
10	16	1100	64·8	15·8	15·5
10	16	1200	64·2	15·1	14·4
10	16	1300	63·5	14·5	13·5
10	16	1400	62·8	14·0	12·6
10	16	1500	62·1	13·6	11·9
10	16	1600	61·4	13·2	11·2

Velocity knots	HP	Prop. RPM	Per cent. efficiency	Diam. in.	Pitch in.
10	16	1700	60·8	12·7	10·6
10	16	1800	60·3	12·3	10·1
10	16	1900	59·7	11·9	9·6
10	16	2000	59·1	11·6	9·2
10	16	2100	58·5	11·3	8·8
10	16	2200	58·0	11·0	8·4
10	20	800	66·3	19·7	20·5
10	20	900	65·5	18·5	18·7
10	20	1000	64·7	17·5	17·1
10	20	1100	63·9	16·7	15·8
10	20	1200	63·2	16·0	14·7
10	20	1300	62·4	15·4	13·6
10	20	1400	61·6	14·9	12·7
10	20	1500	61·0	14·3	12·0
10	20	1600	60·3	13·8	11·3
10	20	1700	59·7	13·4	10·8
10	20	1800	59·0	12·9	10·2
10	20	1900	58·4	12·6	9·7
10	20	2000	57·8	12·2	9·3
10	20	2100	57·1	11·9	8·9
10	20	2200	56·6	11·6	8·6
10	25	800	65·5	20·7	21·0
10	25	900	64·7	19·5	19·0
10	25	1000	63·8	18·5	17·4
10	25	1100	62·9	17·7	16·0
10	25	1200	62·1	17·0	14·8
10	25	1300	61·3	16·3	13·8
10	25	1400	60·5	15·6	12·9
10	25	1500	59·8	15·0	12·2
10	25	1600	59·1	14·5	11·5
10	25	1700	58·4	14·1	10·9
10	25	1800	57·7	13·6	10·3
10	25	1900	57·0	13·3	9·8
10	25	2000	56·4	12·9	9·4
10	25	2100	55·9	12·6	9·1
10	25	2200	55·3	12·3	8·8
10	30	800	64·9	21·6	21·3
10	30	900	63·9	20·4	19·3
10	30	1000	63·0	19·4	17·6
10	30	1100	62·0	18·6	16·2
10	30	1200	61·1	17·8	15·0
10	30	1300	60·4	17·0	14·0
10	30	1400	59·6	16·3	13·1
10	30	1500	58·8	15·7	12·3
10	30	1600	58·0	15·1	11·6
10	30	1700	57·2	14·7	11·0
10	30	1800	56·6	14·3	10·5
10	30	1900	56·0	13·9	10·0
10	30	2000	55·4	13·5	9·7
10	30	2100	54·8	13·2	9·3
10	30	2200	54·2	12·9	9·0
10	35	800	64·3	22·5	21·6
10	35	900	63·2	21·2	19·5
10	35	1000	62·2	20·2	17·8
10	35	1100	61·2	19·3	16·3
10	35	1200	60·4	18·4	15·1
10	35	1300	59·6	17·5	14·1
10	35	1400	58·7	16·9	13·2

Velocity knots	HP	Prop. RPM	Per cent. efficiency	Diam. in.	Pitch in.
10	35	1500	57·9	16·3	12·4
10	35	1600	57·0	15·7	11·7
10	35	1700	56·4	15·2	11·1
10	35	1800	55·7	14·8	10·7
10	35	1900	55·1	14·4	10·2
10	35	2000	54·4	14·0	9·9
10	35	2100	53·7	13·7	9·5
10	35	2200	53·2	13·4	9·2
10	40	800	63·7	23·2	21·8
10	40	900	62·6	22·0	19·7
10	40	1000	61·5	21·0	17·8
10	40	1100	60·6	19·9	16·4
10	40	1200	59·7	18·9	15·2
10	40	1300	58·8	18·1	14·2
10	40	1400	57·9	17·4	13·3
10	40	1500	57·0	16·8	12·4
10	40	1600	56·3	16·2	11·8
10	40	1700	55·6	15·7	11·3
10	40	1800	54·9	15·3	10·8
10	40	1900	54·2	14·9	10·4
10	40	2000	53·5	14·5	10·0
10	40	2100	52·9	14·1	9·6
10	40	2200	52·3	13·7	9·3
10	50	800	62·7	24·7	22·1
10	50	900	61·4	23·4	19·9
10	50	1000	60·4	22·0	18·1
10	50	1100	59·4	20·8	16·7
10	50	1200	58·4	19·9	15·4
10	50	1300	57·4	19·1	14·3
10	50	1400	56·5	18·4	13·5
10	50	1500	55·8	17·7	12·8
10	50	1600	55·0	17·1	22·2
10	50	1700	54·2	16·6	11·6
10	50	1800	53·4	16·2	11·1
10	50	1900	52·8	15·7	10·7
10	50	2000	52·1	15·2	10·3
10	50	2100	51·4	14·8	9·9
10	50	2200	50·7	14·4	9·5
10	60	800	61·7	25·9	22·3
10	60	900	60·6	24·3	20·1
10	60	1000	59·5	22·9	18·3
10	60	1100	58·4	21·7	16·8
10	60	1200	57·3	20·8	15·5
10	60	1300	56·4	19·9	14·6
10	60	1400	55·5	19·2	13·8
10	60	1500	54·6	18·5	13·1
10	60	1600	53·8	18·0	12·5
10	60	1700	53·0	17·4	11·9
10	60	1800	52·3	16·8	11·4
10	60	1900	51·5	16·3	10·9
10	60	2000	50·8	15·8	10·5
10	60	2100	50·2	15·4	10·1
10	60	2200	49·7	14·9	9·7
10	70	800	61·0	26·9	22·5
10	70	900	59·8	25·1	20·3
10	70	1000	58·6	23·7	18·5
10	70	1100	57·4	22·6	16·9
10	70	1200	56·4	21·6	15·8

Velocity knots	HP	Prop. RPM	Per cent. efficiency	Diam. in.	Pitch in.
10	70	1300	55·5	20·7	14·9
10	70	1400	54·5	19·9	14·0
10	70	1500	53·6	19·3	13·3
10	70	1600	52·8	18·6	12·7
10	70	1700	52·0	17·9	12·1
10	70	1800	51·2	17·4	11·6
10	70	1900	50·4	16·8	11·1
10	70	2000	49·9	16·3	10·7
10	70	2100	49·4	15·8	10·3
10	70	2200	48·9	15·4	9·9
12	20	1200	66·6	15·5	16·3
12	20	1300	66·1	14·8	15·3
12	20	1400	65·6	14·2	14·4
12	20	1500	65·1	13·7	13·6
12	20	1600	64·6	13·2	12·9
12	20	1700	64·1	12·8	12·2
12	20	1800	63·6	12·5	11·6
12	20	1900	63·1	12·1	11·1
12	20	2000	62·6	11·9	10·6
12	20	2100	62·1	11·6	10·2
12	20	2200	61·7	11·4	9·7
12	25	1000	67·0	18·0	19·3
12	25	1100	66·4	17·0	17·8
12	25	1200	65·9	16·2	16·6
12	25	1300	65·3	15·5	15·6
12	25	1400	64·8	14·9	14·7
12	25	1500	64·2	14·4	13·8
12	25	1600	63·7	14·0	13·1
12	25	1700	63·1	13·6	12·4
12	25	1800	62·6	13·2	11·8
12	25	1900	62·0	12·9	11·2
12	25	2000	61·5	12·6	10·7
12	25	2100	61·0	12·3	10·3
12	25	2200	60·6	11·9	9·9
12	30	1000	66·5	18·7	19·6
12	30	1100	65·9	17·7	18·2
12	30	1200	65·3	16·9	16·9
12	30	1300	64·6	16·2	15·8
12	30	1400	64·0	15·6	14·9
12	30	1500	63·4	15·1	14·0
12	30	1600	62·8	14·7	13·2
12	30	1700	62·2	14·3	12·5
12	30	1800	61·6	13·9	11·9
12	30	1900	61·1	13·5	11·3
12	30	2000	60·6	13·1	10·8
12	30	2100	60·1	12·7	10·4
12	30	2200	59·6	12·4	10·0
12	35	900	66·6	20·5	21·7
12	35	1000	66·0	19·3	19·9
12	35	1100	65·3	18·4	18·4
12	35	1200	64·7	17·5	17·1
12	35	1300	64·0	16·8	16·0
12	35	1400	63·4	16·3	15·0
12	35	1500	62·7	15·7	14·1
12	35	1600	62·1	15·3	13·3
12	35	1700	61·4	14·9	12·6
12	35	1800	60·9	14·4	12·0

Velocity knots	HP	Prop. RPM	Per cent. efficiency	Diam. in.	Pitch in.
12	35	1900	60·4	13·9	11·5
12	35	2000	59·8	13·5	11·0
12	35	2100	59·3	13·2	10·5
12	35	2200	58·8	12·9	10·1
12	40	800	66·9	22·6	24·1
12	40	900	66·2	21·1	22·0
12	40	1000	65·5	19·9	20·1
12	40	1100	64·8	18·9	18·6
12	40	1200	64·1	18·1	17·3
12	40	1300	63·4	17·4	16·2
12	40	1400	62·7	16·8	15·2
12	40	1500	62·0	16·3	14·2
12	40	1600	61·4	15·8	13·4
12	40	1700	60·8	15·3	12·7
12	40	1800	60·2	14·8	12·1
12	40	1900	59·7	14·3	11·6
12	40	2000	59·1	14·0	11·0
12	40	2100	58·5	13·6	10·6
12	40	2200	57·9	13·3	10·1
12	50	800	66·3	23·7	24·7
12	50	900	65·2	22·2	22·4
12	50	1000	64·7	21·0	20·5
12	50	1100	63·9	20·0	19·0
12	50	1200	63·1	19·2	17·6
12	50	1300	62·4	18·5	16·4
12	50	1400	61·6	17·9	15·3
12	50	1500	60·9	17·2	14·4
12	50	1600	60·3	16·6	13·6
12	50	1700	59·7	16·0	12·9
12	50	1800	59·0	15·5	12·3
12	50	1900	58·4	15·1	11·7
12	50	2000	57·7	14·7	11·1
12	50	2100	57·1	14·3	10·7
12	50	2200	56·6	14·0	10·3
12	60	800	65·7	24·7	25·1
12	60	900	64·8	23·2	22·8
12	60	1000	64·0	22·0	20·8
12	60	1100	63·1	21·0	19·2
12	60	1200	62·3	20·2	17·8
12	60	1300	61·4	19·5	16·5
12	60	1400	60·7	18·6	15·5
12	60	1500	60·0	17·9	14·6
12	60	1600	59·3	17·3	13·8
12	60	1700	58·6	16·7	13·0
12	60	1800	57·9	16·2	12·4
12	60	1900	57·2	15·8	11·8
12	60	2000	56·6	15·4	11·3
12	60	2100	56·1	15·0	10·9
12	60	2200	55·5	14·6	10·5
12	70	800	65·1	25·6	25·4
12	70	900	64·2	24·1	23·1
12	70	1000	63·3	22·9	21·1
12	70	1100	62·4	21·9	19·4
12	70	1200	61·4	21·1	17·9
12	70	1300	60·7	20·1	16·7
12	70	1400	59·9	19·3	15·6
12	70	1500	59·2	18·5	14·7
12	70	1600	58·4	17·9	13·9

Velocity knots	HP	Prop. RPM	Per cent. efficiency	Diam. in.	Pitch in.
12	70	1700	57·7	17·3	13·1
12	70	1800	56·9	16·8	12·5
12	70	1900	56·3	16·4	12·0
12	70	2000	55·8	15·9	11·5
12	70	2100	55·2	15·5	11·1
12	70	2200	54·6	15·2	10·7
14	20	1700	66·8	12·5	13·3
14	20	1800	66·5	12·1	12·7
14	20	1900	66·1	11·8	12·2
14	20	2000	65·8	11·4	11·7
14	20	2100	65·5	11·1	11·2
14	20	2200	65·1	10·8	10·8
14	25	1500	66·9	14·1	15·0
14	25	1600	66·5	13·6	14·3
14	25	1700	66·1	13·1	13·6
14	25	1800	65·8	12·7	13·0
14	25	1900	65·4	12·4	12·4
14	25	2000	65·0	12·0	11·9
14	25	2100	64·6	11·7	11·4
14	25	2200	64·3	11·5	11·0
14	30	1400	66·7	15·3	16·2
14	30	1500	66·3	14·7	15·3
14	30	1600	65·9	14·1	14·5
14	30	1700	65·5	13·7	13·8
14	30	1800	65·1	13·3	13·2
14	30	1900	64·7	12·9	12·6
14	30	2000	64·3	12·6	12·1
14	30	2100	63·9	12·3	11·6
14	30	2200	63·5	12·0	11·1
14	35	1300	66·7	16·5	17·4
14	35	1400	66·3	15·8	16·4
14	35	1500	65·8	15·2	15·5
14	35	1600	65·4	14·7	14·7
14	35	1700	65·0	14·2	14·0
14	35	1800	64·5	13·8	13·4
14	35	1900	64·1	13·4	12·8
14	35	2000	63·6	13·1	12·2
14	35	2100	63·2	12·8	11·7
14	35	2200	62·7	12·5	11·2
14	40	1200	66·8	17·7	18·9
14	40	1300	66·3	16·9	17·7
14	40	1400	65·9	16·2	16·6
14	40	1500	65·4	15·6	15·7
14	40	1600	64·9	15·1	14·9
14	40	1700	64·4	14·7	14·2
14	40	1800	64·0	14·2	13·5
14	40	1900	63·5	13·9	12·9
14	40	2000	63·0	13·5	12·3
14	40	2100	62·5	13·2	11·8
14	40	2200	62·1	13·0	11·3
14	50	1100	66·7	19·6	20·7
14	50	1200	66·1	18·6	19·3
14	50	1300	65·6	17·8	18·0
14	50	1400	65·1	17·1	17·0
14	50	1500	64·5	16·5	16·0
14	50	1600	64·0	16·0	15·2
14	50	1700	63·5	15·5	14·4

Velocity knots	HP	Prop. RPM	Per cent. efficiency	Diam. in.	Pitch in.
14	50	1800	63·0	15·1	13·7
14	50	1900	62·4	14·7	13·1
14	50	2000	61·9	14·4	12·5
14	50	2100	61·4	14·1	11·9
14	50	2200	61·0	13·7	11·5
14	60	1000	66·7	21·5	22·7
14	60	1100	66·1	20·3	21·0
14	60	1200	65·5	19·4	19·6
14	60	1300	64·9	18·6	18·3
14	60	1400	64·4	17·9	17·2
14	60	1500	63·8	17·3	16·3
14	60	1600	63·2	16·7	15·4
14	60	1700	62·6	16·3	14·6
14	60	1800	62·0	15·9	13·8
14	60	1900	61·5	15·5	13·2
14	60	2000	61·0	15·0	12·6
14	60	2100	60·5	14·6	12·1
14	60	2200	60·0	14·2	11·6
14	70	900	66·9	23·6	25·1
14	70	1000	66·2	22·2	23·0
14	70	1100	65·6	21·0	21·3
14	70	1200	65·0	20·1	19·9
14	70	1300	64·3	19·3	18·6
14	70	1400	63·7	18·6	17·4
14	70	1500	63·1	18·0	16·4
14	70	1600	62·5	17·5	15·5
14	70	1700	61·8	17·0	14·7
14	70	1800	61·3	16·5	13·9
14	70	1900	60·7	16·0	13·3
14	70	2000	60·2	15·5	12·7
14	70	2100	59·7	15·1	12·2
14	70	2200	59·2	14·7	11·7
16	25	2100	66·9	11·5	12·3
16	25	2200	66·6	11·2	11·8
16	30	1900	66·9	12·7	13·6
16	30	2000	66·6	12·3	13·0
16	30	2100	66·3	12·0	12·5
16	30	2200	66·0	11·7	12·0
16	35	1800	66·8	13·5	14·4
16	35	1900	66·5	13·1	13·8
16	35	2000	66·1	12·7	13·2
16	35	2100	65·8	12·4	12·7
16	35	2200	65·5	12·1	12·2
16	40	1700	66·7	14·4	15·2
16	40	1800	66·4	13·9	14·6
16	40	1900	66·0	13·5	13·9
16	40	2000	65·7	13·1	13·4
16	40	2100	65·4	12·8	12·8
16	40	2200	65·0	12·5	12·4
16	50	1500	66·8	16·2	17·2
16	50	1600	66·4	15·6	16·4
16	50	1700	66·0	15·1	15·6
16	50	1800	65·7	14·6	14·9
16	50	1900	65·3	14·2	14·2
16	50	2000	64·9	13·8	13·6
16	50	2100	64·5	13·5	13·1
16	50	2200	64·1	13·2	12·6

Velocity knots	HP	Prop. RPM	Per cent. efficiency	Diam. in.	Pitch in.
16	60	1400	66·7	17·5	18·5
16	60	1500	66·3	16·9	17·5
16	60	1600	65·8	16·3	16·6
16	60	1700	65·4	15·7	15·8
16	60	1800	65·0	15·3	15·1
16	60	1900	64·6	14·8	14·5
16	60	2000	64·2	14·5	13·8
16	60	2100	63·8	14·1	13·3
16	60	2200	63·3	13·8	12·8
16	70	1300	66·7	18·9	20·0
16	70	1400	66·2	18·1	18·8
16	70	1500	65·8	17·4	17·8
16	70	1600	65·3	16·8	16·9
16	70	1700	64·9	16·3	16·1
16	70	1800	64·4	15·8	15·3
16	70	1900	64·0	15·4	14·6
16	70	2000	63·5	15·0	14·0
16	70	2100	63·1	14·7	13·4
16	70	2200	62·6	14·4	12·9
20	50	2000		13·4	15·8
20	50	2400		12·3	13·4
20	50	2800		11·3	11·7
20	50	3200		10·6	10·4
20	50	3600		9·9	9·4
20	50	4000		9·4	8·6
20	75	2000		14·9	16·1
20	75	2400		13·5	13·8
20	75	2800		12·5	12·0
20	75	3200		11·6	10·7
20	75	3600		10·9	9·7
20	75	4000		10·3	8·9
20	100	2000		15·9	16·4
20	100	2400		14·5	14·0
20	100	2800		13·4	12·3
20	100	3200		12·4	11·0
20	100	3600		11·7	9·9
20	100	4000		11·1	9·0
20	125	2000		16·8	16·6
20	125	2400		15·3	14·2
20	125	2800		14·1	12·5
20	125	3200		13·1	11·2
20	125	3600		12·3	10·0
20	125	4000		11·7	9·1
20	150	2000		17·5	16·9
20	150	2400		16·0	14·5
20	150	2800		14·7	12·7
20	150	3200		13·7	11·2
20	150	3600		13·0	10·1
20	150	4000		12·2	9·3
20	175	2000		18·2	17·0
20	175	2400		16·5	14·6
20	175	2800		15·2	12·8
20	175	3200		14·2	11·3
20	175	3600		13·4	10·3
20	175	4000		12·6	9·4
20	200	2000		18·8	17·2
20	200	2400		17·0	14·8

Velocity knots	HP	Prop. RPM	Per cent. efficiency	Diam. in.	Pitch in.
20	200	2800		15·7	12·8
20	200	3200		14·7	11·4
20	200	3600		13·8	10·4
20	200	4000		13·1	9·5
25	50	2000		12·9	18·7
25	50	2400		11·7	15·6
25	50	2800		10·7	13·7
25	50	3200		10·0	12·2
25	50	3600		9·4	11·0
25	50	4000		9·0	10·0
25	75	2000		14·1	18·8
25	75	2400		12·8	16·1
25	75	2800		11·9	14·1
25	75	3200		11·1	12·5
25	75	3600		10·5	11·2
25	75	4000		9·9	10·3
25	100	2000		15·1	19·2
25	100	2400		13·8	16·4
25	100	2800		12·7	14·3
25	100	3200		11·9	12·7
25	100	3600		11·2	11·4
25	100	4000		10·6	10·4
25	125	2000		16·0	19·5
25	125	2400		14·5	16·6
25	125	2800		13·5	14·4
25	125	3200		12·6	12·9
25	125	3600		11·8	11·6
25	125	4000		11·2	10·6
25	150	2000		16·7	19·7
25	150	2400		15·2	16·8
25	150	2800		14·1	14·6
25	150	3200		13·1	13·0
25	150	3600		12·4	11·8
25	150	4000		11·7	10·8
25	175	2000		17·3	19·9
25	175	2400		15·9	16·9
25	175	2800		14·6	14·8
25	175	3200		13·6	13·2
25	175	3600		12·8	11·9
25	175	4000		12·1	10·9
25	200	2000		17·9	20·1
25	200	2400		16·4	17·0
25	200	2800		15·1	14·9
25	200	3200		14·1	13·3
25	200	3600		13·2	12·0
25	200	4000		12·5	11·0
30	50	2000		12·8	22·3
30	50	2400		11·4	18·7
30	50	2800		10·5	16·1
30	50	3200		9·7	14·0
30	50	3600		9·1	12·3
30	50	4000		8·6	11·4
30	75	2000		13·8	22·5
30	75	2400		12·5	18·8
30	75	2800		11·5	15·9
30	75	3200		10·7	14·1
30	75	3600		10·0	12·8
30	75	4000		9·5	11·7
30	100	2000		14·7	22·5
30	100	2400		13·3	18·6
30	100	2800		12·2	16·2
30	100	3200		11·4	14·5
30	100	3600		10·8	13·0
30	100	4000		10·2	11·9
30	125	2000		15·5	22·4
30	125	2400		14·0	18·8
30	125	2800		12·9	16·5
30	125	3200		12·1	14·7
30	125	3600		11·4	13·2
30	125	4000		10·8	12·0
30	150	2000		16·2	22·2
30	150	2400		14·6	19·0
30	150	2800		13·5	16·7
30	150	3200		12·6	14·8
30	150	3600		11·9	13·4
30	150	4000		11·3	12·1
30	175	2000		16·7	22·5
30	175	2400		15·1	19·3
30	175	2800		14·0	16·8
30	175	3200		13·1	15·0
30	175	3600		12·4	13·5
30	175	4000		11·7	12·3
30	200	2000		17·2	22·7
30	200	2400		15·6	19·4
30	200	2800		14·5	17·0
30	200	3200		13·5	15·1
30	200	3600		12·8	13·5
30	200	4000		12·1	12·4

Propellers for yachts

When choosing a propeller for a yacht, not only is its performance under power of interest but also its drag when sailing. At speeds of 5 or 6 knots propeller drag is usually less if the shaft is locked rather than allowed to free-wheel. With a 2-bladed propeller in an aperture, one can line up the propeller with the keel or deadwood to reduce drag. The less the total blade area the less the drag, so narrow-bladed, 2-blade propellers are often seen on yachts. Such propellers give a poor performance under power especially against a head sea and wind. If one is more interested in performance under power than the drag under sail, then a 3-bladed propeller with a reasonable blade area is usually best.

The choice boils down to the amount of blade area for engine horsepower. A compromise figure is 5 sq. ins. per horsepower; a sailing man interested in minimising drag would choose down to $3\frac{1}{2}$ sq. ins per horsepower and a motor sailer man up to 10 sq. ins. per horsepower. The figure of square inches is the total blade area of all blades (on one side only), the horsepower figure to use is the maximum that the engine can give when coupled to that propeller.

The propeller tables can be used for 2-bladed propellers but add half-an-inch to the diameter and to the pitch.

Propellers for particular engines (displacement speeds only)

The following table gives propeller sizes for popular car and truck engine conversions. It gives a 'size' for various reduction ratios and for various chosen full throttle r.p.ms. A propeller can be considered as a brake on the engine; the bigger the 'size' of the propeller the greater the braking effect and hence the lower the full throttle r.p.m. For fast boats obviously one wants to extract the full horsepower of the engine, in which case the propeller should allow the engine to rev up to its maximum r.p.m. at full throttle. But on displacement boats the engine is often really too powerful for the boat anyway and choosing a propeller such that the full throttle r.p.m. is *less* than the maximum means a quieter and more economical cruising speed because the revs for any one boat speed will also be *less*.

As an example the makers of the Perkins 4108 say that the engine can be overpropped down to a full throttle r.p.m. of 2500 (from a maximum of 3600). From the table, with 2:1 reduction, the propeller 'size' is 31.9. This figure is the sum of diameter and pitch in inches, and the pitch should be 60% of the diameter. Thus to get the diameter, divide the 'size' by 1.6. If the size is 31.9 then the diameter should be 20 ins and the pitch 11.9 ins (the sum being 31.9). If this diameter is too great then an inch can be lopped off and added to the pitch.

N.B. These propeller sizes are correct only for displacement speeds of 6-8 knots.

Engine Particulars

Engine	Max. HP at RPM	Full throttle HP at different RPMs: 1500	2000	2500	3000	3500	4000
DIESELS							
PERKINS 4.108 1.76 litre 4-cylinder	47 @ 3600	20	29	36	42	46	49
PERKINS 4.236 3.86 litre 4-cylinder	72 @ 2500	51	64	72			
PERKINS 6.354 5.8 litre 6-cylinder	115 @ 2800	75	93	107	119		
BLMC 1.5 litre 4-cylinder	37 @ 3500	18	24	30	34	37	
BMC 2.2 litre 4-cylinder (not now in production)	55 @ 3500	25	34	42	50	55	
BLMC 2.5 litre 4-cylinder	62 @ 3500	32	43	52	58	62	
BLMC 3.8 litre 4-cylinder	66 @ 2400	46	60	69			
BLMC 5.7 litre 6-cylinder	100 @ 2400	72	90	104			
FORD 2401E 2.36 litre eg. Tempest 4/58 & Sabre	58 @ 3600	25	34	43	49	57	
FORD 2402E 3.54 litre eg. Tempest 6/87 & Sabre	87 @ 2500	37	50	63	75	86	
FORD 2712 4.15 litre eg. Tempest 4/80, Sabre, Parsons, Mermaid	80 @ 2500	55	70	80			
FORD 2715E 6.22 litre eg. Tempest 6/120, Sabre, Parsons, Mermaid	120 @ 2500	79	104	120			
FORD 2701E 4 litre 4-cylinder eg. old Parsons Pike Mk. II	72 @ 2500	47	62	72			
FORD 2704E 5.95 litre 6-cylinder eg. old Parsons Barracuda Mk. II	109 @ 2500	72	97	109			
FORD 592E 3.6 litre 4-cylinder, old Parsons Pike & Sutton Merak	63 @ 2250	45	58	65			
FORD 590E 5.4 litre 6-cylinder, Sutton Saiph	96 @ 2250	69	89	100			
MERCEDES OM 636 1.76 litre 4-cylinder	40 @ 3300	19	26	32	38	41	
PETROL ENGINES							
TEMPEST (ex NEWAGE) VEDETTE Mk. 8 BLMC 1100 c.c. 7.5:1 C.R.	28 @ 3000	15	20	25	28		
NEWAGE Navigator BMC 1622 c.c. 7.2:1 C.R.	38 @ 3000	22	30	36	38		
BMC 948 c.c. OHV 7.2:1 C.R. Minor 1000 1956 A35 cars	34 @ 4800		14	19	24	28	31
BMC 998 c.c. 8.3:1 C.R. modern engine	42 @ 5000		19	24	29	33	37
BMC 1498 c.c. 8.3:1 C.R. JB, J2, J4 vans	50 @ 4200		31	34	39	43	48
BMC 1622 8.3:1 C.R. eg. Morris Oxford	61 @ 4500		30	40	48	54	60
FORD 100E 1172 c.c. side valve 7:1 C.R.	36 @ 4500		16	21	26	30	33
FORD 105E 1000 c.c. O.H.V. 7.5:1 C.R. (Old Wortham Blake Fisherboy engines)	40 @ 4500		20	26	30	34	37
FORD 115E 1200 c.c. (Old Wortham Blake Fisherboy engines)	48 @ 4500		24	30	36	41	45
FORD 109E 1300 c.c. Parsons Sea Urchin Mk. II (Old Wortham Blake Fisherboy engines)	50 @ 4500		24	31	38	43	47
FORD 122E 1500 c.c. Sea Urchin Mk. III (Old Wortham Blake Fisherboy engines)	57 @ 4500		30	38	45	50	54
FORD 2251E 1100 c.c. (Crossflow Wortham Blake Fisherboy engines C.R. 8:1)	40 @ 4500		19	24	29	34	38
FORD 2251E 1300 c.c. (Crossflow Wortham Blake Fisherboy engines C.R. 8:1)	48 @ 4500		22	28	34	40	45
FORD 2254E 1600 c.c. (Crossflow Wortham Blake Fisherboy engines C.R. 8:1)	58 @ 4500		27	34	42	49	55
FORD 2261E 1100 c.c. (Crossflow C.R. 9:1)	39 @ 4000		19	24	30	35	39
FORD 2264 1600 c.c. (Crossflow C.R. 9:1)	60 @ 4000		31	39	47	54	60

Prop Sizes (diam. plus pitch in inches)

Choose your desired full throttle engine rpm on this line

DIRECT DRIVE

	1500	2000	2500	3000	3500	4000
PERKINS 4.108	25.6	22.5	20.3	18.67	16.8	15.7
PERKINS 4.236	29.5	25.3	22.5			
PERKINS 6.354	31.4	27.1	24.3	22.4		
BLMC 1.5 litre	24.2	21.4	19.1	17.5	16.1	
BMC 2.2 litre	25.7	22.7	20.4	18.7	17.4	
BLMC 2.5 litre	27.1	23.5	21.2	19.3	17.8	
BLMC 3.8 litre	28.9	25.0	22.3			
BLMC 5.7 litre	31.2	26.9	24.2			
FORD 2401E	25.7	22.7	20.5	18.7	17.5	
FORD 2402E	27.8	24.2	22.0	20.2	19.0	
FORD 2712	29.9	25.2	23.0			
FORD 2715E	31.7	27.7	25.0			
FORD 2701E	29.0	25.2	22.5			
FORD 2704E	31.2	27.3	24.4			
FORD 592E	28.8	24.9	22.1			
FORD 590E	31.0	26.9	24.0			
MERCEDES	24.4	21.7	19.3	17.9	16.5	
TEMPEST	23.4	20.8	18.5	16.8		
NEWAGE	25.1	22.2	19.8	17.9		
BMC 948 c.c.		19.2	17.8	16.3	15.3	14.3
BMC 998 c.c.		20.6	18.4	17.0	15.8	14.9
BMC 1498 c.c.		22.3	19.6	17.9	16.6	15.6
BMC 1622		22.2	20.2	18.6	17.3	16.5
FORD 100E		19.8	18.0	16.6	15.5	
FORD 105E		20.9	18.6	17.1	15.9	
FORD 115E		21.4	19.1	17.7	16.5	
FORD 109E		21.4	19.2	17.9	16.6	
FORD 122E		22.2	20.0	18.4	17.1	
FORD 2251E		20.7	18.4	17.0	15.9	
FORD 2251E		21.1	18.9	17.5	16.4	
FORD 2254E		21.8	19.6	18.2	17.0	
FORD 2261E		20.7	18.4	17.1	16.0	
FORD 2264		22.3	20.1	18.6	17.3	

1.5:1 REDUCTION

	1500	2000	2500	3000	3500	4000
PERKINS 4.108	33.2	29.5	26.5	24.0	22.3	20.7
PERKINS 4.236	37.9	33.0	29.2			
PERKINS 6.354	40.9	35.2	31.3	28.4		
BLMC 1.5 litre	31.7	27.5	25.0	22.7	20.9	
BMC 2.2 litre	33.3	29.3	26.6	24.2	21.4	
BLMC 2.5 litre	34.7	30.6	27.6	24.9	22.7	
BLMC 3.8 litre	37.2	32.6	29.0			
BLMC 5.7 litre	40.5	35.0	31.2			
FORD 2401E	33.3	29.3	26.8	24.2	22.4	
FORD 2402E	35.7	31.5	28.5	26.0	24.2	
FORD 2712	38.4	33.6	29.7			
FORD 2715E	41.3	35.8	32.0			
FORD 2701E	37.3	32.8	29.2			
FORD 2704E	40.5	35.4	31.4			
FORD 592E	37.0	32.4	28.6			
FORD 590E	40.5	34.9	30.9			
MERCEDES	32.0	27.9	25.3	23.1	21.2	
TEMPEST	30.8	26.6	24.0	22.0		
NEWAGE	32.7	28.7	25.9	23.1		
BMC 948 c.c.		25.0	22.9	21.4	19.8	18.5
BMC 998 c.c.		26.3	23.9	22.1	20.4	19.1
BMC 1498 c.c.		28.8	25.6	23.2	21.4	20.1
BMC 1622		28.6	26.4	24.1	22.2	21.0
FORD 100E		25.6	23.4	21.7	20.1	18.7
FORD 105E		26.6	24.3	22.2	20.6	19.1
FORD 115E		27.5	25.0	22.9	21.2	19.8
FORD 109E		27.5	25.2	23.1	21.4	20.0
FORD 122E		28.6	26.1	23.8	22.0	20.6
FORD 2251E		26.3	23.9	22.1	20.6	19.2
FORD 2251E		27.0	24.6	22.7	21.1	19.9
FORD 2254E		28.1	25.6	23.5	21.9	20.6
FORD 2261E		26.3	23.9	22.2	20.6	19.3
FORD 2264		28.8	26.2	24.0	22.2	21.0

2:1 REDUCTION

	1500	2000	2500	3000	3500	4000
PERKINS 4.108	40.1	35.2	31.9	29.0	26.6	24.7
PERKINS 4.236	45.3	39.6	35.2			
PERKINS 6.354	48.7	42.5	37.6	34.2		
BLMC 1.5 litre	38.0	33.1	29.7	27.4	25.1	
BMC 2.2 litre	40.2	35.1	31.7	29.3	26.8	
BLMC 2.5 litre	42.1	36.6	33.1	30.1	27.4	
BLMC 3.8 litre	44.5	39.1	35.0			
BLMC 5.7 litre	48.3	42.2	37.4			
FORD 2401E	40.2	35.2	31.9	29.2	27.0	
FORD 2402E	43.0	37.8	34.3	31.4	29.2	
FORD 2712	45.9	40.2	35.9			
FORD 2715E	49.2	43.3	38.3			
FORD 2701E	44.7	39.3	35.2			
FORD 2704E	48.3	42.8	37.7			
FORD 592E	44.4	38.8	34.6			
FORD 590E	47.9	42.1	37.2			
MERCEDES	38.2	33.6	30.0	28.0	25.5	
TEMPEST	37.0	32.2	28.6	26.4		
NEWAGE	39.2	34.4	30.8	28.0		
BMC 948 c.c.		30.6	27.5	25.7	23.9	22.3
BMC 998 c.c.		32.0	28.3	26.5	24.6	23.0
BMC 1498 c.c.		34.6	30.4	28.1	25.8	24.1
BMC 1622		34.4	31.4	29.2	26.8	25.0
FORD 100E		31.2	27.9	26.0	24.2	22.6
FORD 105E		32.2	28.8	26.7	24.7	23.0
FORD 115E		33.1	29.7	27.7	25.6	23.8
FORD 109E		33.1	29.8	28.0	25.8	24.0
FORD 122E		34.4	31.2	28.8	26.4	24.6
FORD 2251E		32.0	28.3	26.6	24.7	23.1
FORD 2251E		32.7	29.2	27.4	25.4	23.8
FORD 2254E		33.8	30.4	28.4	26.4	24.6
FORD 2261E		32.0	28.3	26.7	24.7	23.2
FORD 2264		34.6	31.3	29.0	26.8	25.0

3:1 REDUCTION

	1500	2000	2500	3000	3500	4000
PERKINS 4.108		45.8	41.3	37.8	34.7	32.3
PERKINS 4.236	59.4	51.1	45.3			
PERKINS 6.354	63.4	54.5	49.0	44.4		
BLMC 1.5 litre	49.5	43.2	38.7	35.2	32.4	
BMC 2.2 litre	52.3	45.8	41.0	37.8	34.9	
BLMC 2.5 litre	54.7	47.6	42.5	38.8	35.8	
BLMC 3.8 litre	58.3	50.6	44.9			
BLMC 5.7 litre	63.0	54.1	48.7			
FORD 2401E	52.3	45.8	41.2	37.6	35.2	
FORD 2402E	56.1	49.0	44.0	40.9	38.1	
FORD 2712	60.2	51.9	46.2			
FORD 2715E	64.0	55.7	50.0			
FORD 2701E	58.6	50.8	52.1			
FORD 2704E	63.0	54.9	56.2			
FORD 592E	58.1	50.3	44.3			
FORD 590E	62.5	54.0	48.3			
MERCEDES	49.8	43.7	39.1	35.9	33.0	
TEMPEST	48.0	41.7	37.6	34.0		
NEWAGE	51.1	44.8	39.9	35.8		
BMC 948 c.c.		39.2	35.8	33.1	30.8	28.8
BMC 998 c.c.		41.3	37.3	34.2	31.8	29.8
BMC 1498 c.c.		45.0	39.5	36.0	33.3	31.3
BMC 1622		44.8	40.6	37.4	34.8	32.6
FORD 100E		40.2	36.5	33.6	31.2	29.2
FORD 105E		41.7	37.8	34.4	32.0	29.8
FORD 115E		43.2	38.7	35.5	33.0	30.9
FORD 109E		43.2	38.9	35.9	33.3	31.2
FORD 122E		44.8	40.3	37.0	34.2	32.0
FORD 2251E		41.3	37.3	34.2	32.0	30.0
FORD 2251E		42.4	38.3	35.2	32.9	30.9
FORD 2254E		44.0	39.5	36.6	34.1	32.0
FORD 2261E		41.3	37.3	34.4	32.1	30.0
FORD 2264		45.0	40.5	37.3	34.8	32.6

CHAPTER ELEVEN

Noise

To quieten an engine fitted in a boat does not cost very much, but does require an understanding of the basic principles of noise reduction. Car engines, relatively speaking, are quiet engines because this aspect is of importance in the motoring world. They also score over many marine engines in that they have at least four cylinders.

Before setting down the principles of noise reduction, how and where is the noise produced? There are two main causes, the exhaust note and the mechanical noise coming from the body of the engine. The exhaust noise is easy to reduce: fit a large silencer or even two, and lead the exhaust pipe overboard. An acceptable level of exhaust noise is quite easily achieved. The noise coming from the body of the engine is the subject of this chapter.

Noise and vibration go together. When an engine is running, every part of it is caused to vibrate at various frequencies by the explosions inside the cylinders. The surface of each part in contact with the air causes the air to vibrate and these vibrations in the air constitute noise. Anything connected to the engine is also caused to vibrate. Thus, if the engine is rigidly mounted to the engine bearers, it is inevitable that the hull will be set into vibration (50). It is obvious from this that even if the engine itself is heavily soundproofed noise will still come from the hull, cabin, and floorboards. It is therefore a

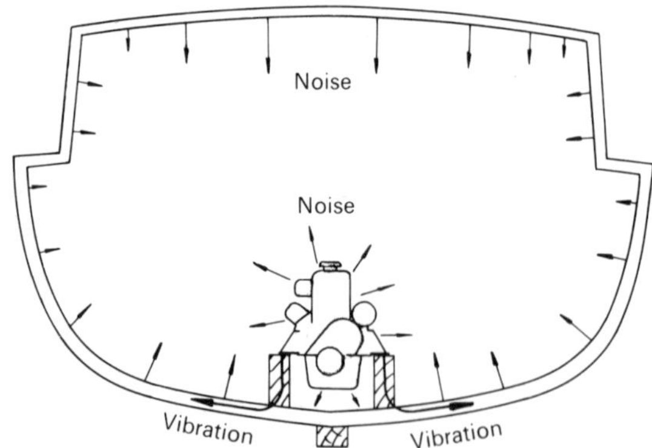

50 A rigidly mounted engine causes the whole boat to act like a noise box

prerequisite that the engine is flexibly mounted, i.e. isolated from the hull. On the other hand, if you do not want to flexibly mount the engine for some reason, then it is still worth soundproofing the engine casing, as a noticeable reduction can be made, but it can never be as effective as when flexible mounts are fitted. In fact, when a car engine is mounted on its normal rubber mounts in a boat, the noise level, even with a completely exposed engine, will be quite acceptable. Imagine, then, what quietness can be achieved by following through with the recommendations of this chapter.

It is important to install the engine on the correct mounts. If they are too soft or too hard they may well *increase* the noise and vibration transmitted to the hull. Obviously the thing to do is to use the standard car rubber mounts—there is no reason why they should be unsuitable providing the propeller thrust is taken by a separate thrust bearing (see Chapter Five).

All the connections to the engine must be flexible. The petrol pipe should have a length of armoured flexible tubing, while the exhaust pipe should either have a flexible section or be mounted like a car's, with bonded rubber/steel mountings or supported so that movement is possible. If the pipe is held down some way from the engine, it will usually be found that the flexibility of the long pipe run itself will be sufficient. Carburettor air intake 'hiss' can be silenced by fitting the normal car-type air filter. The amount of noise produced by induction is considerable—try running your car without the air filter.

Noise reduction consists of putting a barrier between the engine and the ear. An engine casing or box is the obvious way to do this, but for complete effectiveness it is essential to completely surround the engine inside a practically airtight casing—no air paths must be left open along which noise could travel. For instance, holes for the gear lever or starting handle must be covered up. It is no good just fitting a casing down to the floorboard level and forgetting about the bilge. Noise will leak out into the bilge and up through gaps in the floorboards just as water will escape out of a hole in a pipe. Sometimes the engine bearers can be made the sides of a lower box (51) and blanking pieces fitted at each end of the engine between the bearers to form the ends. The bottom of the boat will then form the bottom of the enclosure.

The first essential is thus to completely box in the engine; this is called 'insulation'. Now if the 'box' was made of sheet steel it would be found that the noise was just as great, if not greater. This leads to

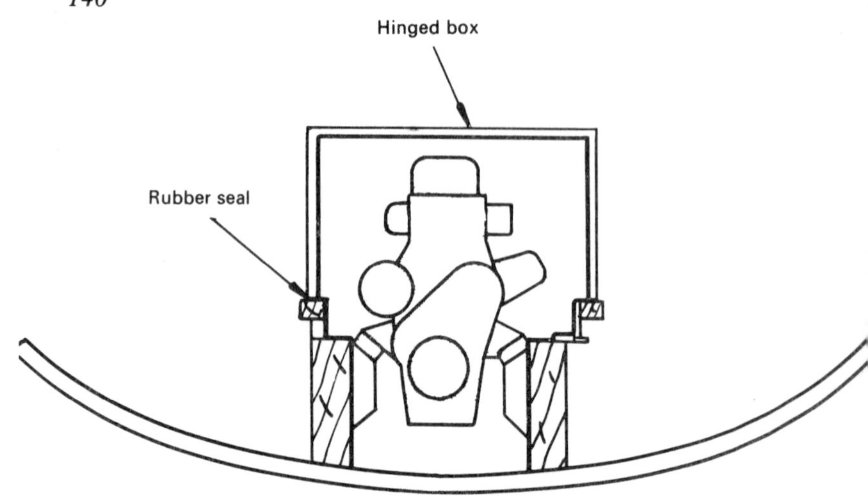

51 Using the engine bearers and hull bottom to form part of the engine 'capsule'

the next topic: noise absorption. Inside a steel box the noise waves emanating from the engine will strike the hard steel sides and be reflected like light from a mirror successively from surface to surface. The noise inside the box will build up as in an echo chamber to a far higher level than if the box were not there at all. The inside surfaces of the box need to be lined with a material which reduces the degree of reflection so that the noise waves do not bounce off so easily. This type of material is called the absorber, and materials which are soft or hairy are usually better than harder substances. Polyurethane foam, felt, glass wool are all good absorbers, but not polystyrene foam. Lining the inside surfaces with an absorber will reduce the noise *inside* the box and consequently the noise heard outside the box. The insulator (the plywood or steel box) will have less work to do.

The criterion for a good sound insulator (the ply or steel box) is sheer mass. The weight per square foot is the governing factor and consequently lead sheet is often used as the insulator.

Having fitted the insulator (the casing) and the absorber (the soft lining inside) the noise now heard will be caused by the sound striking the insulator and making it vibrate. (This is how noise passes through a solid partition.) The whole exterior surface of the casing will be vibrating and causing sound waves to be sent on their journey to the ear. Apart from making the casing heavier and heavier this vibration can only be made less by damping the panels comprising the casing. This is done with material which resists vibration within itself—for instance, lead and bituminous compounds like those used on motor cars to dampen door panels, etc.

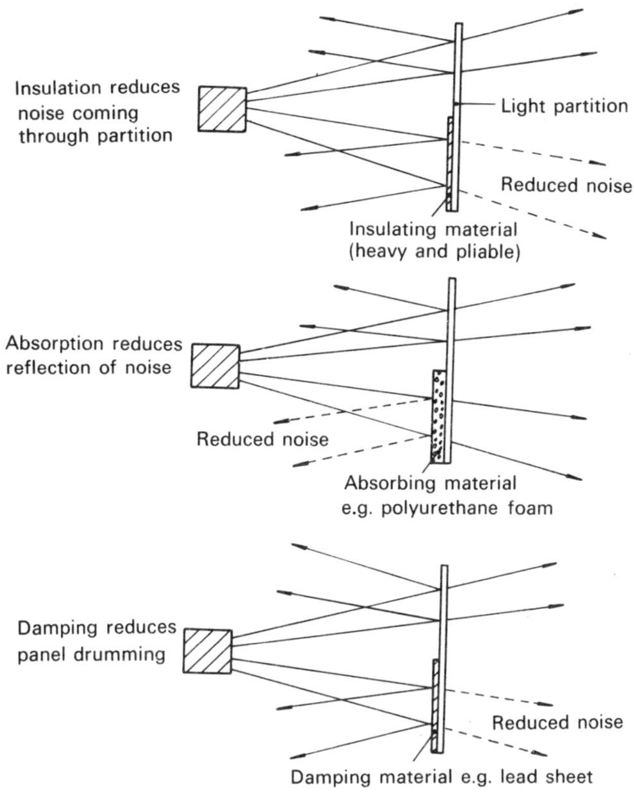

52 The three basic ingredients of noise reduction

We have then three aspects of noise reduction: insulation, absorption and vibration damping (52). If the principles involved are understood the rest is relatively easy. This business of absorption and insulation is usually confused and sometimes one sees attempts which show ignorance in this respect. For instance, I bought a boat some time ago which had an engine casing which was lined on the inside with glass wool. This was fine, but then the wool had been covered with sheet asbestos, thus presenting to the noise waves as hard a surface as the original casing, which was plywood. Also, there were large holes cut out for the starting handle and air ventilation, so that the overall result was the same whether the casing was in place or not.

Practical details

It was mentioned above that it is necessary to complete the capsule *beneath* the engine. This is a fiddly job, especially in a wooden boat, but lead sheet is a good material because of its noise properties and because it can be pressed into shape. Lead flashing as used for roofs is entirely suitable and easily obtained from a builder's merchant. It does not cost all that much. A glassfibre boat is simpler to treat, as loosely fitting pieces of plywood can be glassed to the hull. Bear in mind accessibility to the engine.

Above the floorboard or engine bearer level a normal 'box' can be constructed from $\frac{1}{2}$ in. plywood, sheet steel or glassfibre. The lower edges of the box should be seated on a soft rubber strip to avoid noise leaks. If the engine is installed below the floor level, then the inspection hatches must be sealed in a similar way. PVC-covered magnetic sealing strips as used on some refrigerators make a useful seal.

Where the exhaust pipe passes through the casing, asbestos tape and a large rubber grommet should be used. Electric cables, the petrol pipe and the controls should all be sealed where they pass through the casing. This attention to detail is essential as even the smallest crack has a disproportionate effect on the noise level. It is as though the noise were searching every nook and cranny to get out.

To prevent the casing panels from vibrating, lead sheeting can be glued on the inside. This also considerably increases the mass and hence transmission reduction of the panel, without increasing the thickness very much. If the casing is of steel, bitumastic compounds can be used in lieu of lead to dampen the panels, making them 'dead' when tapped. There are few proprietary insulation boards suitable for boat engine cases, but a lead/plywood sandwich is most effective, besides being cheap and easily made at home.

On the other hand, there are many proprietary absorption materials. Apart from glassfibre wool or mat, also used as a thermal insulator in lofts, and polyurethene foam, there are such intended products as Acoustilam and Quietclad made specifically for boats, (see Appendix). Some have self-adhesive backing. The greater the thickness of the absorbing material the greater the effectiveness, but this effect tails off above about 2 in.; $\frac{1}{2}$ in. thickness is the practical minimum. The effectiveness of an absorbing material can be increased at lower frequencies by covering it with *perforated* hardboard or aluminium. This also helps to keep the glass wool in place and provide a clean surface.

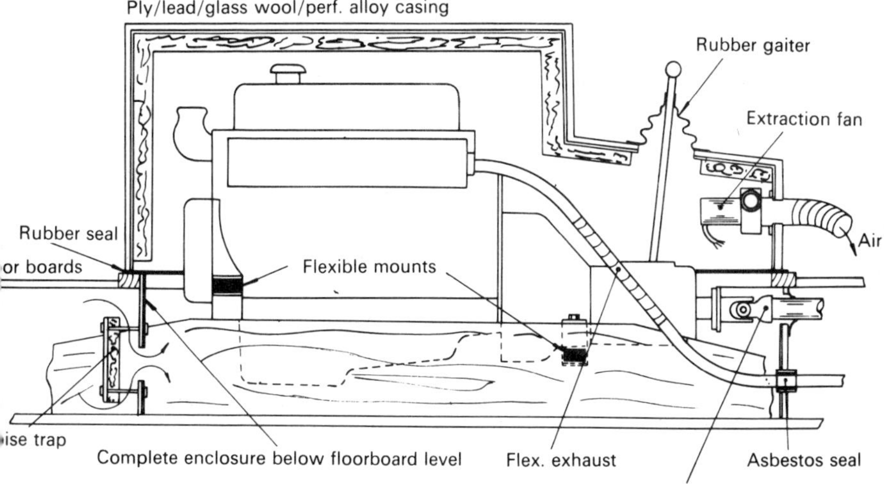

53 The complete soundproofed installation

Although I have mentioned polyurethene foam it must be remembered that this is inflammable, and I strongly recommend glass, slag or mineral wool instead, especially for petrol engines. Similarly, perforated aluminium sheeting is more desirable than pegboard. It is not essential to cover the whole of the inside surface of the enclosure with absorbing material—a coverage of about 80% of the total surface area is sufficient.

The only item not yet discussed is the ventilation fan. Of course, if the engine is encapsulated as I have been stipulating, it would soon stop through lack of air or through overheating. The noise-absorbing wool or foam will also act as excellent thermal insulation, the metal of the engine will slowly heat the air inside the casing, and the engine will suck in hot air and effectively 'de-rate' itself.

The only answer to this is to fit an extraction fan and an air inlet. There is one very important safety point to make here. In the case of a petrol engine it is vital to have a fan, and just as vital to have a non-sparking fan. Suppose that while stationary the carburettor overflowed because of a bit of dirt under the needle. It takes only a drop of petrol to produce an explosive mixture in the confines of an engine box. When you came to operate the starter motor, the commutator of which is bound to produce sparks, a violent explosion would occur. Similarly, if the electric fan is not 'spark-proofed' (flameproof motor casing and plastic fan) it may well set off any explosive mixture. This

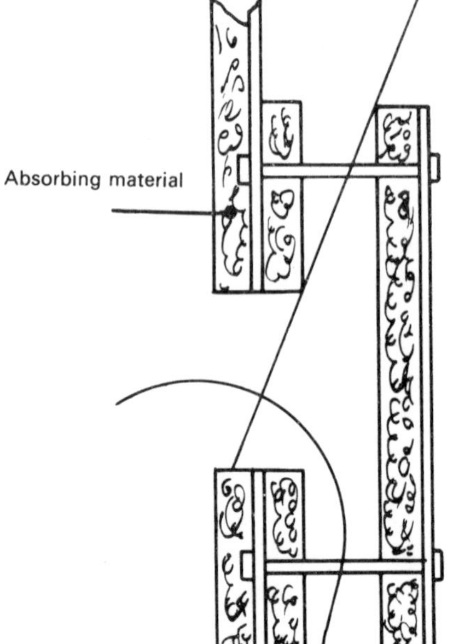

54 Simple noise trap

never happens in cars because any petrol leaks or vapour simply drop away to the road.

Before starting the engine, it is a safe policy to either lift the engine cover or switch on the fan for a minute to suck out any explosive gases. Better still, the ignition can be arranged electrically to be inoperative with the extractor fan off. Thus the fan *has* to be switched on before the ignition and starter motor circuits can be completed.

The ducting to the fan needs to be lined on the inside with a sound-absorbing material, otherwise noise will get out through the duct. An inlet must, of course, be fitted and this can be in the form of a noise trap (54). The engine must be adequately cooled when totally enclosed, even if a fan is fitted. This virtually implies engine oil cooling and a water-cooled exhaust manifold. Radiator cooling is out of the question. The fan should not be mounted on a panel of the casing as the panel would be caused to vibrate and radiate noise.

Diesel fuel does not form explosive gases at ordinary temperatures, so is a much safer fuel than petrol.

To sum up the requirements for good noise reduction, the following rules should be adhered to:

1 Flexibly mount the engine and have a flexible drive and exhaust pipe, etc.
2 Enclose the engine as completely as possible.
3 Line the inside surfaces with an anti-vibration material such as lead sheet.
4 On top of this add sound-absorbing wool or foam covered with a perforated lining.
5 Fit an extraction fan and an air inlet with soundproofed ducting.

Engine cassettes and rafts

While simple techniques like those discussed so far can make an extremely quiet installation on a larger boat (40 foot or so) it is not so easy on a small craft where people's ears are inevitably closer to the engine. (But one good example in the professional world is the Swedish Albin 25 motor cruiser).

Despite rubber mounts, structure-borne noise is usually the culprit especially with a diesel. In a yacht it may be possible to attach the rubber mounts to the ballast keel which because of its vast mass,

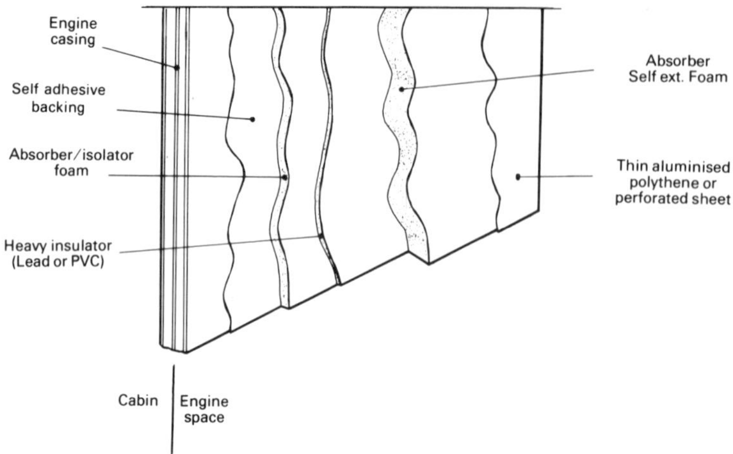

54A Typical lay-up of noise reducing sheet material

many times that of the engine's weight, will hardly react to the vibration of the engine, thus very little vibration is passed to the hull. This method has been successful on several large yachts.

Another trick is to flexibly mount the engine on a heavy rigid raft which in turn is rubber mounted to the hull. The mass or weight of the raft needs to be large (approaching that of the engine) which is a disadvantage although two engines may be mounted on the same raft.

Some small production motor boats (notably the Orrskar and Tresfjord 28 — Norwegian motor cruisers) employ a 'cassette' which is a raft combined with an acoustic hood. The engine is installed on rubber mounts in a sound-proofed box with connections for services (water, fuel etc) rather like those generator sets that can be supplied housed in an acoustic box. This box is then rubber mounted to the hull. This concept gives very good results in the case of the above mentioned boats. The arrangement is not easy to engineer into an existing boat — the layout needs to be worked out at the design stage.

All too often the results of noise reducing techniques are disappointing. People are lured into buying expensive noise reducing material retailed by the boat industry, the materials themselves being

Table showing typical absorption values of different materials within the audible frequency range.

	Thickness	Frequency cycles/second 125	250	500	1000	2000	4000
		Absorption %					
Glass fibre mat	1″	10	25	45	60	70	70
	2″	20	45	65	75	80	80
Mineral wool	2″	25	55	70	75	80	90
Felt	$\frac{7}{8}$″	-	15	40	75	85	-
Polyurethene flex foam	2″	25	50	85	95	90	90
Exp. polystyrene	1″	10	25	55	20	10	15
Rubber sponge	$\frac{1}{4}$″	-	5	5	10	35	-
Insulating fibre board	$\frac{1}{2}$″	10	15	25	30	30	40
Cork	1″	5	10	20	55	60	55
Plywood	$\frac{1}{2}$″	15	25	20	15	10	5
Perforated asbestos acoustic board	$\frac{1}{2}$″	15	45	50	50	55	65
Glass fibre covered with perforated metal sheet	1″	10	35	60	90	35	15
Soft sheet rubber	$\frac{1}{4}$″	-	5	5	10	5	-
Axminster carpet	$\frac{1}{4}/\frac{3}{8}$″	-	5	15	30	45	55

very well engineered but the results in a boat depend so much on how the material is fitted. Those that are insulating as well as absorbing need to be fitted in an airtight fashion all around the engine enclosure — something that is often impossible on an existing boat.

Putting the engine in a box *before* installing it in a boat of course makes the task of achieving good insulation so much easier, while the structure-borne noise is much reduced by the double isolation achieved by the two sets of rubber mountings.

CHAPTER TWELVE

Conversion to Paraffin

The successful conversion of a petrol engine to run on paraffin is very attractive from a financial point of view. Any of the types of vaporising oil cost about the same as diesel fuel. The best grade of paraffin, or kerosene as it is sometimes called, is TVO (Tractor Vaporising Oil), but this often cannot be obtained nowadays. The refined grades of lighting and heating paraffin are quite suitable. Lamp oil should be avoided. This is one of the problems of running an engine on this fuel—it is not usually available at the waterside.

Compared to petrol, paraffin is a 'dirty' fuel in that it forms soot and carbon more readily, thus necessitating more frequent de-coking, plug cleaning and lubricating oil changes. To start the engine, petrol is still required, and only when the engine is warm will it run satisfactorily on paraffin. This entails a dual fuel system with two tanks, two pipes and a two-way cock. If the conversion of the engine to run on paraffin is not done well, vaporisation when idling for any length of time will cease and the engine will stall. The carburettor has then to be drained and the engine started afresh on petrol. Similarly, restarting after a five minute stop, at a lock for instance, may be dicey on paraffin, so that it could mean that one has to remember to switch over to petrol shortly before stopping, so that the carburettor is full of petrol ready for the next start. This has to be done in any case if stopping for more than a few minutes.

Some people revolt against the smell of paraffin, especially if it is not being burned very well and there is a following wind, causing the exhaust gases to drift into the cockpit.

Paraffin has a lower calorific value compared to petrol, and in consequence the power output of the engine will be less. Also it is usually found that a high compression ratio engine (over, say, 7 : 1) does not run well on paraffin. 'Pinking' is quite likely and the compression ratio has to be reduced, so again the power drops. This rules out paraffin engines for fast boats, and it also creates difficulties with modern car engines with their compression ratios of 9:1.

For the successful converter, fuel bills will be cut to a half of the petrol costs. The consumption does go up a little per horsepower produced, but a consumption of about 0·7 pints per HP per hour is usually achieved. There are not many manufacturers on the market nowadays who offer paraffin engines from which conversion parts could be utilised. As far as I know, no car engine conversion firm produces parts for running on paraffin.

Conversion

The best advice is to tackle the conversion by trial and error. Obviously a separate tank is required for the paraffin. The petrol tank can be much smaller, perhaps only a gallon in capacity and gravity fed, while the paraffin is pump-fed from the larger and lower tank. The two pipes from the tanks join at a two-way cock at the carburettor. The transfer from petrol to paraffin is then achieved by switching over the cock, but it will take a minute or two before all the petrol in the float chamber is used up.

A larger carburettor jet opening will be required when running on paraffin in order to give a richer fuel–air mixture. The best setting can only be found by trial and error, until the engine is running evenly with the least rich setting, on both the slow-running and main jets, in the case of a fixed jet carburettor. Smelling and observing the exhaust gases will also help to decide whether the fuel is being burned correctly. A strong paraffin smell indicates unburnt fuel, the result of which is lubricating oil dilution because of unburned paraffin trickling down into the crankcase. After a long period of running this can be detected by the level in the sump rising rather than falling. The lubricating value of paraffin is not very great, so this is something to be avoided. Valve burning, heavy carbon deposits and plug fouling are symptoms of incorrect combustion.

One way in which vaporisation can be more readily achieved is to pre-heat the paraffin before it reaches the carburettor. This can be achieved by wrapping the copper fuel pipe around the original exhaust manifold, the exhaust pipe or even a hot water pipe (55). Other methods include fitting a shroud over the bare exhaust manifold and making the carburettor suck hot air from inside by means of an extension pipe from the carburettor intake. On a similar theme a long box can be fitted around the hot exhaust pipe and the carburettor made to suck from the air inside. Alternatively, a heating box can be fitted directly onto the carburettor and the exhaust gases can then be led into and out of this box. The insertion of a pipe through the box then leads hot air to the carburettor.

The best method of all involves heating the paraffin/air mixture as it passes from the carburettor to the engine. Droplets of fuel are then effectively vaporised. One way is to fit a heating box between the carburettor and the engine. A $\frac{1}{8}$ in. thick welded steel box about 6 in. cube is suitable for small car engines. Another and better way is to fabricate a new exhaust manifold rather like a water-cooled manifold but with internal air pipes leading to the intake ports. Surrounded by hot exhaust gases, the ingoing air and paraffin mixture is heated over a large surface area. This method can only be applied where the exhaust and inlet ports are on the same side of the engine.

Clean combustion is also helped by maintaining a high engine temperature (as high as possible) of 180°F unless a direct salt water cooling system is employed. Only a few minutes are required after starting the engine for the changeover to paraffin to be made without the engine faltering.

Usually better results are obtained with a lowered compression ratio. The old marine paraffin engines popular some years ago had compression ratios of about 5 : 1. Again a trial and error basis is the best policy, but the ratio can be reduced by fitting an extra cylinder head gasket. Most manufacturers offer high or low compression versions of their engines (the lower compression for export), the difference being obtained either by the depth of the piston crown or the depth of the cylinder head. Another way of reducing the compression ratio is by inserting a compression plate sandwiched between two cylinder head gaskets.

The simple conversion does have the disadvantage that one has to remember to switch over to petrol before stopping, otherwise the carburettor float chamber has to be drained. Draining can be arranged by drilling and tapping the bottom of the chamber and fitting a small cock. Unless a remote cable control is arranged for the two-way petrol paraffin cock the engine box lid has to be lifted and the tap groped for. A way to overcome this is to have two SU electric pumps (car type), one in each feed pipe, with switches on the instrument panel (55). Changeover is accomplished by switching off one pump and switching on the other. The SU type of pump has a natural non-return action, so syphoning from one tank to the other cannot occur. On the other hand, if the tanks are above the level of the carburettor, then both fuels will tend to flow whether the pumps are switched on or not. The tanks must therefore be below the level of the

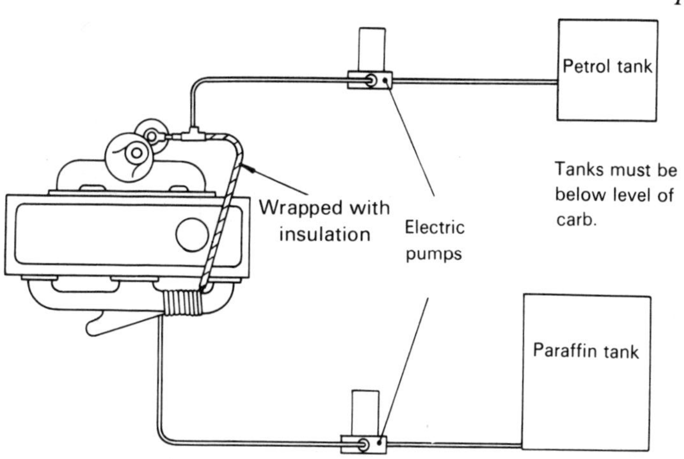

55 Using SU electric pumps for paraffin conversion

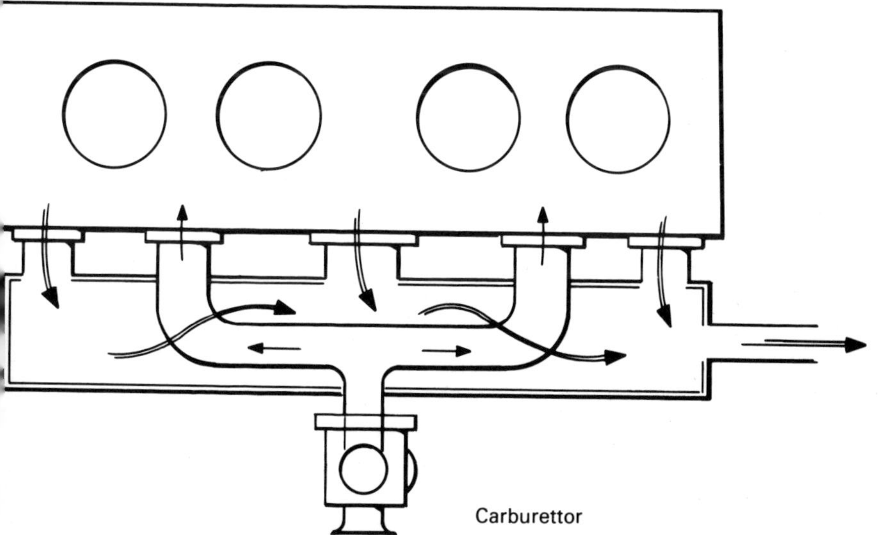

55A Replacing the exhaust manifold with a fabricated vapouriser box through which passes the paraffin/air mixture ensures that the paraffin is vapourised and does not enter the engine in large droplets. Professional conversions use this method

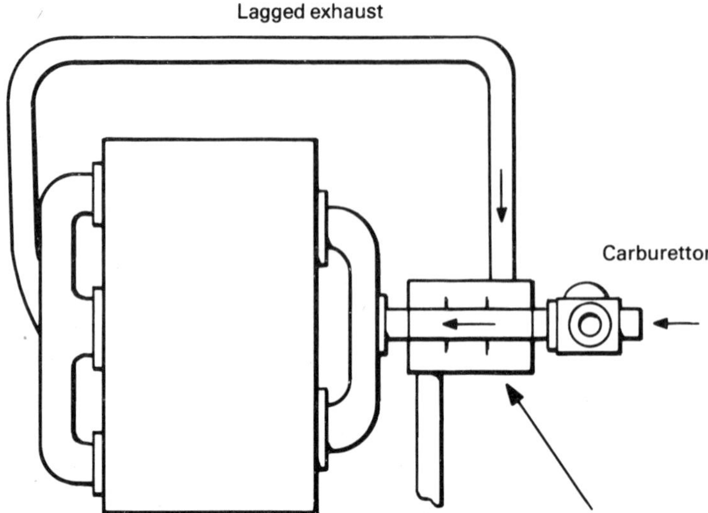

55B An alternative and simpler method but not as effective as (55A)

carburettor. No two-way tap is required on this system; the two fuel pipes merge into one at the carburettor.

Some of the old types of marine paraffin engines had double carburettors, i.e. two float chambers (one for each fuel) and two jets. Thus petrol or paraffin was instantly available at the jet at a turn of the changeover lever; there was no necessity to change over to petrol before stopping. This arrangement is possible with the SU variable jet carburettor because there is a flexible pipe (on most SU carburettors) feeding fuel from the float chamber to the jet. If a two-way cock is fitted in this line and another float chamber bolted alongside the original, then the appropriate fuel can be fed directly to the jet. With a variable jet carburettor the choke control actually 'opens out' the jet orifice, so here is a simple way of enriching the mixture when switching over to paraffin—the choke knob is pulled out by an amount determined by experiment. In the fixed jet type of carburettor (e.g. Zenith) it would not be as easy to intercept the fuel on its way to the main and slow running jets. It is not usually necessary to alter the ignition timing when running on paraffin, at least at low compression ratios.

CHAPTER THIRTEEN

Actual conversions and installations

This chapter is devoted to actual amateur and professional conversions and the snags encountered. I have chosen widely different methods of conversion and installation to illustrate the many combinations possible with the varying types of cooling system, drive, etc.

BMC 948 cc 'A' type (A40)

This is installed in a 22 ft clinker Thames cruiser and gives a very quiet and smooth drive at a gentle 5 knots and 1400 r.p.m. Consumption is half a gallon an hour. The engine was obtained from a crashed car complete with starter, dynamo, gearbox, etc., and was in such good condition that little needed to be done before installation. A brass sump pump was fitted and a galvanised tray fitted between the engine bearers. Blocks of wood with sloping tops were coach-screwed on to the inside faces of the engine bearers to take the forward rubber mounts and a $1\frac{1}{2} \times \frac{1}{8}$ in. steel flat bar was fitted to span the engine bearers and take the single rubber mount underneath the gearbox. This form of mounting prevents discernible vibration in the hull, and gives a low noise level inside the boat despite the fact that virtually no soundproofing is fitted. Because the engine is cooled by the original radiator and fan plenty of air gaps and holes have been provided in the engine case. The radiator sits across the engine bearers. It was found that cooling was not quite sufficient at first; the temperature crept up above 175°F after a long spell of running, although the water never actually boiled. An extra blade was fitted to the fan, the thermostat taken out and the bypass blocked off. After four years the cooling again became slightly insufficient, due probably to the furring up of the radiator and water passages in the engine. As the A40 radiator does not have a very deep core it was replaced with one having a deeper core giving more cooling area. Being a completely self-contained arrangement there is never trouble from weed and polythene bags in the river. The warm air is blown into the cabin, which is hardly ever found to be a nuisance—quite the contrary, in fact.

The gearbox was converted to give 1·4 : 1 ahead and 1 : 1 astern. Astern is simply fourth gear and ahead is third gear. The other gears are blocked off. Opposite rotation is achieved with a chain and sprockets fitted in lieu of the third gears, so in fact ahead drives through the chain. This has never given any trouble. The car-type universal shaft is used, driving to a half coupling on the propeller shaft, while the propeller thrust is taken by a wheel hub bearing from a sports car, which has double Timken roller bearings. This unit is rigidly bolted to a substantial member running across the boat just forward of the stern tube gland.

The normal A40 manifold is fitted together with a car-type exhaust silencer and pipe leading to the transom. Most of the exhaust line is lagged with asbestos tape. A car petrol tank is fitted in the bows and a copper pipe leads through the bilges to the engine. At first the engine was gravity fed and this caused endless trouble through air locks. For one thing, the pipe enters the tank on one side and then bends down into a sump, thus forming a syphon which had to be started. Also the run of the pipe was tortuous. Eventually, after dozens of frustrating stoppages, a mechanical petrol pump was fitted to the engine, which solved the problem.

The throttle consists of a motor mower-type lever and cable. As the actual throttle butterfly movement from idle to full ahead (1750 r.p.m) was so small, a long lever (12 in. arm) had to be fitted to reduce the sensitivity of the throttle. The battery and all electrics are standard car types. A battery master switch and petrol cock at the tank are fitted.

The clutch is operated by the left foot when sitting at the steering position, and is a car-type hydraulic system. A strong wooden lever about 2 ft long is linked to the gearbox lever so that their motions are identical. Pushing the lever forward gives ahead and aft astern. During the winter the water is drained out of the block and radiator to preclude trouble from frost. The engine oil is not deliberately cooled, but the cooling effect of air from the fan over the sump must be considerable.

Austin 7

Although such an old type of engine, it is surprising how often it is used in boats. Spares are still obtainable, apparently. This engine is fitted in a double ended ex-lifeboat hull used on the canals. To avoid the engine taking up space in the cabin it was fitted over the propeller shaft and a chain drive adopted (56). The engine itself was in fair condition, but Cord piston rings were fitted, the combustion spaces decarbonised and the valves ground in. It is rigidly mounted on a frame of $1\frac{1}{2}$ in. angle bar and the chain tension adjusted by packing up the engine. A $\frac{1}{2}$ in. pitch chain is carried on 25 teeth sprockets (4

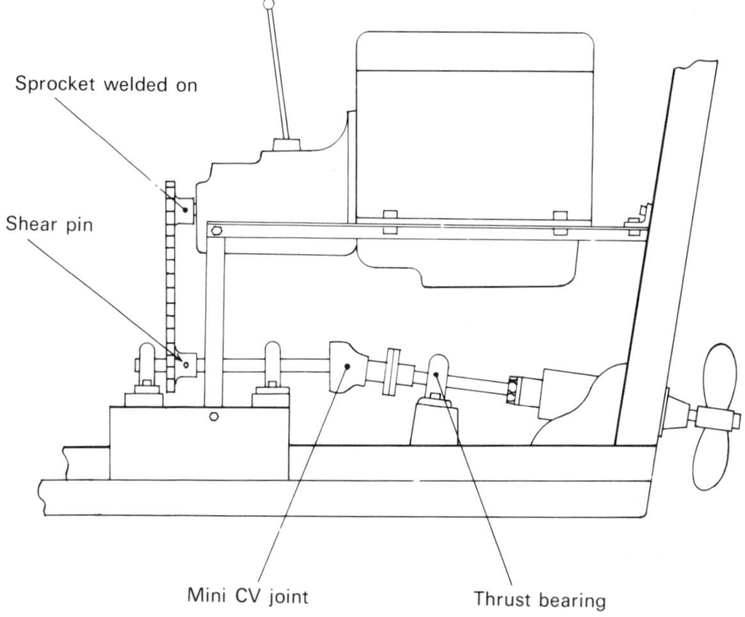

56 Up-and-over chain drive

in. diameter) and easily transmits the 6–8 HP necessary for canal cruising. A Stuart Turner stern tube, thrust block and shaft are fitted, the other bearings being standard RHP plummer blocks. A Mini constant velocity joint is used complete with the drive shaft. Although the CV joint allows an angular discrepancy between the two shafts, it still required accurate lining up of the plummer blocks in the vertical and sideways planes. The rubber drive coupling on the Mini might have been a better coupling, being a rubber spider joint. The gearbox is used unconverted, and at first fourth gear was used for ahead (1 : 1) and reverse for astern. This meant that the power astern was small, but later on the chain drive which was originally

1 : 1 was modified with a smaller lower sprocket. This meant that to give the same propeller shaft revs the gearbox could be run in second gear. Consequently the astern ratio was not very different from the ahead ratio, thus giving better astern power.

Direct cooling is employed with a Parsons bronze pump driven off the camshaft by means of a short length of water hose secured with hose clips. A cooling coil in the sump and a water injected exhaust silencer are fitted, but several sophistications are also employed. A bypass from the outlet of the pump passes straight overboard and is controlled by a tap. There is also a tap in the pipe leading to the silencer, and by adjusting these two taps it is quite easy to maintain the temperature at 170°–180°F. Being fresh and not salt water this high temperature is permissible.

A further refinement is a two-way seacock whereby with the cock in the down position the suction is taken from a pipe leading to the bilges, thus pumping the bilges. The clutch is shifted by a hydraulic car clutch mechanism adapted for the Austin 7, and foot operated.

Hand starting is possible from the output end of the gearbox as the engine is high enough to allow the handle to be swung and because a short piece of tube is welded to the sprocket and spirally slotted to receive the starting handle. Reverse must be engaged to start, to avoid one turning the engine over the wrong way.

Ford 122E (1500 cc)

This is a straightforward conversion using Wortham Blake's excellent conversion kits. The Jabsco pump is driven off the camshaft. A modified timing cover is supplied with a mounting plate for the pump. The pump spindle has a slot across its end face which engages with a dog in a driving plate, which in turn is bolted on to the chain wheel using the original bolts. A replacement sump is supplied, zinc sprayed and chromic painted and complete with a cooling coil of copper pipe. The original pump and fan pulley have been taken off and the hole in the block blanked off with a plate fitted with an elbow connection. There is a similar plate to fit in lieu of the thermostat and top hose.

A water-cooled exhaust manifold is supplied and is fitted with the standard gasket. The copper water piping comes already bent to shape with nipples fitted, thus making an easy job of the circuit. Each of the three lengths of pipe have a rubber hose section to avoid cracking from vibration. The water is circulated in the sequence of sump, pump, exhaust manifold, block.

Engine mounting feet bolt on to the side of the block. The marine gearbox which can be fitted instead of the original box is supplied with an adaptor housing incorporating aft mounting feet and is made from seawater resistant light alloy. The box gives direct drive ahead and astern by operation of a single long lever. A 2 : 1 reduction gearcase, which would be necessary for slower boats and where the full power of the engine is to be used, bolts on to the end of the gearbox. Propeller thrust can be taken by the reduction box or the gearbox.

This simple, effective conversion cools the engine sufficiently for full power operation—56 HP at 4500 r.p.m. As converted, the engine is only suitable for solid mounting, but the car-type flexible mounts could be used instead if the car gearbox was retained. Flexible mounts, however, are available for the fully converted engine.

The marine gearbox adds greatly to the bill and is the most costly item. Without the marine gearbox an excellent marine engine could be had for about one-fifth of the cost of a new marine unit. Bearing in mind the facts presented in Chapter Four on gearboxes, it would be best, if the marine box were not fitted, to have a thrust bearing on the propeller shaft and a double articulated drive. This would free the car gearbox of propeller thrust (it would not be capable of taking 56 HP) and side load and deflection on the oil seal. The usual gearbox conversion and use of the clutch, together with this drive and flexible mounts, would be a good alternative to the full conversion. More modern Ford petrol engines are nowadays used as the basis for conversion particularly the 1600 cc cross flow engine.

VW engine

The following installation drives a 16 ft club rescue boat along at a fair speed. Air cooling is an advantage in winter to avoid frost troubles and helps to warm up wet rescued crews. As the engine was too wide to drop between the engine bearers a pulley drive was used to drop the drive down to the propeller shaft level (57). The ratio of the drive is 1 : 1 using 5 in. pulleys and five belts (Fenner

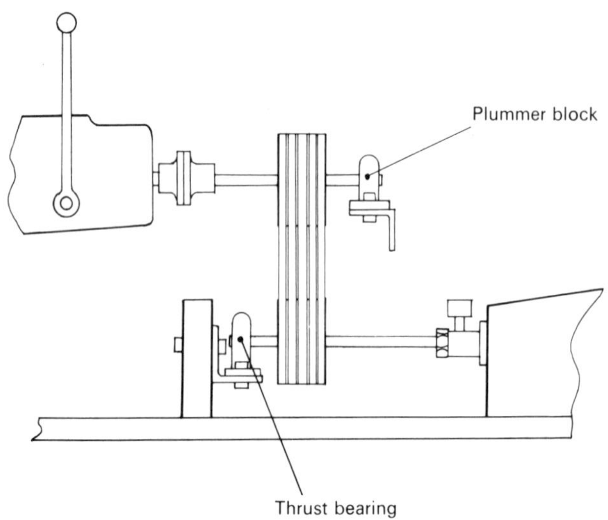

57 Raised drive using vee-belts

Spacesaver). These have never given any trouble from slipping, as they were correctly chosen for the power to be transmitted. The propeller thrust and side load from the belts are taken by a Fenner double taper roller bearing. The engine was mounted rigidly on a steel angle bar frame which sits on the original engine bearers. Belt tension is adjusted by packing up the angle bar frame. A Wortham Blake gearbox was fitted onto the original VW bell housing after made-up adaptor plates had been bolted to the flywheel with the normal clutch bolts. The splined gearbox stub shaft supplied with the gearbox bolts on to the adaptor plates which cause the stub shaft to protrude into the gearbox the correct amount.

Of course with the VW engine there are none of the cooling conversion problems of a water-cooled engine, although in this installation the engine is completely open, apart from a glassfibre open-ended hood. The complete VW exhaust is used extended back to the transom skin fitting with a large-bore steel pipe. All the normal VW car equipment is fitted (dynamo, starter, etc.) and hand starting is possible by means of a lug welded on the angle bar frame forward of the engine through which the starting handle can be poked.

There have been no cooling or drive problems, but naturally the noise level is rather high. Full power is never needed because the hull is not capable of more than 7 knots or so. The hull is quite open, but if a VW engine were fitted in a cabin boat or boxed in quite elaborate measures would have to be taken to duct the hot air away and prevent it recirculating into the blower.

$3\frac{1}{2}$ litre Morris Commercial

This is a large old petrol engine installed in a 28 ft steel ex-lifeboat based on the Thames. The engine is keel cooled and is converted to run on TVO (or paraffin). Timber 6 × 3 in. engine bearers were fitted to the hull and the engine rubber mounted on these. The stern tube has Cutless rubber bearings, and the $1\frac{1}{2}$ in. diameter steel propeller shaft is coupled to a marine gearbox through a flexible coupling. The propeller thrust is taken through the coupling to the gearbox. The engine and gearbox are mounted separately (the gearbox rigidly), while the drive between the two is via a Hardy Spicer articulated shaft. This is coupled to the flywheel by an adaptor plate, the original clutch and gearbox, of course, not being retained. Two tanks are fitted, one for TVO (the larger of the two) and one for petrol. Each feed line to the engine has an electric SU pump, and the TVO pipe is wrapped around the original exhaust manifold. About 7 ft of $\frac{5}{16}$ in. pipe is in contact with the manifold, thus preheating the fuel and aiding vaporisation in the carburettor. The SU pump when switched off prevents fuel being fed to the carburettor under gravity or syphoning back to the tank. The changeover from petrol after starting is achieved by simply switching the TVO pump on and the petrol pump off. The compression ratio of the engine was reduced from $5\frac{1}{2}:1$ to $5:1$.

A Lombard keel cooler is fitted. This consists of two 6 ft lengths of 1 in. diameter tube fitted alongside the keel. Water is circulated in a closed circuit, except for the header tank, by a belt-driven pump. After passing through the block the water is fed into an exhaust cooler fitted just below the exhaust manifold and then back to the keel cooler. A cabin heater is fed with hot water from this system and is controlled by a tap.

Being such a large low-compression engine, it only needs to revolve at 1000 r.p.m. to push the boat along at a comfortable 6 knots. As the cost of paraffin is far less than petrol the boat is very economical. The ease of switching from one fuel to another obviates one of the disadvantages of paraffin.

Ford 100E

This conversion used to be carried out by Leigh Marine (now defunct). A Jabsco seawater pump is driven off the end of the camshaft. There is a small flanged stub shaft which bolts on to the chain wheel and the pump itself is mounted on a bracket. A rubber hose is led to the lower block inlet, where a blanking plate with a hose connection is fitted. There is also a blanking plate with a hose connection fitted at the head, and a rubber hose leads from here to the water-cooled exhaust manifold. This is fabricated from galvanised tube of various diameters and galvanised tees, elbows and connectors. Engine L-shaped feet are bolted to the block. The coil and regulator are mounted on a bracket at the aft end of the head.

The car-type gearbox is retained and converted to give $1\frac{3}{4}:1$ ahead and 2 : 1 astern. This was achieved by turning off the driving gear on the primary shaft until it cleared its mate on the layshaft, and welding the uppermost second gear (three-speed box) to the primary shaft. The layshaft thus revolves faster and gives a lesser and more suitable reverse ratio. Ahead is first gear. Across the aft end of the box is bolted a thick plate which acts as the aft engine feet, houses the oil seal and holds in place the aft bearing which takes the propeller thrust. Seamaster engines (the name of the Leigh conversion) are usually bolted down rigidly with the propeller thrust taken on the after gearbox bearing. No bearing or oil seal trouble has ever been experienced, even when an engine has had to work hard—they are capable of 36 HP at 4500 r.p.m. The drive is taken by the car-type Hardy Spicer universal coupling. The spline is pinned so that reverse thrust can be taken, and a sleeve over the shaft coming out of the coupling can be bored out to fit the propeller shaft.

The clutch movement is combined with the gear lever in a similar fashion to (24). However, a quadrant is used to transfer the vertical motion from the gear lever to a horizontal motion, thus operating the clutch lever. This, with practice, allows easy gear changing with one hand and fine control by deliberately slipping the clutch.

BMC 2·2 diesel

The BMC 2·2 is a very popular engine ashore and afloat although the engine itself is not now in production. The particular installation described here gives the 21 ft glassfibre boat a speed of 14 knots, by virtue of the shape of the hull. It is a 'fast displacement' hull, round-bilged but with a wide flat underside to the transom, and a fine entry forward, a 'Seaworker' hull now moulded by, among others, Colvic Craft. The high speed is achieved using the full 43 HP of the engine, so the engine had to be fully marinised. Cooling is by a Polar heat exchanger, a cooling coil in the sump and a water-cooled exhaust manifold by Norris. Seawater is circulated by a Jabsco 2620-200 pump belt driven off the crankshaft. The fresh water side retains the original pump and thermostat housing and is also fitted with a Polar header tank mounted on the engine. Running temperature is an efficient 180°F. The exhaust is run dry through galvanised water piping kept at least an inch clear of any glassfibre or timber and lagged with asbestos string for the first few feet.

The standard rubber mounts are fitted, which give a very low level of vibration in the hull and help noise reduction. Drive to the half coupling on the propeller shaft is taken through a Hardy Spicer propeller shaft. A Fenner double taper roller bearing is fitted on the propeller shaft to take the propeller thrust. Reasonable astern power is achieved by the conversion of the gearbox. The driving gear on the primary shaft was ground down and the third gear on the main shaft welded to the primary shaft. Ahead is second gear now having a ratio of $1\frac{3}{4}:1$, and astern, reverse, with a ratio of almost $3\frac{1}{2}:1$. The clutch is incorporated into the gear lever in a similar fashion to the Leigh conversion.

A 20 gallon steel tank in the stern locker feeds fuel through a copper pipe to a glass filter bowl and hence to a CAV paper filter mounted on the engine. Fuel consumption at full throttle is only 2 gallons an hour, cruising consumes one gallon an hour. As this boat is used for family cruising a great deal of attention has been given to noise reduction. Apart from the rubber mounts, the engine is enclosed in a casing with removable top and sides which extends right down to the fibreglass skin of the hull. To give the engine sufficient ventilation a Delco car-type extractor fan is fitted and interlocked with the key starter, so that it is always running when the engine is running. The fan extracts from the bilges and an inlet vent in the form of a noise trap (54) is fitted in the aft end of the casing. The inside surfaces of the $\frac{1}{2}$ in. plywood casing are lined with $\frac{1}{16}$ in. lead sheet, and glassfibre wool $1\frac{1}{2}$ in. thick faced with pegboard.

A novel feature is the cabin heater. Before the hot water from the heat exchanger goes overboard it passes through a brass car heater unit complete with paddle-type fan. This unit is fitted on the inside of the cabin bulkhead partly covered by mahogany plywood, and draws air through a hole in the bulkhead. Even when switched off the unit gives off warmth useful for drying wet clothes, etc.

A rev counter is fitted on a panel above the wheel, together with a temperature gauge (in the fresh water circuit), an oil pressure gauge and an ammeter.

Leyland (BLMC) 1·5 diesel

Because of the rapid increase in the cost of petrol the diesel engine is now a very firm favourite. One of the most popular engines for conversion is the BLMC 1·5 litre. It is virtually the smallest 4 cylinder diesel available. Small enough in physical size to be considered as an auxiliary in a yacht and yet powerful enough (37 HP at 3600 r.p.m.) to propel quite large seagoing motor boats. With the wide availability of conversion parts, marinisation is now converging towards a standard form, and the CT Marine conversion described here of this particular engine, is typical.

A kit of parts can be supplied to marinise the engine. Fittings to adapt to a marine gearbox or an Enfield outdrive can be supplied. The total cost, including a gearbox or outdrive is less than half of that of a new 1·5 marine engine. But then there is also the cost of obtaining a basic engine complete with starter and alternator etc.

A Bowman combined heat exchanger/water cooled exhaust manifold is the biggest item in the kit and is simply bolted in place after reversing the original inlet manifold. Both manifolds share the same original studs and it takes two people to manoeuvre the combined weight. A Jabsco pump complete with pulley is bolted to a pre-drilled cast aluminium engine foot, itself bolted to the engine as is the corresponding foot on the other side of the engine. A pulley to drive the pump is fitted on the crankshaft pulley simply by the existing large securing bolt. The original thermostat housing is discarded (but the thermostat itself retained) and replaced by a new one merely to facilitate pipe runs. Hose and hose clips (supplied) readily complete the fresh water and salt water circuits.

A cast aluminium bell housing bolts directly to the block after the existing stud holes in the block have been tapped out $\frac{5}{16}$ in. Whitworth. This bell housing has integral mounting feet and also six bolt holes to correspond to a Borg Warner gearbox.

The only complication to the whole conversion is the drilling and tapping of the flywheel to take a drive plate. Five or six holes are involved; CT Marine will do the job if the flywheel is taken to them. Also three pins on the face of the flywheel have to be removed by a sharp tap with a hammer. For an Enfield outdrive a stub shaft with a Dunlop Metalastic coupling can be supplied which bolts to the flywheel. The stub shaft fits onto the input of the outdrive. In the case of a Borg Warner box all that is required is to bolt the damper drive plate to the flywheel. The splined input shaft of the gearbox mates directly with this.

Four rubber mounts are supplied capable of taking the propeller thrust. There is also a sump pump and fittings, a throttle bracket, an air filter and a wiring loom.

A kit like this enables a conversion to be achieved every bit as good as a professional one. All the parts are designed to make life as easy as possible for the converter. But of course one pays for this service.

If the basic engine is obtained cheaply one may be loath to spend several hundred pounds on a conversion kit and a gearbox. Since the main expenses are occasioned by the gearbox and the heat exchanger/manifold much money can be saved by converting the original gearbox and having direct cooling or keel cooling. It may also be possible to use the original exhaust manifold and the original rubber mounts. The overall cost can de-escalate dramatically, but correspondingly the amount of time and effort spent on conversion increases.

Golf diesel

This 1.5 litre diesel was specially designed for the Volkswagen Golf car and as such has made a name for itself as being the first diesel to compete in terms of performance and noise with a petrol engine. In the Golf car it gives the same performance as the 1100 cc petrol Golf, is as quiet and smooth as a petrol engine above about 30 mph and gives over 50 m.p.g. It runs freely to 5,000 r.p.m. (giving 50 HP at this speed) and cries out to be marinised. There are several companies in Europe which produce marinised Golfs; Bootmotor of Berlin and Pon Nautic of Holland are two, (the latter is imported into England by Carvel Developments Ltd., of Bedford). Hawker Siddeley Marine Ltd produce a version rated at either 43 HP at 4,000 r.p.m. or 35 HP at 3,000 r.p.m. The engine features an overhead camshaft driven by a toothed belt which drives the Bosch injection pump. The cylinder head is of aluminium.

The Golf can be compared to the Leyland 1.5 litre which as marinised by the numerous professionals weighs around 600 lbs including a reduction gearbox, whereas the Petter Golf conversion weighs 384 lbs. It is therefore an attractive engine for a small (say 16 foot) speedboat or in a twin installation it should make a 20 footer plane. But its quietness and its light weight also make it attractive as a yacht engine or for a displacement motor cruiser.

The car engine mounting points come at awkward positions so in a boat it is likely that new brackets and conventional marine rubber mounts will have to be used. Bowman do a combined manifold/heat exchanger for the Golf and Jabsco make a water pump to fit on the front end driven off the camshaft. One of the reasons for the engine's quietness is a high running water temperature (80–94° C) and pressure (up to 19 p.s.i.) both points to be borne in mind when marinising the cooling system. An oil cooler is essential for this engine when installed in a boat. A separate expansion tank (as fitted on the car), mounted on a bulkhead close to the engine but about a foot higher than the top of the engine, is the best way to keep the system free of air locks.

The paper element fuel filter on the car installation is mounted off the engine and the fuel system is self-bleeding (at least it is with the Bosch injection equipment – some earlier Golfs had CAV equipment which was not self-bleeding). The self-bleeding design is extremely useful, when changing filters for example. A magnetic cut-off valve on the injection pump means that there is no need for a stop control cable, the starter key can operate the cut-off valve so that starting and stopping is achieved just as on a petrol engine. Heater plugs are fitted one to each cylinder and these are switched on via the starter key. On the car they are automatically switched off after about 20 seconds at which point the engine will start instantly from cold. The whole fuel and starting system can be used on a boat with the addition of an extra fuel filter with a sediment/water bowl.

A large air intake housing containing a paper element filter is another reason for the engine's quietness so this feature should be retained. Since the engine in the car drives the front wheels, the gearbox housing includes a differential and hence two output flanges one to each wheel. Consequently gearbox conversion is far more difficult than with back-wheel-drive car engines. A 63 amp/hour battery is fitted to the car; on a boat a slightly larger capacity would be advisable.

Volkswagen also produce, as industrial engines, a 5 and a 6 cylinder version of the Golf giving 65 and 75 HP respectively.

CHAPTER FOURTEEN

Corrosion

Seawater is highly corrosive. The salt causes it to be an electrolyte i.e. capable of passing electric current. This means that two different metals in seawater and in contact with each other (or connected through an electrical path) will act like a battery and the metal lower in the Series (see below) will be corroded, the other one being protected or even plated with the first. Avoid using dissimilar metals underwater or within the water cooling circuit. An aluminium propeller on a bronze shaft or an aluminium thermostat housing on a seawater-cooled engine would in both cases cause the aluminium to be corroded extremely rapidly. Always use fasteners of a material as high or higher in the Series than the material of the fitting – never lower – because if there is any attack it will be spread out over a large area of fitting rather than a small area of fastener.

Seacocks should be in gunmetal or silicon bronze or aluminium bronze, never manganese bronze or brass. The latter two materials suffer from de-zincification which means that in seawater the zinc in the metals leaches out leaving a weak porous mass of copper. Propeller shafts are often of manganese bronze and these should be galvanically protected by wiring them up to a zinc anode. This can stop de-zincification. Indeed a zinc anode should be fitted and wired up as per the makers' instruction if any underwater fitting is of steel, iron, brass, manganese bronze or stainless steel. The zinc anode must not be painted. It will erode away in preference to the sterngear and will last a year or two if it has been sized correctly.

Good materials for underwater use are gunmetal, silicon bronze, aluminium bronze, nickel aluminium bronze, copper and copper nickel.

Stainless steel

Stainless steel even Type 316 suffers from deep and local pitting whenever it is wet but shielded from a flow of water e.g. under barnacles or in wet wood or where a propeller nut, for example, bears against the propeller hub. Never use stainless through-hull fasteners underwater. If a stainless shaft or rudder is used it should be protected with zinc anodes. The best commonly available type of stainless steel is 316 (used to be known as EN58J). Type 304 is a 'lower' grade.

In clean freshwater corrosion is far less of a problem and brass seacocks can be used and even mild steel shafts. But if the water is slightly polluted then corrosion can rear its ugly head again. On a seagoing boat stainless steel hose clips are very worth while.

A water injection bend is often an area of high corrosion because hot seawater is squirted into the pipe. If it impinges onto the wall of the pipe then rapid corrosion can be expected. The direction of the jet of water should be *down* the centre of the pipe ideally achieved on a bend. Cast iron and stainless steel are the usual metals for this bend, the latter usually giving a better life.

Laying-up

When the boat is laid-up for the winter corrosion can be kept at bay by flushing through the engine (if it is direct cooled) with fresh water and then water mixed with inhibiting oil (e.g. Esso Cutwell or Rust Ban 392, Shell Dromus oil B or BP Energol SB4). These oils are not anti-freeze so the jacket should be drained for the winter after flushing. There are also oils for inhibiting the crankcase – they give off an anti-corrosion vapour (e.g. Esso Rust Ban 623, Shell Ensis, BP Energol Protective oil 30). In mild winters it is sufficient to renew the oil (with the normal type of oil) run the engine briefly and then seal the exhaust (at the injection bend) intake the crankcase ventilation orifices thus sealing the whole engine.

For cold climates there are also fuel preservative oils for diesels on which the engine is run until the pump and injectors are full (e.g. Shell Fusus A, BP Energol LM). A spray of WD40 or Supertrol over the external areas of the engine will help to stop condensation and rusting.

The Galvanic series

A metal lower down in the Series will be attacked by one higher up if there is an electrical path between them (even damp wood can provide that path). Stainless steel and Monel do not attack as much as their position might indicate (hence stainless bolts in an aluminium fitting are OK). The metals fall in the following order:-

Stainless steel (316)
Monel
Stainless steel (304)
Silver bronze
Nickel aluminium bronze
80/30 copper nickel
Lead
90/10 copper nickel
Gunmetal
Silicon bronze
Manganese bronze
Aluminium brass
Solder
Copper
Tin
Brass
Aluminium bronze
Steel & iron
Aluminium
Zinc
Magnesium

Appendix A

Part 1 Engine Marinisers who supply parts or kits for DIY

Lancing Marine
51 Victoria Road
Portslade
Sussex Tel 0273 410025

Marinising kits, engines, marine gearboxes, outdrives, jet units, Ford, Perkins, Bedford, Mercedes, Gardner, VW Golf and BLMC diesels; Ford, BMC Rover and Jaguar petrol engines. Propellers and sterngear. Many installation components.

CT Marine Ltd
9 Paxton Place
London SE27 9SS Tel 01 761 7325

Kits and engines. Ford petrol 1100 and 1600 cross flow engines, Ford 4 and 6 cylinder diesels. British Leyland 1.5, 1.9, 2.5 and 5.7 litre diesels. Hurth, PRM and Borg Warner gearboxes, and Enfield outdrives.

T Norris Industries Ltd
Wood Lane
Isleworth
Middlesex TW7 5ER Tel 01 560 3453

BMC and Ford diesel engine conversion kits. Bowman heat exchangers, couplings, stern gear, silencers, diesel exhaust hose, gearboxes.

Diesel Conversion Products
The Moorings
Salisbury Road
St Margaret's Bay
Nr Dover Tel 0304 853131

Conversion kits for BLMC and Ford 4D and 6D and Perkins 6354 Diesels and virtually any car engine to special order. Water cooled manifolds for unusual engines a speciality.

Lehman Power Ltd
1 Fison Way
Thetford
Norfolk Tel 0842 65566

Ford diesel engines and conversion components.

Polar Engineering Ltd
Pear Tree Lane
Dudley, W. Midlands
Tel 0384 337950

Polar type heat exchangers and water cooled exhausts and combined heat exchangers for popular diesels (Leyland, Ford, Perkins).

Lipscombe and Hessey
11 Victoria Road
Etonwick
Windsor Tel Windsor 64413

Conversion parts, engines, spares, installation equipment, old engine spares.

Petramill Ltd
Kingsway
Goole
North Humberside Tel 0405 2177

Marinising parts and kits.

Auto Engineering (Marine Division)
Warren Avenue
Industrial Estate
Milton
Portsmouth Tel 0705 731468

Engine reconditioning, metal spraying, marinisers.

High Power Marine Ltd
Griffin Lane
Thorpe St Andrew
Norwich Tel 0603 39371

Conversion kits made up to order for specific application for Perkins BMC and Ford diesels, also Scania, Gardner and BMW.

Reeves Marine Services
113–115 Sterte Road
Poole
Dorset BH15 2AE Tel 0202 675000

Conversion equipment for Leyland and Ford diesels and Ford 1100–1600 cc petrol engines. Stern gear.; Hydrive, PRM, Borg Warner, Hurth, Watermota marine gearboxes. Wortham Blake sole stockists.

Paul Sykes Organisation Ltd
Wakefield Road
Barnsley
South Yorkshire Tel 0226 298911

New and used diesels suitable for conversion.

MIT Queensborough Shipyard
South Street
Queensborough
Kent Tel 0795 661255

Marinisation parts, new diesels. Leyland, Thornycroft, Poyaud.

C-Power (Marine) Ltd
PO Box 27
Gainsborough
Lincolnshire Tel 0427 5356

Marinising parts.

Cranes and Commercials Exports Ltd
Elm Street
Northam
Southampton S01 1GA Tel 0703 332011

Used and reconditioned diesels suitable for conversion, engine spares.

Watermota Ltd
Abbotskerswell
Newton Abbot
South Devon
Tel 0626 66444

Marinising parts and installation equipment.

Sillette Ltd
13a Tabor Grove
Wimbledon
London SW19 Tel 01 947 8424

Conversion parts for Ford petrol engines and the smaller BL diesels and Perkins 4108.

Tecmarine Ltd
Dap Dune Wharf
Wharf Road
Guildford
Tel 0483 505995

Marinising parts, propellers, sterngear.

John Dell & Co
Marine House
Popham St
Nottingham
Tel 0602 582829

Ford and BL marinisation kits

AJW Engineering Services
Polean Industrial Estate
Looe PL13 2AL
Tel 05036 3388

Gearboxes, marinising parts, sterntubes, etc.

Part 2 Equipment

Outdrives

Enfield Industrial Engines Ltd, Somerton Works, Cowes, Isle of Wight. Tel Cowes 0983 294711

Ocean Outdrives

P W Clarke & Sons, 11 Church Close, Whittlesford, Cambridge. Tel 0223 833279

Sonic

Silette Ltd, 13a Tabor Grove, Wimbledon, London SW19. Tel 01 947 8424

Sternpower

Sternpower Marine Drives, 51 Victoria Road, Portslade, Sussex. Tel 0273 410025

MARINE GEARBOXES

Borg-Warner

Borg-Warner Ltd, Eldon Way, Langford Road, Biggleswade, Beds. Tel 0767 313684

Hurth

C/T Marine Ltd, 9 Paxton Place, London SE27 9SS Tel 01 761 7325

PRM

Newage Transmission Ltd, Barlow Road, Coventry CV2 2LD. Tel 0203 617141

SELF-CHANGING GEARS

Self-Changing Gears Ltd, Lythalls Lane, Coventry CV6 6FY. Tel 0203 88881

TMP

Thamesway Marine Products Ltd, 96 Thames St, Weybridge. Tel 0932 43072

Twin Disc

Marine & Industrial Transmission Ltd, Queensborough Shipyard, South Street, Queensborough, Kent. Tel 07956 61255

Technodrive

Freedom Marine, Westfield Lane, Etching Hill, Near Folkestone, Kent. Tel 0303 862215

ZF

ZF Gears (Great Britain) Ltd, Abbeyfield Road, Lerton, Nottingham. Tel 0602 869211

Watermota J Type
Watermota Ltd, Abbotskerswell, Newton Abbot, South Devon. Tel 0626 66444

Hydrive
Reeves Marine Services, 113/115 Sterte Road, Poole, Dorset BH15 3AE. Tel 0202 675000

WATER JET UNITS

Castoldi
Bluebird Marine Ltd, London Road, Bolney, Sussex. Tel 044482 303

Hamilton & Saifjet
Lancing Marine, 51 Victoria Road, Portslade, Sussex. Tel 0273 410025

Outjet
West Beach Motors Ltd, Stephenson Way Industrial Estate, Formby, Liverpool. Tel 07048 70039

PP Jets
R G Parker (Engineering) Ltd, Units 5–7 Ailwin Road, Moreton Hall, Bury St Edmunds, Suffolk. Tel 0284 701568

Riva Calzoni
Sulzer Bros (UK) Ltd, Farnborough, Hants. Tel 0252 44311

UA
UA Engineering Ltd, Canal Street, Sheffield. Tel 0742 21167

FILTERS

CI – European and American Engines, 82–84 Somerton Road, Liswerry, Newport, Gwent. Tel 0633 277129

FLEETGUARD filter units, water separators, coalescers. Also engine oil – postal monitoring service. Laboratory analysis of engine oil from sump can indicate condition of engine. Useful as a warning for impending trouble but also when buying a used engine.

Lucas CAV Ltd, PO Box 36, Warple Way, Acton, London W3. Tel 01 743 3111

Many varieties of fuel filters for diesel and petrol engines, including a *Waterstop* type that can trigger a warning light if water caught in the filters rises above a pre-set level.

PROPELLERS, STERN TUBES, PROP SHAFTS

T. Norris (Industries) Ltd, 6 Wood Lane, Isleworth, Middlesex.

Bruntons (Propellers) Ltd, Sudbury, Suffolk.

Watermota Ltd, Newton Abbot, Devon.

Brenco Sterngear, Brightlingsea Engineering Co. Ltd, 8 Colne Road, Brightlingsea, Essex. Brightlingsea 3368.

NEI Clarke Chapman Engineering Ltd, 72 Quayside Road, Bitterne Manor, Southampton S02 4AO. Tel 0705 39366/8.

Hamble Propeller Foundry, 116 Botley Road, Swanwick, Hants. Tel Locks Heath 4284

C. J. Russell (Brentford) Ltd, Hampton Works, Sheen Lane, Mortlake. Tel 01878 1214

J. Crowther (Royton) Ltd, Eden Works, Honeywell Lane, Oldham, Lancashire. Tel 061 652 423415

Reeves Marine Services, 113–115 Sterte Road, Poole, Dorset. Tel 0202 675000

Delta Marine Ltd, 70 Warwick Street, Birmingham B12 0NH. Tel 021 552 1718

Saildrives

The following leg units are available without an engine:-

Perkins Engines Ltd, Peterborough. Tel 0733 67411. Similar unit to Bukh and suitable for an engine such as the 4108.

Barnes Marine Units, Riverside Road, Wroxham NR12 8UD. Tel Wroxham 2625

Enfield Industrial Engines Ltd, Somerton Works, Cowes, Isle of Wight. Tel 0983 294711

Sonic Sillette Ltd, 13a Tabor Grove, Wimbledon London SW19. Tel 01 947 8424

NOISE REDUCTION MATERIALS

T. MAT Marine Noise Control, Sulivan Way, Loughborough, Leicestershire. Tel 0509 217171 Foam or mineral wool/lead or PVC sandwich.

ACOUSTEX Aqua Marine Manufacturing, 381 Shirley Road, Southampton Tel. 0703 778121 Foam with thin foil facing. Self adhesive

SONAZORB Marine Power (Poole) Ltd. West Quay Road, Poole, Tel 0202 676469 Aluminium polythene/foam/polymer/foam

COUSTILAM Bestobell Acoustics, Farnham Road, Slough, Berkshire. Tel Slough 35135 Faced Foam/lead/foam sandwich.

QUIETCLAD Halyard Marine Ltd, 2 Portsmouth Centre, Quartremaine Road, Portsmouth. Tel 0705 671841 Mineral wool/lead/mineral wool faced with neoprene or PVC.

HEAT EXCHANGERS

Kemper & Van Twist Diesel BV. 3300 AO. Dordrecht, Holland. Tel 078130155 Heat exchangers, oil coolers, keel coolers.

Polar Engineering Ltd, Pear Tree lane, Dudley, W. Midlands. Tel 0384 337950

E. J. Bowman (Birmingham) Ltd, Aston Brook Street East, Birmingham. Heat exchangers - many types and special types, to fit, for instance, BLMC 1.5 and 2.5; Ford 2500, 2711/2E, 2713/4/5E and 2704ET diesels; Ford V4 and V6 petrol engines. Combined heat exchanger and oil cooler for the Bedford 220 and 330 and Perkins 4-108 diesels. Combined heat exchanger and water cooled exhaust manifold for the Perkins 4-108 diesel (all these heat exchangers have integral header tanks). Also many types of oil coolers, separate header tanks, sump pumps, charge air coolers for turbo-charged engines, and water-cooled manifolds for Bedford 220 and 330, Ford 2711/2E and 2713/4/5E diesels. Heat exchanger/exhaust manifold for Golf diesel.

SILENCERS AND EXHAUSTS

Whitehouse Flexible Tubing Ltd, Britten Street, Redditch, Worcestershire. Tel Redditch 62394 & 64036

Marine Power (Poole) Ltd, West Quay Road, Poole, Dorset.

ENGINE COOLING ALARMS

ELMIC FLOW SENSOR. Detects a drop in flow rate in a pipe and operates a light or buzzer.

Elmic Ltd, Southend Arterial Road, Romford, Essex RM3 OXB

COOLGUARD. Engine water-loss alarm.
Tritillian Products Ltd. 160 London Road, Newbury, Berkshire RG132 2AX
Tel 0635 49012

ROBOMATIC. Monitors up to 5 functions of oil/water level, pressures and temperatures and gives audible or visual alarm or engine shut-down. Stewart Automotive Equipment, Sherbourne Drive, Windsor, Berkshire SL4 4AE

PUMPS

JABSCO PUMPS. Cleghorn, Waring & Co (Pumps) Ltd. 9–15 Hitchin Street. Baldock, Hertfordshire. Tel 0462 893838

Impellor type pumps for engine cooling
Frank Henry, 271 Canterbury St, Gillingham, Kent. Tel 0634 50203

PROPS VARIABLE PITCH

KMF Kirsor Motor-og Propelfabrik, Norvangen 12. 4220 Korsor, Denmark.

British Agents – Sabb, Emsworth Marine Engineering Ltd, The Yacht Harbour, Emsworth, Hampshire. Tel 024 34 71152

Watermota Ltd, Newton Abbot, Devon.
V.P. propeller for up to 15 hp.

Barnes Marine Units, Riverside Road, Wroxham, NR12 8UD. Tel Wroxham 2625

FLEXIBLE COUPLINGS MOUNTINGS CHAIN WHEELS & PULLEYS

BABBITT flexible mounts and couplings, King Marine & Industrial Sales, Gaters Hill, Mansbridge Road, Southampton. Tel West End 7705

Eurovib (Acoustic Products) 1 Shortlands Road, Kingston-upon-Thames, Surrey. Flexible engine mounts.

GKN Aquadrive double CV joint drive shaft for boats and rubber mountings. Halyard Marine Ltd – 2 Portsmouth Centre, Quartremaine Road, Portsmouth PO3 5QT. Tel 0705 671641

J. H. Fenner & Co Ltd, (branches in main towns)
V belts, pulleys, Taper-lock bushes, flexible couplings, chain drives, bearings.

Cementation (Muffelite) Ltd, Hersham, Walton-on-Thames, Surrey.

Reynolds (branches in main towns, also engineering suppliers). Chain drives, flexible couplings. *Also see under Chandlers and Engine Marinisers.*

R & D Marine Ltd, Meadow Works, Clothall Road, Baldock, Hertfordshire SG7 6PD. Tel 0462 892391

Flexible engine mounts, flexible couplings, damper plates.

SPRING STARTERS

Lucas Marine Ltd. Marinised hand wound spring starter that fits in lieu of or as well as an electric starter. See local Lucas distributor.

PLASTIC SEACOCKS

Action Hose Couplings, Unit 20, Bordon Industrial Estate, Bordon, Hampshire. Tel 04203 3600
'Banjo' Lloyds approved ball valve type seacock.

VARIOUS UNMARINISED ENGINES, Ex-ministry & Army

Watsons Eastern Motors Ltd, Aldeburgh, Suffolk.
Single cylinder industrial engines up to 8 hp and electrical equipment.
Various larger engines from time to time.

L W Vass Ltd. Tel Ampthill 403255

West London Engineering, Tel 01 969 7978

Dixon Kerly Ltd. Tel Maldon 5330

'Exchange and Mart'.

FAN EXTRACTORS

Simpson Lawrence (from chandlers). Plastic blower – 120 cu.ft/min.

E B Blowers Eraser International Ltd, Unit M, Portway Industrial Estate, Andover, Hants. Tel 0264 51347 *Also see under Chandlers.*

HYDRAULIC DRIVES

A R S Marine Ltd, Chedgrave, Loddon, Norfolk. Tel 0508 20555
Volvo-based drives for up to 200 hp.

KEEL COOLERS

Golden Arrow Marine Ltd. Newhaven, Sussex.

THRUST BEARINGS

R.H.P. Bearings (from engineering suppliers, e.g. Associated Engineering Ltd. or Brown Bros. Ltd)
N.P. Series pillow blocks

Fenner (from local branches)
Fenner S.C. plummer blocks, similar to RHP pillow blocks.
Fenner Series E Plummer blocks with Timken roller bearings for 1¼ in shafts upwards.

CHANDLERS HAVING GENERAL INSTALLATION EQUIPMENT

A.N. Wallis & Co. Ltd, Greasley Street, Bulwell, Nottingham.
VETUS equipment.

ZINC ANODES

M.G. Duff & Partners Ltd. Chichester Yacht Basin, Birdham, Sussex. Specialists in cathodic protection.

Part 3 Horsepower

There are so many horsepower ratings and standards in common use that the situation is very confusing. However the quantity 'horsepower' is easily defined:

$$\text{Imperial hp} = \frac{\text{Torque (ft lbs) x engine rpm}}{5252}$$

This is measured in practice simply by making the engine drive a dynamometer (a brake) (hence brake horsepower BHP) and measuring the torque developed and the rpm. The metric horsepower is slightly less 'powerful' than the Imperial and is referred to as CV or PS.

$$1 \text{ Imperial hp} = 1.0139 \text{ PS (or CV)}$$

Horsepower can also be expressed in KW:

$$1 \text{ Imperial hp} = 0.746 \text{ KW}$$

Now the important 'power' that drives a boat along is the actual horsepower that is delivered to the propeller – not the power at the crankshaft nor at the gearbox coupling. Losses occur as the power flows down the drive shaft. A direct drive marine gearbox loses about 5%, a reduction gear loses another 3%, a propeller shaft loses another 3%. Outdrives and saildrives lose about 7%; hydraulic drives lose at least 25%. Engines lose power at high ambient air temperatures and low barometric pressures (or high altitudes). It is the air *inside* the engine box that the engine sucks that matters – not the external air temperature.

There is great confusion over ratings and standards. Standards intended for marine engines have only been introduced recently. They are based on ISO (International Standard) 3046. There is BS (British Standard) 5514 and DIN (German Standard) 6271. None of these are commonly used as yet. One standard that is used – BS AU141a – is actually intended for diesel engines in road vehicles. On test the horsepower is measured at the crankshaft with an air temperature of 20°C and the horsepower figure given either as a 'gross power output' with the engine only driving ancilliary items essential for its operation (e.g. the oil pump) or as an 'installed power output' when items such as the alternator (as fitted to the road vehicle) are added. Another standard, BS 649, takes a higher temperature (29.4°C) and ancillaries must be installed; and an 'overload' and a 'continuous' rating is involved. Here is another point – engines are often rated either continuously or intermittently, the rpm and/or the horsepower being adjusted to suit.

DIN 6270, and 70020 (an automotive rating) are taken at 20°C with ancillaries included. DIN 6270 has either a continuous rating (A) or an overload (B).

So horsepower ratings to BS 649, DIN 6270 and DIN 70020 should be

roughly comparable and provide a close idea of the power available at the crankshaft when installed in a boat. It is then necessary to knock off the losses horsepower ratings because the engine was allowed to be stripped and operated in very favourable conditions but the new SAE code J816B gives a much more realistic figure.
operated in very favourable conditions but the new SAE code J816B gives a much more realistic figure.

Marine engine manufacturers often give SHP figures (shaft horsepower) and these can usually be relied upon (despite being to no recognised standard) as giving a horsepower that will actually be produced at the gearbox flange when the engine is installed in a boat.

Car and truck engine horsepower figures will usually be to DIN or BS from which must be deducted percentages as mentioned above to arrive at the power at the propeller. It is this power that must be used in the propeller tables or for speed estimation.

Weights and Measures

TEMPERATURES

°F	°C	°F	°C	°F	°C
32	0	95	35	158	70
41	5	104	40	167	75
50	10	113	45	176	80
59	15	122	50	185	85
68	20	131	55	194	90
77	25	140	60	203	95
86	30	149	65	212	100

1 mil = 1 'thou' = 0.001 in = 25um = 25 microns = 0.025 mn
1 metre = 3.28 feet
1 ins = 25.4 mn
1 kg = 2.2 lbs
1 metric tonne = 1000 kg = 2205 lbs
1 Imp ton (US 'long' ton) = 2240 lbs
1 'short' ton = 2200 lbs

1 knot = 1.15 mph = 1.69 ft/sec
1 km/hour = 0.54 knot = 0.62 mph

1 Imp gallon = 8 Imp pints = 1.2 US gall = 4.55 litres
Petrol weighs about 7.2 – 7.5 lbs per Imp gallon
Water weighs 10 lbs per gallon
Diesel weighs about 8.4 lbs per gallon
1 KW = 1000 Watts (W)
1 Imp hp = 550 ft lbs/sec = 746 W = 1.0139 metre hp (CV)
Watts = amps x volts
1 atmosphere = 14.5 psi = 1000 m bar (approx)
1 psi = 0.07 kg/cm^2

APPENDIX C

Literature

Marine Engine Know-how
Perkins Engines Installation manual. Highly recommended and not just for Perkins diesels.

Construction of Small Craft
SBBNF Rules including safe engine installation. Boat Industry House, Vale Road, Oatlands Village, Weybridge, Surrey.

The Care and Repair of Marine Petrol Engines
by Loris Goring, published by Adlard Coles Ltd, Granada Publishing, Frogmore, St Albans, Hertfordshire.

The Care and Repair of Small Marine Diesels
by Chris Thompson, published by Adlard Coles Ltd.

APPENDIX D

Engine oil classification

The API classification is usually found written on the side of oil cans. Each category of oil is given two letters. The first letter indicates S for petrol engines and C for diesels. The second letter indicates the grade, the quality increasing alphabetically. E.g. SF and CD are top quality lubricating oils.

Index

Notes

Notes

Notes

Notes

Notes